THROUGH
A GLASS DARKLY

THROUGH A GLASS DARKLY

Looking at Conflict Prevention, Management, and Termination

Stephen J. Cimbala

Westport, Connecticut
London

Library of Congress Cataloging-in-Publication Data

Cimbala, Stephen J.
    Through a glass darkly : looking at conflict prevention, management, and termination / Stephen J. Cimbala.
        p. cm.
    Includes bibliographical references and index.
    ISBN 0-275-97184-8 (alk. paper)
        1. United States—Military policy.   2. Military policy—Case studies.   3. Military history, Modern—20th century.   4. International relations—Case studies.   5. Cold War.   6. World politics—1989–   I. Title.
    UA23.C5435   2001
    327.1'6'0904—dc21   00-064953

British Library Cataloguing in Publication Data is available.

Library of Congress Catalog Card Number: 00-064953
ISBN: 0-275-97184-8

First published in 2001

Praeger Publishers, 88 Post Road West, Westport, CT 06881
An imprint of Greenwood Publishing Group, Inc.
www.praeger.com

Printed in the United States of America

The paper used in this book complies with the Permanent Paper Standard issued by the National Information Standards Organization (Z39.48–1984).

10 9 8 7 6 5 4 3 2 1

Contents

Acknowledgments

I gratefully acknowledge the following persons for their intellectual contributions to my understanding of issues covered in this manuscript and/or for critiquing parts of it: John Arquilla, Pavel Baev, Paul Davis, Ben Fischer, William Flavin, Raymond Garthoff, Lester Grau, Colin Gray, Jacob Kipp, Edward Kolodziej, Peter Rainow, James Scouras, Timothy Thomas, Graham Turbiville, and Col. Peter Vercruysse.

I am especially grateful to Dr. James Scouras for permission to make use of his analytical model and some of his data. He bears no responsibility for their application here nor for any of my arguments or opinions.

I am also especially grateful to Gen. Peter Schoomaker, Commander-in-Chief (CINC), U.S. Special Operations Command, for his permission to meet with persons at United States Special Operations Command (US-SOCOM) for very enlightening exchanges of information and perspective. James Majors made me feel especially welcome in Tampa.

Ben B. Fischer's contributions to my understanding of pertinent Cold War history deserve special mention. He has been generous with his insights and cues for important sources.

Col. William Flavin, U.S. Army (Ret.), has patiently shared with me his expertise on U.S. special operations and low-intensity conflict, his experience in planning special operations for the North Atlantic Treaty Organization, and his considerable grasp of military history and civil-military relations. I shall never be able to repay his forced march over the battlefields of Waterloo accompanied by his expert play-by-play during it.

I gratefully acknowledge administrative support for this project from

Penn State Delaware County Campus staff members Charele Raport, George Franz, and Edward Tomezsko.

The encouragement and support for this project by Dr. James Sabin, Greenwood Publishing Group, is very much appreciated.

This book is for Betsy, Chris, and David, whom I love and cherish beyond the ability of words to convey.

Arguments and opinions expressed in this study do not represent those of the U.S. Department of State, the Department of Defense, the Pennsylvania State University, or any persons named above.

Introduction

War, crisis, and peacekeeping are both objective and subjective experiences. They are objective in the sense that some event, variously described by observers and participants, actually took place. War, crisis, and peace operations are also subjective. How participants and observers understand the experience of war, crisis, or peacekeeping depends on the perspective that they bring to bear on it.[1] In everyday experience, we all know that two people, having seen the same thing, will report it differently. For example, President John F. Kennedy once sent two senior advisers to Vietnam to assess the situation there and required that they report to him immediately upon their return to Washington. One adviser reported that all was going well in Vietnam and that future prospects for the prosecution of the war by the government of South Vietnam were bright. The second adviser expressed little confidence in the ability of the South Vietnamese regime to fight the Viet Cong or to maintain the allegiance of most of the people under its rule. Kennedy remarked: "You two did visit the same country, didn't you?"

How participants in a decision or event comprehend and report that experience also varies through time. The past is seen differently from the present and the future. For example, leaders' memoirs are not as burdened by the time and attention span limitations as are their contemporaneous notes. On the other hand, memoirs written long after an experience has occurred are subject to selective and biased recall. In this study, we examine three cases of conflict prevention, management, or termination that took place during the Cold War. After reviewing these past cases, we consider three issue areas related to national security that will challenge the conflict prevention, management, and termination ca-

pacities of the U.S. government in the twenty-first century. Having completed both tasks, we will infer certain lessons learned for theorists,
policymakers, and military planners from these cases. Thus the study
combines *retrospective* with *prospective* policy analysis.[2]

The past cases include one from the early Cold War years (the Cuban
missile crisis of October 1962); the 1983 nuclear "war scare" between the
United States and Soviet Union; and the Gulf war (Operation Desert
Storm) of 1991. The present or future cases include the possibly malign
side effects of the overlap of an old war form (mass destruction) with a
newer one (information-based warfare); nuclear proliferation, or the
spread of nuclear weapons to currently nonnuclear countries or even to
nonstate actors such as terrorists; and third, the conduct of military
peacekeeping and other "operations other than war" in order to put out
the fires lit by failed or failing states. Each of the cases corresponds to a
particular type of problem (conflict prevention, management, or termination) in the past or in the present and future. Thus:

Past Cases

1. *Conflict Prevention*: the Cuban missile crisis.

2. *Conflict Management*: the 1983 nuclear "war scare."

3. *Conflict Termination*: the Gulf war of 1991.

Present/Future Cases

4. *Conflict Prevention*: nuclear deterrence and information warfare.

5. *Conflict Management*: nuclear weapons spread.

6. *Conflict Termination*: military operations "other than war."

The terms *conflict prevention, conflict management*, and *conflict termination* can be defined as follows, for purposes of this study:

Conflict *prevention* is the avoidance of an outbreak of war that is (1)
undesired by policymakers on either side; (2) to some extent unexpected
in the way in which it develops; (3) involves a very short time for decision on the part of the disputant parties before political disagreement
spills over into actual fighting. Note that conflict prevention, as in the
case of conflict management and termination, can describe both a *process*
or set of actions toward an intended purpose and an *outcome* or result
of a decision-making process. Of course, conflict prevention is a matter
of degree. If the July crisis of 1914 had been contained as a dispute
between Austria-Hungary and Serbia, World War I would have been
avoided (at least temporarily), although fighting between Austria and
Serbia took place.[3]

Conflict *management* is the control and limitation of a set of disagreements among state or nonstate actors in order to (1) mitigate the extent

of misperception of one another's motives on the part of states or non-state actors who are potentially or actually in military conflict; (2) regulate or otherwise *limit* the amount and kind of destruction attendant to warfare or other conflict and attempt to *reduce* the intensity of disagreements that keep conflict going, using techniques such as peacekeeping, peace enforcement, humanitarian rescue, and other means; (3) create an international, regional, or local climate of expectations that war is politically undesirable or morally unacceptable (sometimes called a "security community") and that its military consequences would leave all or most disputants worse off than they were without war.[4] Once a conflict has broken out, the effort is to terminate the conflict (see below) and restore this prewar climate of expectations supportive of peace.

Conflict *termination* means bringing to an end actual military fighting and, preferably, also concluding the political issues that gave rise to the fighting. It sometimes occurs that it is necessary to arrange a cease-fire or armistice among field forces before the final political terms of settlement can be concluded (as in World War I in November 1918). Conflict termination may be agreed to by the disputants or imposed by outsiders, including by international organizations or by state actors singly or in combination. As applied to unconventional wars within states, conflict termination can only reach so far. It rarely can bring an immediate halt to all the shooting and looting that takes place among competing ethnic, national, religious, or clan factions. Conflict termination is a short-term process for the most part: It cannot guarantee against a replay of fighting unless the political, social, and cultural issues that gave rise to the conflict are ameliorated or unless one of the major disputants ceases to exist (Germany in World War II; Carthage in the Second Punic War).[5]

The definitions given for conflict prevention, management, and termination, as noted earlier, involve both an aspect of process and an aspect of outcome or result. One important matter about process deserves further comment. Generally speaking, prevention and termination of conflict are short-term processes compared to conflict management. Prevention attempts to avoid sin; management, to live with sin while minimizing its side effects; and termination, to halt sin in progress. By way of analogy between military conflict and sex: Conflict prevention is abstinence; conflict management is safe (or relatively safe) sex; and conflict termination is the search for an AIDS vaccine.[6]

How were the cases selected? The past and present-future cases were selected according to the following criteria: (1) the author has considerable interest in the topic, based on past research; (2) the controversies and conflicts were, or are, high on the agenda of U.S. and allied national security policy (that is, the stakes were high, and the outcome mattered a great deal in the past, or the stakes are high now and the outcomes matter a great deal in the present and future); and (3) enough evidence exists of an other-than-anecdotal sort to form a reasonably coherent picture of events.

Not all readers will agree with the arguments that follow. If they did, they would be self-evident points hardly worth writing about. On the other hand, the willingness to engage controversial issues in war and policy is fraught with risk in today's academic and policy worlds. When people's favorite shibboleths about public affairs and about military policy are under scrutiny, they react emotionally. Scholars are no less emotional about their preferred theories than are policymakers in defending their past decisions.

To save time and energy for the disgruntled, readers of the following pages will be especially prone to apoplexy if they believe any, or all, of the following things: (1) The U.S.–Soviet nuclear relationship during the Cold War was overdetermined in the direction of peace and stability, and the actual likelihood of an outbreak of war was insignificant; (2) the Gulf war of 1991 was a triumphant march of American technology over technologically inferior foes and can serve as a paradigm for future conflict termination; (3) the United States should be optimistic about its likelihood of success in conducting future military interventions for peacekeeping; (4) since no nuclear war took place during the Cold War, it demonstrates that nuclear deterrence will also be shock resistant even in the twenty-first century and despite proliferation; and (5) information-based warfare will supersede the interest of states in weapons of mass destruction and allow the United States to exploit "information dominance" against future adversaries both large and small.

SEQUENCE OF TOPICS

In Chapter 1, we revisit the Cuban missile crisis of 1962 as a case of conflict prevention. It was a partial success. Nuclear war or any war between the United States and the Soviet Union was avoided. But a conflict took place in the Caribbean that reverberated to the top of the political and military pyramids in Moscow and in Washington. And that conflict was resolved just short of war. Many tense moments in the crisis, as recalled by participants and established by scholars, left the outcome in the balance until the very end of a tense 13 days. Our study shows how poorly both U.S. and Soviet leaders understood one another's definitions of the military-strategic and political situation. Each side, from the latter 1950s until the early 1960s, felt pressured by the other to make political concessions and to keep pace in a nuclear arms race. Each felt the other was racing for nuclear superiority and a possible first-strike capability. Ironically, the missile crisis took place because each side engaged in defensive moves (as seen by itself) that were perceived as aggressive or offensive (as seen by the other side).

In contrast to the Cuban missile crisis, the 1983 "war scare" between the United States and the North Atlantic Treaty Organization (NATO) and the Soviet Union (discussed in Chapter 2) was not punctuated by a dramatic beginning (such as the discovery of the Soviet missiles in Cuba) or a decisive ending (Khrushchev's announcement after two weeks of tension that he would remove the missiles). Evidence of the 1983 war scare only appeared in retrospect, and the crisis itself took place over a prolonged period: from about 1979 through late 1983. It was prompted, as was the Cuban missile crisis, by geopolitical rivalry compounded by ideological distrust and mutual misperception. A combination of events and decisions, each seen by the United States as separate decisions or actions, caused some Soviet political leaders and intelligence agencies to conclude that the United States and NATO were plausibly preparing for a nuclear first strike against the Soviet Union. Moscow tasked its foreign and military intelligence agencies to engage in unprecedented cooperation in order to detect any signs of U.S. or allied preparedness for nuclear attack. The intelligence bureaucratic mind-set, having been prepared to collect evidence of Western perfidy or desperation, set about trying to find the evidence in order to confirm the unfounded assumption.

If Cuba 1962 was a case of conflict prevention, and the 1983 war scare a case of conflict management, then the Gulf war of 1991 qualifies for study as a possible case of conflict termination. Conflict termination is accomplished according to U.S. and UN policy objectives narrowly defined: to expel Iraq from Kuwait and to restore the prewar regime in Kuwait. However, in broader terms the conflict between the United States and Iraq continued long after the 43 days of battle in January and February 1991. Saddam Hussein remained in power in Baghdad to attempt to rebuild his shattered military, to further oppress his own people, and to stonewall UN arms inspectors seeking to discover his hidden weapons of mass destruction. In Chapter 3, we consider aspects of both the military campaign against Iraq in Operation Desert Storm and the political situation leading to an apparent failure of deterrence that opened the door to Iraq's invasion of Kuwait. These political and military considerations are part of the backdrop by which the partially successful conflict termination must be understood.

In Chapter 4, we move from the retrospective to the prospective analysis of the relationship between the use of force and policy in conflict prevention, management, and termination. The case in Chapter 4 is the arrival of "third-wave" civilization and information-based warfare (a part of which is "information warfare"). The Gulf war of 1991 was a sneak preview of some of the features of information-based warfare: smart weapons for long-range precision strike, such as cruise missiles; intelligent command and control systems to link sensors, shooters, and information bases; and superior "eyes in the sky" in the form of satellites for navigation and reconnaissance, and airborne warning control planes that tracked all enemy sorties within hundreds of miles and vectored friendly forces against them in nearly real time. Hubristic forecasts emerged from the Pentagon after 1991 of a future U.S. military that would achieve "dominant battlespace awareness" against future opponents.

However, it has turned out that the age of information-based warfare has not displaced the age of mass destruction. Nuclear weapons have not gone away, and in fact, more states than hitherto seem to want to acquire them. Even with regard to relations between the United States and Russia, the combination of nuclear deterrence and information warfare (attacks on computers and their related communications systems) could lead to a variety of failures in decision making, prompting a crisis or an inadvertent war.

As anticipated in Chapter 4 and as discussed in Chapter 5, the spread of nuclear and other weapons of mass destruction (biological and chemical) holds the potential for a significant failure in international conflict management. Complacency about nuclear proliferation, based on the slow rate of nuclear weapons spread during the Cold War, is not warranted in the twenty-first century. The present international system, compared to the Cold War system, is both polycentric and multidimensional. It is polycentric in the sense that there are no longer two main centers of political influence and military power as in the Cold War years of U.S. and Soviet predominance. In addition, the current international system is multidimensional. Military power is not necessarily transferable across other power dimensions: Economic power, social status, ethnicity, religion, and other factors become sources of power in their own right. To some extent, this is a reversion to the norm of international history and away from the abnormal condition of the Cold War. Nevertheless, the polycentric and multidimensional international system now creates a higher demand for weapons of mass destruction and a larger number of possible suppliers: Both suppliers and demanders are motivated by diverse political, economic, social, and cultural factors.

One school of thought during the Cold War argued that since nuclear deterrence had seemed to work well between 1945 and 1991, it would continue to do so even in the face of additional nuclear weapons spread. And some point to the 1998 official acknowledgments by India and Pakistan of their status as nuclear powers, and to the de facto nuclear status of Israel, as evidence for the argument that proliferation is compatible with stability. On the other hand, we have not lived in the post–Cold War world for very long: Our sample of stable or unstable behaviors among nuclear armed states in that world is very small. In addition, U.S. officials fear the spread of nuclear and other weapons of mass destruction (WMD) among states with special grievances against the existing order or with local and regional scores to settle: Iran, Iraq, North Korea, Syria, and Libya.

One does not have to believe that all of these regimes are "rogues" in order to make less-than-optimistic assumptions about their probable behavior once they have attained nuclear status. It is enough to have observed their past behavior. Fixation on the problem of rogues may obscure the more fundamental risks inherent in further nuclear weapons spread: (1) Some recent and aspiring nuclear powers are also building or buying ballistic missiles and other delivery systems, including some with the range and payload capacity to threaten the forward deployment and crisis response of U.S. forces or American allies; (2) some recent and aspiring nuclear states have uncertain or unknown relationships between their military and civil authorities; and (3) some of the same states have economic disasters or political instabilities from which they need to distract their restless citizens, and provoking a major foreign policy crisis might appeal to besotted elites under siege.

WMD proliferation is one of the major security challenges of the new world order. The other is the breakdown of states and the unleashing of civil strife in which primordial values (race, religion, ethnicity) are overlapped with economic and social grievances. We know of no fully adequate term to describe this new world disorder—but it poses the major problem of conflict termination for the first part of the twenty-first century, in numbers and in the degree of inherent difficulty. Civil wars tend to go on forever and to be fought with the bitterest of motives. But it does seem clear that U.S. and other developed state militaries, at the behest of the United Nations or on their own, will be tasked to intervene in civil wars or other forms of humanitarian chaos more frequently in the next few decades than they were in the preceding quarter century. The 1990s witnessed U.S. excursions into multinational peace operations in Somalia, Haiti, Bosnia, and Kosovo (Serbia). In each case, considerable controversy attended the deployments of U.S. forces, and the Somalia deployment ended in a military setback and political fiasco.

The U.S. military is divided with respect to its interest in unilateral or multinational peace operations, as explained in Chapter 6. It knows that expertise in "peace wars," as we have called them, will be demanded, owing to policymakers' interest in showing a high American profile in this activity. On the other hand, military planners and commanders recognize the considerable costs in time, commitment, and training in deploying peace operations forces. Commanders also recognize that peace wars call for a combination of sociopolitical and military skills that not all warriors are able, or willing, to acquire. In addition, the situational context for peace operations deployments may find the U.S. military caught between competing factions of n'er-do-wells in a culture that is unfamiliar and with rules of engagement that disallow prevention of some of the most provocative violations of human rights. However culturally aware and socially conscious the young warriors of the future U.S. armed forces may be, there are some situations of human horror that it may be impossible or imprudently costly for outsiders to resolve. In addition, although the U.S. Congress has showed a surprising amount of tolerance for extended peace operations in the 1990s, its toleration appears to depend on low casualty rates and public apathy.

LOOKING AHEAD

Whether a new paradigm of warfare has emerged, in the aftermath of the end of the Cold War and the U.S. triumph in Desert Storm, is a subject of considerable debate among scholars and policymakers. New paradigm advocates come from two directions. Both kinds of new paradigm advocates see a bleak future for the territorial state as the most competent and legally sovereign wielder of military power. One school of thought suggests that the nation–state will become less relevant as a maker of war, or as a stake in war, because of politics. Subnational forces such as guerrillas, terrorists, or ethnic and religious warriors will, with increasing frequency in the next century, bring the territorial nation–state under siege. Failed and failing states will topple like dominoes into a basket of instability, buffeted by external environmental and economic forces that further weaken the walls of sovereignty.[7]

Another school of thought is equally pessimistic about the twenty-first-century capacity of the state to monopolize the use of force and to protect its economic and political borders. The second pessimistic school is based on assumptions about the impact of technology on politics. According to adherents of this version of the jeopardized state, the information revolution will make armed forces based on hierarchy and mass less important compared to forces built around "smart" sensors, weapons, and command/control and reconnaissance systems. Networks will defeat hierarchies.[8] Those who advocate this line of reasoning contend that the Gulf war of 1991 was the first information war in which the victor prevailed due to superiority in brainpower over its foe. Saddam Hussein's army was rendered into something resembling Falstaff's army as a result of U.S. and allied superiority in what is now called "C4ISR" (command, control, communications, computers and intelligence, surveillance and reconnaissance) systems, together with long-range precision strike and stealth weapons platforms.

Both schools of thought offer reasoned arguments for the apparent end of state dominance of the military art, but the implications of these arguments do not necessarily lead in consistent directions. The ethnic and religious warriors who dot the landscape from Somalia to Afghanistan challenge Western cultural ways of thinking about war. They threaten to drive war down into the bowels of the international order by fighting in such a manner that the difference between "civilian" and "military" is for practical purposes obliterated. Thus, warring Somali clans used women and children as hostages against U.S. and other peacekeepers in 1992 and 1993. In Sierra Leone and in Liberia in the 1990s, political anarchy caused continual flip-flopping of military formations for hire, equipped with whatever weapons could be had from the black market and loyal to the most charismatic or ambitious political aspirant of the day. In Bosnia from 1992 to 1995, ethnic cleansing and religiously based warfare finally reduced the status of UN peacekeepers to that of a rich menu of targets. NATO was required to step in, in support of the Dayton Peace Agreement, with an Implementation Force of some 60,000 troops in order to get the competing factions to disarm and canton their weapons. NATO was also authorized to deploy with explicitly intimidating rules of engagement: If we are shot at (by whomever), we will shoot back, and with devastating power. Therefore, anarchy in Bosnia was ended (temporarily, at least) only by the willingness of the largest *state* armies to engage and disarm the hostiles.

The reality of the information revolution cannot be denied, but its implications, like those of "low-intensity" or irregular warfare, are not at all obvious. Technology can equip state and nonstate actors' forces with more options: Information-*assisted* warfare is surely with us. But warfare based on entirely new military principles and fought by networks instead of hierarchies is not necessarily the dominant trend of the twenty-first century. This is so for several reasons. First, war, even information-based war, remains political and involves strong feelings of nationalism and culture. Cyberwar and netwar without political content cannot engage the support of the public, and in democracies, this factor may limit policymakers' and commanders' options. Second, those on the receiving end of U.S. or allied cyberwar may decide to respond with an asymmetrical strategy: For example, weapons of mass destruction (nuclear, biological, or chemical weapons) or the use of atrocities and other nonhumanitarian measures for leverage against the public psyche of the West. Third, the United States, as the most information-based economy and society, may for that very reason be the most vulnerable to infowar. Being rich in honey may attract honeybees.

It would be premature, therefore, to expect that high-technology warfare or anomic varieties of "grunt" war will make conventional warfare, as fought by professionally trained armies that are accountable to state governments, obsolete. The greater likelihood is that new varieties of conventional and unconventional, including cyber- and virtual wars, will mark the twenty-first-century competition for power and influence among international state and nonstate actors. In addition, there is an ironic symbiosis between the state, supposedly in decline, and the nonstate forces that are thought to be superseding it. The antistatists need the state as a reference point, much as Karl Marx needed the capitalists, Republications need Democrats, and Greeks at the time of Alexander needed Persians. The threat posed by the "other" is a necessary solidifier of the resolve that makes both state and nonstate actors endure beyond the ephemeral wisps of today's headlines. Even in a world whose technology and culture are becoming ever more "virtual," virtual armies cannot blow up buildings, destroy real tanks, or shed blood. Nor can the virtual forces show true virtue in combat. The human element in war, however circumscribed by smart technology and the simulacra of war, will remain decisive, not derivative.

NOTES

1. Richards J. Heuer, Jr., *Psychology of Intelligence Analysis* (Washington, D.C.: Center for the Study of Intelligence, Central Intelligence Agency, 1999), pp. 7–16, lucidly explains this problem and applies it to intelligence estimation. Heuer's work on strategic deception, especially with regard to perceptions management, is also pertinent; see his "Soviet Organization and Doctrine for Strategic Deception," ch. 2 in Brian D. Dailey and Patrick J. Parker, eds., *Soviet Strategic Deception* (Lexington, Mass.: D. C. Heath, 1987), pp. 21–53. Also relevant are studies of strategic military surprise; see, for example, Richard K. Betts, *Surprise Attack: Lessons for Defense Planning* (Washington, D.C.: Brookings Institution, 1982).

2. For an excellent example of retrospective and prospective policy analysis, see Gordon A. Craig and Alexander L. George, *Force and Statecraft: Diplomatic Problems of Our Time* (New York: Oxford University Press, 1983). An uncommon appreciation for the relationship between war and policy, and therefore between military strategy and policy analysis, appears in Colin S. Gray, *Modern Strategy* (Oxford: Oxford University Press, 1999), esp. pp. 55–67.

3. Much of the literature on crisis "management" applies mostly to our category of conflict prevention, although it overlaps as well with conflict management. See Ole R. Holsti, "Crisis Decision Making," in Philip E. Tetlock et al., eds., *Behavior, Society and Nuclear War* (New York: Oxford University Press, 1989), I: 8–84, and Alexander L. George, ed., *Avoiding War: Problems of Crisis Management* (Boulder, Colo.: Westview Press, 1991) for pertinent concepts and issues. Some discussions of deterrence hold insights pertinent to the problem of war prevention; see, for example, Robert Jervis, Richard Ned Lebow, and Janice Gross Stein, *Psychology and Deterrence* (Baltimore, Md.: Johns Hopkins University Press, 1985).

4. See Edward A. Kolodziej, "Thinking about Coping: Actors, Resources, Roles and Strategies," ch. 15 in Edward A. Kolodziej and Roger E. Kanet, eds., *Coping with Conflict after the Cold War* (Baltimore, Md.: Johns Hopkins University Press, 1996), pp. 363–394, and I. William Zartman, "Bargaining and Conflict Reduction," ch. 11 in ibid., pp. 271–290. Also pertinent to the management of conflict is some of the literature on coercive diplomacy and bargaining, especially in crisis. See, for example, Alexander L. George, "The Development of Doctrine and Strategy," in Alexander L. George, David K. Hall, and William E. Simons, *The Limits of Coercive Diplomacy* (Boston: Little, Brown, 1971), pp. 1–35.

5. On war termination, see Fred Charles Ikle, *Every War Must* End, rev. ed. (New York: Columbia University Press, 1991), esp. pp. 1–16 and 38–58. On bargaining for war termination, see Paul Pillar, *Negotiating Peace: War Termination as a Bargaining Process* (Princeton, N.J.: Princeton University Press, 1983); Paul Bracken, "Institutional Factors in War Termination," ch. 7 in Stephen J. Cimbala and Sidney R. Waldman, eds., *Controlling and Ending Conflict: Issues before and after the Cold War* (Westport, Conn.: Greenwood Press, 1992), pp. 183–196; and Stephen J. Cimbala, "The Political Aspects of War Termination," in ibid., pp. 1–40.

6. See among many possible pertinent sources: Thomas C. Schelling, *Arms and Influence* (New Haven, Conn.: Yale University Press, 1966), pp. 69–108; Alexander L. George, "Strategies for Crisis Management," ch. 16 in George, *Avoiding War: Problems of Crisis Management*, pp. 377–394; Eliot A. Cohen and John Gooch, *Military Misfortunes: The Anatomy of Failure in War* (New York: Vintage Books, 1991); Alexander L. George and William E. Simons, eds., *The Limits of Coercive Diplomacy*, 2nd ed. (Boulder, Colo.: Westview Press, 1994), esp. chs. 1 and 2; Stephen J. Cimbala, "Military Persuasion and the American Way of War," *Strategic Review*, no. 4 (Fall 1994), pp. 33–43; Cimbala, *Military Persuasion* (University Park, Pa.: Penn State Press, 1994); Richard Ned Lebow, *Nuclear Crisis Management: A Dangerous Illusion* (Ithaca, N.Y.: Cornell University Press, 1987); and Cimbala, *Coercive Military Strategy* (College Station: Texas A & M University Press, 1998).

7. For appraisals of this perspective, see Martin van Creveld, *The Transformation of War* (New York: Free Press, 1991), and Christopher Bellamy, *Knights in White Armour: The New Art of War and Peace* (London: Hutchinson, 1996).

8. Expert assessments of this perspective appear in John Arquilla and David Ronfeldt, eds., *In Athena's Camp: Preparing for Conflict in the Information Age* (Santa Monica, Calif.: RAND, 1997). See also John B. Alexander, *Future War: Non-Lethal Weapons in Twenty-first-Century Warfare* (New York: St. Martin's Press, 1999), and Steven Metz, *Armed Conflict in the 21st Century: The Information Revolution and Post-Modern Warfare* (Carlisle Barracks, Pa.: U.S. Army War College, Strategic Studies Institute, April 2000).

Part I

Past Cases

Chapter 1

Bargaining at the Brink:
Otherness and the Cuban
Missile Crisis

INTRODUCTION

The Cuban missile crisis of October 1962 has been the subject of numerous academic and policy studies. The basic narrative of events surrounding the crisis is by now well known to specialists and to lay readers. Interpretation of these events is another matter. Historians, policy analysts, and even former crisis participants have locked horns over the reasons for the Soviet decision to deploy offensive, nuclear-capable missiles in Cuba. The arguments will probably continue well beyond the end of the next millennium.

New perspective is needed on the Cuban missile crisis more than new facts. Some have seen the crisis as an inevitable military showdown that the United States "won" due to its larger numbers of nuclear warheads and delivery systems (missiles and bombers). Others have described the confrontation as a result of Cold War politics. In this view, each Cold War "superpower" constantly sought to manipulate political and military events to its advantage: The Cuban missile crisis resulted from Khrushchev's strategic miscalculation by going too far and risking too much. Additional explanations have been given based on the personalities of the two heads of state involved in the crisis: U.S. President John F. Kennedy and Soviet Premier Nikita S. Khrushchev.

The factors already mentioned certainly played a part in bringing about the Cuban missile crisis at the time that it occurred. But another aspect of the crisis deserves further study: How well did the two states and their political and military leaders understand one another's perspectives about ends, means, and military strategy in the years leading up to the crisis and during the critical 13 days of military confrontation in October 1962? What follows is an attempt to answer that question: of the validity of each side's image of the other, or sense of "otherness." Valid images held by states about one another's goals, means, and strategies lead to accurate predictions of their behavior; invalid images, to errors and disaster, including outbreaks of crisis and war.

PERSPECTIVE TAKING BEFORE AND AFTER CUBA

The U.S.–Soviet relationship throughout the Cold War years was marked by simplification on each side of the political objectives and military doctrine of the other. As only one example, U.S. policy analysts and government officials described Soviet military doctrine from the 1960s through the 1980s, including military doctrine for the use of strategic nuclear weapons, first-strike oriented and aimed at seeking victory through nuclear war. Deterrence, in the Soviet view as described by much of the U.S. defense community, rested on the ability to fight and win a nuclear war.[1] U.S. analysts who sought to make this case could draw from some statements made by party officials, military-technical literature including important publications in the *Officer's Library Series*, and some evidence of Soviet research and development on future generations of nuclear offensive and defensive weapons. Officials in the Carter and Reagan administrations were especially concerned with Soviet intercontinental ballistic missile (ICBM) capabilities for preemptive attack on U.S. missile silos and command centers and with Soviet ballistic missile defenses already deployed and in development.

Had the same information included a larger component of U.S. perspective taking of the Soviet strategic view, U.S. assessments might not have seemed so ominous. Soviet interest in nuclear offensive and defensive forces could have been interpreted as components of a strategy that emphasized the deterrence of war and the limitation of damage, should nuclear war occur. This interpretation might have been supported by the recognition that Soviet interest in first-strike strategies waned as their military planners became less dependent on preemption for survivability of their land-based forces. Then, too, the Soviet force configuration differed from the American: U.S. capabilities spread over three legs of the strategic "triad" placed most survivable U.S. striking power in submarines and bombers. Soviet retaliatory potential as well as first-strike capability resided in the timely launch of their ICBMs, carrying a disproportionate share of their hard-target warheads. The argument that Soviet ICBMs were targeted against U.S. ICBMs and therefore intended as first-strike weapons ignored the equally plausible inference that second-strike counterforce was considered by Soviet military planners, as by U.S. defense officials, as a requirement for credible deterrence.[2]

It was ironic that during the latter 1950s and early 1960s both the U.S. and Soviet governments were marked by fears of strategic insecurity, based on misperceptions of actual capabilities and of military intentions. Khrushchev's atomic diplomacy of the latter 1950s had sought to exploit U.S. fears that Soviet competency in nuclear rocket weapons greatly exceeded U.S. ability to develop and to deploy those weapons. Khrushchev used extravagant claims of Soviet nuclear superiority to buttress otherwise weak foreign policies and to fend off domestic and foreign critics of his detente policies and military budget cuts.[3] Addressing the Supreme Soviet in January 1960, Khrushchev asserted not for the first time his claim to strategic superiority, argued that world economic trends were moving in favor of socialism, and contended that nuclear war, although certainly devastating for both sides, would result in victory for socialism.[4]

By the fall of 1960, Khrushchev had begun to retreat from some of his more extravagant claims about Soviet nuclear superiority and about the ability of socialism to prevail in nuclear war with comparatively few casualties. His speeches more and more after the fall of 1960 emphasized that the consequences of nuclear war for both sides would be highly destructive. The same thematic focus on the mutually destructive effects of nuclear war appeared in an article in the Communist Party theoretical journal *Kommunist* by General Nikolai Talensky in July of 1960, and Talensky enlarged his presentation of the same themes in a later article in *Mezhdunarodnaya zhizn'* (*International Affairs*).[5] According to Talensky's later article, calculations showed that casualties in a world war would be approximately 500 to 600 million in the main theater of military action (presumably Europe), of an estimated total population of 800 million.[6] One reason for this retreat of Khrushchev and military leaders from previous assertions of nuclear superiority and war-winning capability was the Soviet view that Chinese leaders were far too cavalier about the consequences of nuclear war, challenging the Soviets for leadership of the world communist movement on the basis of ideological claims that disputed Soviet willingness to stand firm in confrontations with the West.

Another reason for a pulling back in Soviet nuclear assertiveness was a recognition by the Soviet leadership that the United States was much more aware by 1960, and thereafter, of the actual state of the strategic nuclear balance of power. Dwight Eisenhower's last State of the Union address provided an opportunity for the U.S. president to note that "the 'missile gap' shows every sign of being a fiction."[7] Almost immediately after the Kennedy administration took office, press reports appeared that claimed, on the basis of Pentagon studies, that there was actually no "missile gap."[8] Citing new U.S. intelligence estimates, press reports in September 1961 acknowledged that actual Soviet ICBM deployments in 1961 would fall far short of the maximum possible number projected in earlier U.S. estimates. Therefore, the new intelligence estimates, according to press reports, eliminated completely any notion of a missile gap unfavorable to the United States.[9]

Nor was this all. Beginning in October 1961, Kennedy administration officials launched an offensive in public diplomacy to dispel the existence of any missile gap favorable to the Soviet Union. Further, U.S. government officials publicly proclaimed that the United States had now (by autumn 1961) attained strategic nuclear superiority over the Soviet Union. The public relations offensive began with the speech by Deputy Secretary of Defense Roswell Gilpatric on October 21, 1961, and was followed by similar statements from other high Kennedy administration officials. Gilpatric noted that the United States, even after absorbing a Soviet surprise first strike, would probably retain second-strike forces that were greater than the forces used by the Soviet Union in its attack. "In short," according to Gilpatric, "we have a second-strike capability which is at least as extensive as what the Soviets can deliver by striking first."[10] The actual balance of forces at the time of the Cuban missile crisis (including forces becoming available at the very end of the crisis period, through October 28) appears in Table 1.1.

As Richard Ned Lebow and Janice Gross Stein have noted, the reaction of Khrushchev and his military advisers to this U.S. public diplomacy was understandably one of concern, even alarm.[11] U.S. intelligence had to have mapped correctly the locations of Soviet ICBMs (SS-6s) in order to determine with such precision that the nuclear strategic balance was so lopsidedly in the U.S. favor. Therefore, Soviet land-based missile forces might be vulnerable to a U.S. first strike. The meaning of U.S. nuclear superiority might be not only the existence of a U.S. relative advantage in nuclear striking power but also the U.S. ability to jeopardize the survival of the Soviet deterrent. The Soviets were quick to respond to the Gilpatric speech. Two days later, Soviet Defense Minister Malinovsky, addressing the Twenty-second Party Congress in Moscow, charged that Gilpatric, with the concurrence of President Kennedy, was "brandishing the might of the United States" and had "threatened us with force."[12] Malinovsky added that "this threat does not frighten us," but obviously it did.

Soviet leaders gave similar and negative appraisals to statements on the subject of nuclear weapons and nuclear war made by U.S. leaders, including President Kennedy, subsequent to the Gilpatric speech. A spring 1962 interview with President Kennedy published in the *Saturday Evening Post* was interpreted in the Soviet press as an attempt to intimidate the Soviet leadership by threatening a U.S. nuclear first strike under some conditions.[13] Taking note of the assertively optimistic trends in U.S. official statements on the nuclear balance of power in July 1962, Khrushchev described the new U.S. appraisals as meaningless. He argued that

Table 1.1
Strategic Nuclear Forces, U.S.–Soviet Balance: Cuban Missile Crisis

	Launchers	Warheads/Launcher	Total Warheads
U.S. ICBMs			
Minuteman 1A	10	1	10
Titan 1	54	1	54
Atlas F	24	1	24
Atlas D	24	1	24
Atlas E	27	1	27
ICBM Totals	139		139
U.S. SLBMs			
Polaris A2	64	1	64
Polaris A1	80	1	80
SLBM Totals	144		144
U.S. Bombers			
B-58	76	2	152
B-47 (y)	338	1	338
B-47 (x)	337	2	674
B-52 (y)	108	3	324
B-52 (x)	447	4	1,788
Bomber Totals	1,306		3,276
U.S. Totals	1,589		3,559
Soviet ICBMs			
SS-7	40	1	40
SS-6	4	1	4
IRBM	16	1	16
MRBM	24	1	24
ICBM Totals	84		84
Soviet SLBMs			
SSN5	6	1	6
SSN4	66	1	66
SLBM Totals	72		72
Soviet Bombers			
Bear-A	75	2	150
MYA-4	58	4	232
Bomber Totals	133		382
Soviet Totals	289		538

Notes: Totals include Soviet MRBMs and IRBMs scheduled for initial deployment in Cuba but not Soviet MRBMs or IRBMs deployed in the Soviet Union. Author's estimates from sources listed in notes.

(x) and (y) indicate different force loadings for B-47 and B-52 aircraft.

the real military balance of power could only be determined in the course of a war.[14] This was obvious backing and filling. The general trend in Soviet statements about the strategic balance from mid-1961 was one of the acknowledgment of, and the acceptance of, parity as the basis for political relations between the two powers.[15]

Khrushchev's rocket rattling of the immediate post-Sputnik period had set the stage for his own humiliation when the facts were revealed about the true nature of the nuclear strategic balance in 1961. Khrushchev's strategy of nuclear bluff was annoying to the United States and helped to provoke a U.S. response that appeared to the Soviet Union as one based on nuclear bullying. The result of Soviet nuclear bluffing followed by U.S. nuclear bullying was that both sides moved further from a shared understanding of the security dilemma created by their military competition—and especially by their strategic forces.

Perspective taking might have suggested to the Americans in 1962 that the Soviets were less concerned with the "bean count" of U.S. compared to Soviet nuclear weapons and more concerned with the broader correlation of social and political forces. The role of nuclear weapons and other forces in Soviet military strategy had been to support Soviet policy, including the spread of revolutionary Marxism-Leninism to states outside of the Soviet bloc (at least, until Gorbachev). This could hardly be accomplished by nuclear adventurism against an opponent with superior forces, as Khrushchev was reminded by the Politburo when it decided it no longer required his services. Soviet political strategy is not always compatible with the most risky or assertive military strategy, as their willingness to adhere to the SALT (Strategic Arms Limitation Talks) I and SALT II agreements, including the Anti-Ballistic Missile (ABM) Treaty, attested.

Soviet perspective taking of the American standpoint might have helped to avoid the misjudgment that the United States would accept the Soviet missile deployments in Cuba. Although we do not know as much as we would like to know about the Soviet interpretion of U.S. failure at the Bay of Pigs, it seems safe to infer that the episode could not have impressed them favorably with U.S. determination and sagacity. Khrushchev must have wondered why Kennedy had authorized the expedition and then failed to rescue the situation when the chips were down. This was a reasonable doubt of Kennedy's resolve on Khrushchev's part: Many Americans doubted it, too. Kennedy's reluctance to follow through in the Bay of Pigs might have seemed to Khrushchev as a characteristic propensity for hesitation in crises, instead of a singular uncertainty on the part of a new president facing an unexpected debacle. Khrushchev also seems to have erred in assuming that Kennedy perceived only a domestic policy problem with regard to possible Soviet missile deployments in Cuba. Soviet assurances to U.S. officials in September 1962 suggested that no offensive missiles or other objectionable weapons would be deployed in Cuba that might complicate matters for the U.S. president during an election campaign.

President Kennedy and his advisers, in turn, were insufficiently sensitive to the problem of how the Soviets might (wrongfully) interpret U.S. domestic policy debates. Kennedy's reassurances to members of Congress that there were no "offensive" Soviet weapons in Cuba and that he would not accept the deployment of offensive weapons in the future drew a fine and legalistic line between offense and defense. Soviet leaders might well have interpreted this distinction as a loophole that could be exploited to justify the deployment of nuclear weapons in Cuba. After all, whether weapons are defined as offensive or defensive is an issue of purpose as much as it is an issue of technology. If, from the Soviet perspective, the purpose of the missile deployments was to contribute to the deterrence of an attack on Cuba, or to the defense of Cuba if attacked, then the weapons could, from that perspective, be described as defensive.

Some U.S. students of the crisis have concluded that only the U.S. ultimatum and threat of an immediate air strike or invasion, conveyed to the Soviet government through Ambassador Anatoly Dobrynin on October 27 by Robert Kennedy, forced Khrushchev to agree to remove the missiles. An equally plausible argument could be made that the game was up for Khrushchev once the United States obtained unambiguous photographic evidence of the Soviet deployments. From then on, Khrushchev's agenda was to save as much political face as possible and to withdraw the missiles while precluding a U.S. attack on Cuba. Obviously, from the standpoint of sheer military power, there was little the Soviet Union could do to prevent the United States from using its *conventional*-force superiority to overthrow Castro. On the other hand, the United States was not eager to repeat the Bay of Pigs fiasco, so any U.S. invasion decision would have had to commit major forces against a significant Soviet and Cuban conventional defense. Khrushchev's missile deployments almost gave the United States a rationale for a difficult and costly military undertaking that Kennedy would have been hard put to justify without the symbolism of Soviet nuclear power deployed in the Caribbean. Khrushchev turned a potentially dissuasive conventional force against all but massive invasion into a lightning rod that would justify exactly that kind of U.S. attack on Cuba.

DETERRENCE AND THE CUBAN MISSILE CRISIS

The significance of deterrence in the Cuban missile crisis was related to the difference between *usable* and *useful* military power. Nuclear weapons were useful for making threats but not usable in combat at an acceptable cost. Nuclear deterrence entered into the picture only as a backdrop to the successful application of conventional deterrence and a willingness to engage in crisis bargaining based on the appearance of reciprocal concession. The credible threat to destroy Soviet offensive missile emplacements in Cuba by air strike and land invasion, and the corollary threat to remove the Castro regime from power, could be accomplished with conventional forces alone. The burden of geographical war widening or nuclear escalation would be Khrushchev's, not Kennedy's.

The favorable outcome for U.S. crisis management should not obscure the fact that nuclear and conventional deterrence failed prior to the crisis. On the basis of what he must have known about the military balance in nuclear and conventional forces, Khrushchev took an extreme risk in placing Soviet missiles in Cuba. The explanation that he did so in order to adjust an unfavorable strategic balance is consistent with U.S. deterrence theory to a point, but at other points, it is not.

A strategic nuclear balance of power tilted 17 to 1 in favor of the United States should have deterred Khrushchev from his Cuban initiative, according to *both* orthodox and heterodox schools of nuclear deterrence strategy. The orthodox school argues that mutual vulnerability and second-strike capability are necessary and sufficient conditions for the preservation of deterrence stability. The heterodox school contends that mutual second-strike capability is not enough for credible deterrence when push comes to shove. The United States, in this second model of credible deterrence, also requires for crisis management a significant relative advantage in nuclear striking power or, in what amounts to the same thing, in capability for damage limitation.[16]

Neither the orthodox nor the heterodox model of deterrence would allow for the kind of challenge Khrushchev made in the face of overwhelming U.S. conventional and nuclear superiority. According to orthodox logic, the United States in 1962 possessed a second-strike capability against the Soviet Union; the Soviet Union did not have a similar capability against the United States. And the heterodox requirements for deterrence were also fulfilled: The United States had significant advantages in nuclear striking power and in the ability to impose a relatively favorable war outcome (if not an absolutely acceptable one). Making reasonable assumptions about the performance parameters of Soviet and U.S. weapons, Table 1.2 shows the plausible outcome of any nuclear exchange in the last days of the Cuban missile crisis.

One can argue that Khrushchev was "irrational" according to the logic of U.S. deterrence theory, but the observation elides the central issue of whether deterrence logic has any explanatory power. Deterrence nomenclature is pervasive in the literature, but demonstrating the explanatory or predictive power of a deterrence model is something else. However,

Table 1.2
U.S. and Soviet Survivable and Deliverable Forces, October 1962

Summary	Numbers
Total Soviet deliverable warheads	41
Total Soviet deliverable EMT	109
Deliverable Soviet reserve warheads	26
Deliverable Soviet reserve EMT	33
% Deliverable Soviet reserve warheads	0.63
% Deliverable Soviet reserve EMT	0.31
Total U.S. deliverable warheads	659
Total U.S. deliverable EMT	655
Deliverable U.S. reserve warheads	591
Deliverable U.S. reserve EMT	587
% Deliverable U.S. reserve warheads	0.90
% Deliverable U.S. reserve EMT	0.90
Correlation of deliverable warheads	16.03
Correlation of deliverable EMT	6.02
Correlation of reserve warheads	6.00
Correlation of reserve EMT	17.50

Notes: This table compares U.S. survivors of a Soviet first strike and Soviet survivors of a
U.S. first strike. It is not therefore a classical "exchange model" but a statistical comparison derived from an exchange model. Information about the exact model used is
available from the author.
EMT = Equivalent megatonnage.

deterrence supported by the credible ability to prevail in battle at an
acceptable cost to the threatener is another matter. The United States was
in this position in Cuba, unless nuclear weapons were brought into the
picture by the Soviet Union in the Caribbean or elsewhere. The United
States had established conventional "escalation dominance" in that it
could remove the missiles forcibly if it chose without nuclear escalation
or geographical war widening. The burden of further escalation was
placed upon Khrushchev, but no step that Khrushchev could have taken,
subsequent to a U.S. invasion of Cuba, could have saved Soviet missile
sites from destruction or, in all likelihood, the Castro regime from military defeat.

Khrushchev attempted to implement his own model of "extended deterrence," but it was more of a political than a military model. The ties

between Cuba, as a standard bearer of socialist community buried within the U.S. sphere of influence, and its Soviet benefactor were not those of a military guarantee. Castro sought an explicit Soviet defense guarantee and wanted to go public with the news of Soviet missile deployments in Cuba, but the Soviet leadership demurred on both counts. Cuba was a prize worth keeping in the Soviet camp so long as the risks of doing so fell well short of actual military conflict with the United States. Khrushchev was not prepared to give Castro a blank check in the form of excessive leverage over Soviet decisions for war and peace in the Caribbean.

Evidence for this comes from Soviet behavior before and during the Cuban crisis, and some of the most interesting recent evidence appears in crisis correspondence between Khrushchev and Castro recently published in the December 2, 1990, issue of *Granma*. In a message to Khrushchev on October 26, 1962 (two days before the crisis was resolved), Castro tells Khrushchev that "aggression is almost imminent within the next 24 or 72 hours" in the form of a U.S. air attack or invasion.[17] Castro then conveys his "personal opinion" that if "the imperialists invade Cuba with the goal of occupying it, the danger that that aggressive policy poses for humanity is so great that following that event *the Soviet Union must never allow the circumstances in which the imperialists could launch the first nuclear strike against it*."[18] Castro added in this message that if the United States actually invaded Cuba, then "that would be the moment *to eliminate such danger forever* through an act of clear legitimate defense, however harsh and terrible the solution would be, for there is no other."[19]

Khrushchev's response to this request for a Soviet nuclear first strike on the United States following any U.S. invasion of Cuba (sent October 28, the day that the Soviet Union agreed to remove the missiles in return for a U.S.-noninvasion-of-Cuba pledge) was to urge Castro "not to be carried away by sentiment and to show firmness."[20] Khrushchev argued in response to Castro that the Soviet Union had settled the issue in Castro's favor by obtaining a noninvasion pledge from the United States and by preventing war from breaking out. Khrushchev also offered the argument that Pentagon "militarists" were now trying to frustrate the agreement that he and Kennedy had reached. This was why, according to Khrushchev's response to Castro, the "provocative flights" of U.S. reconnaissance planes continued. Khrushchev scolded Castro for shooting down a U.S. reconnaissance plane on October 27: "[Y]esterday you shot down one of these, while earlier you didn't shoot them down when they overflew your territory."[21] The Soviet leader implied that such trigger-happiness would play into the hands of those in U.S. government circles who wanted war: "[T]he aggressors will take advantage of such a step for their own purposes."[22]

The United States, despite its apparent military superiority at the nuclear and conventional levels, was as ready to terminate the crisis without war as the Soviet Union. The U.S. objective was not to sever completely the "extended deterrence" connection between the Soviet Union and Cuba. U.S. crisis management objectives did emphasize, nonetheless, two aspects of the U.S. view of the Soviet–Cuban connection. The first was that, from Washington's standpoint, the Cuban–Soviet relationship was perceived as one of client and patron, or dependency. This was emphasized in U.S. insistence upon dealing only with Khrushchev on the conditions for removing the Soviet missiles. Second, the United States and the Soviet Union resolved the crisis on terms that called for UN inspection and verification of the Soviet missile withdrawal. Fidel Castro objected on both counts. He disliked the willingness of Khrushchev to arrange for crisis termination without having consulted Cuba first. And Castro refused to cooperate in permitting UN or other on-site inspection of missile launcher dismantling and removal. The United States and the Soviet Union worked around this obstacle by arranging for the removal and shipment of the missiles in such a way that the process could be verified by U.S. aircraft surveillance and by other means. Castro objected to the terms on which the crisis was ended on the grounds that they implied a relationship between Havana and Moscow of a one-way dependency instead of a two-way exchange.

OTHER INTERPRETATIONS

There are counterarguments to my contention that the results of the Cuban missile crisis of 1962 can be viewed as an escape from inadvertent mutual disaster and, at the same time, as an instance of successful, but risky, coercive military strategy. I assume that Khrushchev's Cuba gambit was not based on the actual desire for a military showdown with the United States but on the reasoning that the United States would choose political demarches instead of military threats to get the missiles out. My argument pushes the U.S.–Soviet nuclear deterrence relationship into the crisis background and ignores the possibility that calculations about nuclear victory or defeat would have mattered to policymakers. The strongest argument in favor of the importance of extended nuclear deterrence in the Cuban missile crisis was the possibility of a trade of U.S. Jupiter missiles in Turkey for Soviet medium-range ballistic missiles (MRBMs) in Cuba.

U.S. Jupiter intermediate-range ballistic missiles (IRBMs) were deployed in Turkey and Italy during the Eisenhower administration. The decisions for U.S. IRBM deployment in Europe were taken in the aftermath of the Suez crisis of 1956, which shook allied NATO confidence in American guarantees of European security, and in the context of post-

Sputnik American concerns about the viability of the U.S. nuclear deterrent.[23] Some arguments used by U.S. proponents of the Thor (in Great Britain) and Jupiter IRBMs were not too dissimilar from those used by the Soviets on behalf of MRBM deployments (and planned IRBM deployments) to Cuba in 1962. U.S. leaders feared after the initial test launches of Soviet ICBMs in 1957 that they needed an interim fix for a perceived status of missile inferiority (although not overall force inferiority, given the size of U.S. bomber forces in the latter 1950s). The Jupiter missiles deployed in Turkey were liquid fueled and used "soft" (aboveground) launchers, which made them vulnerable to first strikes or prompt retaliatory launches.

U.S. leaders saw the Jupiter missile deployments as a concession to the requirements for NATO alliance unity. The host European nation would "own" the missiles and launchers, but the United States would maintain control over warhead dispersal and launch decisions (presumably in consultation with the host state). For the Turkish government, this meant that they had accepted a share of the U.S. nuclear deterrent despite the obvious provocation this would provide for Moscow. The strategic rationale for the Thor and Jupiter deployments was vitiated by technology that made possible sea-based missile deployments and ICBMs based in North America that could cover the same target base in the Soviet Union or in Eastern Europe. The Kennedy administration recognized that the Jupiters in Turkey constituted a technological dinosaur and a potential political provocation. The president had decided in principle to order the removal of the Jupiter missiles from Turkey prior to the development of the 1962 Cuban crisis, but he had not pressed the issue assertively after initial approaches to Turkey were rebuffed by that government.

The Cuban missile crisis thus caught the Kennedy administration with obsolete nuclear missiles deployed in a forward, exposed position, obviously vulnerable to Soviet *conventional* as well as nuclear attacks. Moreover, Soviet attacks against U.S. missiles in Turkey, in response to any U.S. attack on Cuba, could draw the entire NATO alliance into a war with Moscow. Kennedy and Robert McNamara, during deliberations of the ExComm, recognized the political irony that obsolete missiles deployed in Turkey were now potential hostages to Soviet horizontal and vertical escalation. In addition, McNamara was especially conscious of the danger of escalation once a U.S. NATO ally was attacked in the aftermath of fighting in Cuba.

McGeorge Bundy, special assistant to the president (Kennedy) for national security, and James G. Blight transcribed and edited tapes of the October 27, 1962, meetings of the ExComm, and portions of this material appeared in the winter 1987–1988 issue of the journal *International Security*.[24] In these transcripts, President Kennedy continually returns to the theme that the Jupiter missiles offered Khrushchev an attractive way out of his predicament that Kennedy might not be able to refuse. Khrushchev's "second" letter of October 27 toughened the terms suggested in his "first" letter of October 26, wherein he agreed to remove Soviet offensive missiles from Cuba in return for a U.S. noninvasion pledge. The October 27 letter (which may have been composed and sent first for reasons still not fully known) insisted upon a trade of U.S. Jupiter missiles in Turkey for Soviet missiles in Cuba. Kennedy was bothered by the apparent symmetry of the trade, in the eyes of world, allied NATO, and U.S. opinion.

The president's principal advisers, on the other hand, emphasized the potential damage to NATO solidarity, to U.S.–Turkish relations, and to future credibility of extended deterrence in Europe if the United States made an obvious missile trade under the pressure of the Cuban crisis. As the president kept returning to the apparent plausibility of a missile trade, his advisers sharpened their cautionary notes about the impact on NATO and future deterrence. One example is cited below, during Ex-Comm discussions on how to respond to Khrushchev's two apparently contradictory letters:

Kennedy: How much negotiation have we had with the Turks?

Dean Rusk, Secretary of State: We haven't talked with the Turks. The Turks have talked with us—the Turks have talked with us in-uh-NATO.

Kennedy: Well, have we gone to the Turkish government before this came out this week? I've talked about it now for a week. Have we had any conversation in Turkey, with the Turks?

Rusk: . . . We've not actually talked to the Turks.

George W. Ball, Undersecretary of State: We did it on a basis where if we talked to the Turks, I mean this would be an extremely unsettling business.

Kennedy: Well, *this* is unsettling *now*, George, because he's got us in a pretty good spot here, because most people will regard this not as an unreasonable proposal, I'll just tell you that. In fact, in many ways—

Bundy: But *what* most people, Mr. President?

Kennedy: I think you're going to find it very difficult to explain why we are going to take hostile military action in Cuba, against these sites—what we've been thinking about—the thing that he's saying is, "If you'll get yours out of Turkey, we'll get ours out of Cuba." I think we've got a very tough one here.[25]

Kennedy's advisers continue to express hostility to the idea of a missile trade throughout the remainder of this discussion. Rusk comments, "The Cuba thing is a Western Hemisphere problem, an intrusion into the Western Hemisphere." Kennedy adviser Paul Nitze argues that the president should try to get the missiles out of Cuba "pursuant to the private negotiation" (the terms of the first Khrushchev letter). Bundy cautions that a missile trade, if accepted at this stage of the crisis, means that "our position would come apart very fast." Ball notes that if we talked to the Turks about an immediate missile deal, they would take it up with NATO and "our position would have been undermined." He adds that the United States "persuaded them [the Turks] that this *was* an essential requirement," and now Turkey feels that a matter of prestige is involved. Bundy argues that a missile trade would create the impression of trying to sell out U.S. allies for American interests, adding that "that would be the view in all of NATO."[26]

Despite this consensus of his advisers against the concept of a missile trade, Kennedy held open until the very end of the crisis the option of a missile trade. He approved a back-channel initiative from Dean Rusk to the UN Secretary General that would have resulted in a "UN" proposal for a missile trade as the basis for resolving the crisis. The Rusk initiative was developed as an option; the president had not made up his mind at the time whether he would accept a missile trade if Khrushchev refused to deal on the basis of the latter's first letter.[27]

The second counterargument to my assertion that nuclear deterrence remained secondary to conventional deterrence in the Cuban missile crisis is the importance of the perceived role of escalation in bringing the crisis to a conclusion. Pressure to end the crisis in a timely manner came not only from the possibility of a limited war in the Caribbean but also from the possible expansion of the fighting into general U.S.–Soviet conflict. Absent nuclear weapons, the crisis may have been much more prolonged and the terms on which it was resolved more ambiguous.

The counterargument that nuclear deterrence, in addition to conventional deterrence, made a difference in the Cuban missile crisis assumes a connection between nuclear *weapons* and nuclear *deterrence* that is not necessarily proved. Whereas conventional deterrence may have operated asymmetrically to support crisis management in favor of U.S. policy objectives, the impact of nuclear weapons on decision making may have been symmetrical. The Soviet and U.S. leaderships might equally have feared loss of control more than either feared a deliberate first strike by the opponent. Notice that this is different from conventional deterrence, in which leaders' hopes and fears are almost directly correlated with expected battlefield outcomes. Leaders planning a conventional war may still guess incorrectly, with disastrous results. Nevertheless, expected battlefield outcomes in conventional war can be projected with more reliability than they can for nuclear war scenarios, however subject to error the former are necessarily going to be. The disconnection between nuclear deterrence and military victory makes the effort to control crisis a military as much as a political objective.

Evidence for this counter-counterargument would be fears on the part of a side with a great deal of nuclear "superiority" in numbers of second-strike weapons that despite this superiority, loss of control could result in nuclear war with unacceptable outcomes for the superior power. Members of the U.S. ExComm decision-making group, including the president and his leading cabinet officers, do show this perceptual inclination to fear loss of control leading to nuclear escalation despite apparent U.S. strategic nuclear superiority. Secretary of Defense Robert McNamara, estimating the U.S. numerical advantage in strategic nuclear weapons at 17 to 1 in October 1962, nevertheless doubted that this relatively advantageous position was meaningfully related to the attainment of U.S. crisis management objectives without war. In his interview with James G. Blight in May 1987, McNamara explained his reasoning in terms that indicate the irrelevance of relative advantage for a cost-benefit calculus in which unknown risks of absolute destruction are involved:

Look, in my judgment, in fundamental terms, the so-called strategic balance hasn't shifted since 1962. The significant question isn't: How many weapons did we have then and now, relative to the Soviets? The question you should ask is: What did each side have in its arsenal then and now that was, or is, militarily useful? Let me put it another way: What is the likelihood then and now that either side might initiate the use of nuclear weapons and come away with a net gain? The answer to both questions is: Zero! Then and now, for both the U.S. and the Soviet Union, there are no militarily useful nuclear weapons in their arsenals and thus there is no advantage in using them.[28]

Others on the ExComm did not agree with McNamara's pessimism about the irrelevancy of the nuclear balance of power. C. Douglas Dillon, secretary of the treasury under Presidents Kennedy and Lyndon Johnson and a member of the ExComm, shared the view of Paul Nitze and other "hawks" that U.S. nuclear superiority was decisive in forcing Khrushchev to back down. Dillon recalled in 1987 that as the crisis wore on, he became progressively less worried, in contrast to other ExComm participants who became more nervous about possible war and nuclear escalation. Dillon noted that in the Treasury Department he had not been fully current for the last several years on the details of U.S. force structure. He added:

I was not, when I first heard about it, fully aware of the extent of the nuclear superiority that we had. And, when I became aware of that, then I changed my view entirely and, of course, I agree totally with Nitze and think the McNamara thesis that our nuclear superiority made little or no difference is dead wrong. Our nuclear preponderance was essential. That's what made the Russians back off, plus the fact of our total conventional superiority in the region.[29]

Dillon engages in transference here regarding the logics of nuclear deterrence and conventional dissuasion, and as the interview continues, he
advances two supporting points to explain why others, including Mc-
Namara, discounted U.S. nuclear superiority. First, the more experienced
policymakers on the ExComm were hawkish, according to Dillon, because they had been through crisis management and decision-making
situations before. As he explained, "I think simple inexperience led to
an inordinate fear of nuclear damage, the fear of what might happen.
McNamara, in particular, felt that way, I guess, although I wasn't so
conscious at the time that that was his reason."

One reason for the greater concern on the part of McNamara and other
ExComm "doves" about the risks of escalation was undoubtedly the
higher sensitivity of the Defense and State Departments to the implications for Europe and NATO of a failure in crisis containment. McNamara
illustrates this sensitivity to the European implications of risk assessment
when he pushes his ExComm colleagues on October 27 to consider the
aftermath of a U.S. air strike and invasion of Cuba. McNamara persists
in raising the troubling issue of what U.S. responses will be if the Soviets
strike at Jupiter missile bases in Turkey.[30] Most other ExComm members
do not see the point, so McNamara drives home the danger of nuclear
escalation by sketching a plausible scenario. The "minimum" military
response by NATO to a Soviet attack on the Jupiter missiles in Turkey,
according to McNamara, would involve conventional war fighting in and
near Turkey, including strikes by Turkish and U.S. aircraft against Soviet
warships and/or naval bases in the Black Sea area. McNamara emphasizes that such exchanges would be "damned dangerous," and the implication of imminent escalation to nuclear war fighting is obvious.[31] He
then argues that the United States should defuse the Turkish missiles
before any invasion of Cuba (presumably making this public) so that the
Turkish missiles are removed from their hostage status.

In making this argument about the risks of escalation in an alliance
context, McNamara is not necessarily breaking faith with his earlier emphasis on the priority of shared nuclear risk and the irrelevance of putative nuclear superiority. But the acknowledgment of the hostage status
of the Jupiters in Turkey and their potentially catalytic role in crisis or
wartime escalation is an acknowledgment of the mistake made in deploying those missiles. They were deployed, among other reasons, in
order to create deterrrence "coupling" between theater forces and strategic nuclear forces. The assumption was that coupling would make extended deterrence more credible than it would otherwise be by adding
additional levels of U.S. force deployments in Europe between conventional and all-out nuclear war. The same assumption helped to drive U.S.
and allied NATO rationales for the decision taken in 1979 to deploy
Pershing II and ground-launched cruise missiles (GLCMs) in Western

Europe (begun in 1983 and disbanded as a result of the Intermediate-Range Nuclear Forces [INF] Treaty of December 1987).

As the Jupiter missiles in Turkey in 1962 became nuclear crisis management hostages and potential catalysts of escalation, so, too, did the NATO "572" deployments become hostages that slowed the momentum of arms control and detente in Europe during the 1970s. The reason for the irrelevance of Jupiters in 1962, as for the Pershing II and GLCMs in the 1980s, had little to do with their technical characteristics (such as the Jupiters' vulnerability and long launch preparation or the Pershings' range). The political issue is that because nuclear dissuasion cannot be substituted for nuclear deterrence, "intermediate" nuclear weapons do not necessarily support the successful management of crisis and the control of escalation.

Instead, such weapons deployments can contribute to the deterioration of crisis and to the loss of control over escalation. They can do this, as the Jupiters did, by commingling horizontal escalation, or geographical war widening, with vertical escalation, the expansion of conventional into nuclear war fighting. Khrushchev's attack on Jupiter missiles in Turkey would have been a "nuclear" war even if he had only used conventional weapons: Nuclear weapons would be destroyed in the attack and perhaps fired back at the Soviet Union if its conventional first strike were unsuccessful. (The same potential problem faced U.S. air strike planners once Soviet MRBMs in Cuba were thought to be operational.) This "vertical" expansion of the fighting could have been compounded in 1962 by "horizontal" extension of combat to Berlin or Turkey.

Against my arguments here, it might be contended that the issue of intermediate nuclear weapons deployed in Europe was actually irrelevant to the resolution of the Cuban missile crisis. One could take the strict position that the missiles in Turkey were not a clandestine U.S. deployment but a publicly acknowledged agreement under NATO auspices. The Turkish missiles were a red herring introduced into the Cuban missile crisis by Khrushchev, in search of a face-saving exit.

I concede that this argument has some validity, but it misses the distinction between precision of policy objective (getting the missiles out of Cuba without introducing irrelevant issues) and the potential for U.S. nuclear weapons deployed abroad to contribute to inadvertent escalation. Kennedy was right to keep the policy focus on the removal of Soviet missiles from Cuba without a *publicly acknowledged* linkage to subsequent removal of Jupiter missiles from Turkey.[32] On the other hand, transcripts of ExComm deliberations and other evidence suggest that Kennedy also recognized the complications created for his management of the missile crisis by the presence of vulnerable, nuclear-capable missiles deployed so close to Soviet borders. Ironically, the Turkish missiles also served as part of Khrushchev's justification for deploying Soviet MRBMs and

IRBMs to Cuba: He would pose to the Americans a threat similar in scope and in geographical proximity to that presented by U.S. IRBMs in Turkey and in other European countries.[33]

The irrelevance of Turkish missiles can be asserted only on the assumption that what mattered in the resolution of the Cuban missile crisis, and perhaps in the instigation of it also, was the strategic nuclear balance of power. Although some members of the ExComm do assert that this balance was of primary importance, other key policymakers, including the U.S. president and the secretary of defense, did not assume so direct a connection between nuclear superiority and crisis management prevalence. Resolution of the Cuban missile crisis in 1962 may suggest that nuclear deterrence is loosely coupled to crisis management even in a two-sided U.S.–Soviet confrontation and perhaps even less relevant in a multisided crisis among nuclear armed states with less experience in conflict resolution and intracrisis communication.[34]

CONCLUSION

For several years prior to the Cuban missile crisis, U.S. and Soviet images of one another's politicomilitary objectives and strategic preferences were wide of the mark. Each side saw the other as determined to acquire military superiority, including nuclear superiority, for the purpose of political intimidation: nuclear coercive diplomacy. Khrushchev saw his Cuban missile deployments as a defensive measure to redress an unfavorable global balance of strategic nuclear power and to deter a planned U.S. invasion of Cuba. Kennedy saw Khrushchev's missile gambit as an attempt to humiliate the U.S. president in his own backyard and in the face of repeated warnings from U.S. officials that offensive missile deployments in Cuba would not be tolerated.

The Soviet leadership's rocket-rattling diplomacy in the latter 1950s convinced the United States that America had to run fast in order to catch up with a Soviet military headstart in the missile race. The United States overlearned this lesson when the Kennedy administration, having campaigned against Eisenhower's alleged tolerance for a "missile gap" favoring the Soviets, opened the spigot on military spending for strategic nuclear forces. The Kennedy administration then discovered that the alleged missile gap was actually very much in U.S. favor and, having done so, publicly rubbed Soviet nuclear inferiority in the faces of the Kremlin leadership. Khrushchev, in turn, saw missiles sent to Cuba as a proportional response to U.S. deployments via NATO of medium-range ballistic missiles in Europe and aimed at Russia. The Soviet leader convinced himself that, the Soviet missile deployments having been completed, the United States would have to accept them after the fact as irreversible, although regrettable. The United States failed to signal its unambiguous objections to the use of Cuba as a veritable nuclear aircraft carrier by Moscow until the deployments had already begun and the cat had been set among the pigeons.

NOTES

1. The various editions of the Pentagon's *Soviet Military Power* during the Reagan years provide ample evidence for my point here. For an overview of this issue, see Robert L. Arnett, "Soviet Attitudes towards Nuclear War: Do They Really Think They Can Win?" *Journal of Strategic Studies*, no. 2 (September 1979), pp. 172–191.

2. For evidence, see President's Commission on Strategic Forces (Scowcroft Commission), *Report* (Washington, D.C.: The White House, April 1983).

3. John Lewis Gaddis, *We Now Know: Rethinking Cold War History* (Oxford: Clarendon Press, 1997), esp. pp. 222–223 and 235–236 on Khrushchev's strategy for exploiting fictive nuclear superiority.

4. *Pravda*, January 15, 1961.

5. Talensky, in *Kommunist*, said that it was necessary to "emphasize that a future war, if the aggressors succeeded in unleashing it, will lead to such an increase in human losses on both sides that its consequences for mankind might be catastrophic." In his *International Affairs* article, Talensky drew an explicit comparison between the destruction of Soviet cities at the hands of Nazi Germany and the destruction attendant to nuclear rocket war, arguing that the degree of destruction in nuclear war would be "magnified a thousand times" compared to World War II and extended over whole continents. Talensky, *Kommunist*, no. 7 (1960), pp. 31–41, and Talensky, *Mezhdunarodnaya zhizn'*, no. 10 (1960), p. 33, both cited in Arnold L. Horelick and Myron Rush, *Strategic Power and Soviet Foreign Policy* (Chicago: University of Chicago Press, 1966), pp. 78–79.

6. Horelick and Rush, *Strategic Power and Soviet Foreign Policy*, pp. 78–79.

7. Ibid., p. 80.

8. Ibid.

9. Ibid., p. 83.

10. Gilpatric, quoted in ibid., p. 84.

11. Richard Ned Lebow and Janice Gross Stein, *We All Lost the Cold War* (Princeton, N.J.: Princeton University Press, 1994), ch. 2.

12. Horelick and Rush, *Strategic Power and Soviet Foreign Policy*, p. 85.

13. Ibid., pp. 86–87. Kennedy had actually said that he would not rule out the possibility of a U.S. first strike under some conditions, which was consistent with previous U.S. policy guidance for nuclear weapons employment in the Eisenhower administration.

14. Khrushchev, quoted in *Pravda*, July 11, 1962, cited in Horelick and Rush, *Strategic Power and Soviet Foreign Policy*, p. 87.

15. Horelick and Rush, *Strategic Power and Soviet Foreign Policy*, p. 87.

16. I have admittedly collapsed a wide spectrum of opinion into two boxes here. For more complete discussion, see Robert Jervis, *The Meaning of the Nuclear Revolution* (Ithaca, N.Y.: Cornell University Press, 1989); Colin S. Gray, *Nuclear Strategy and National Style* (Lanham, Md.: Hamilton Press, 1986); and David W.

Tarr, *Nuclear Deterrence and International Security: Alternative Nuclear Regimes* (White Plains, N.Y.: Longman Publishing Group, 1991).

17. Letter from Castro to Khrushchev, October 26, 1962, *Granma*, December 2, 1990, p. 3. I am grateful to Ned Lebow for first calling this to my attention.

18. Ibid. Italics supplied.

19. Ibid. Italics supplied.

20. Letter from Khrushchev to Castro, October 28, 1962, *Granma*, December 2, 1990, p. 3.

21. Ibid.

22. Ibid.

23. David N. Schwartz, *NATO's Nuclear Dilemmas* (Washington, D.C.: Brookings Institution, 1983), ch. 4, esp. pp. 62–66 and 73–74. The Gaither Report had also advocated overseas U.S. IRBM deployments even before Sputnik (ibid., p. 65). U.S. Jupiter missiles were formally handed over to the Turks on October 22, the day of President Kennedy's televised address announcing the U.S. discovery of the Soviet missiles in Cuba and the decision to impose the quarantine in response. See James G. Blight and David A. Welch, *On the Brink: Americans and Soviets Reexamine the Cuban Missile Crisis* (New York: Hill and Wang, 1989), p. 172.

24. McGeorge Bundy, transcriber, and James G. Blight, editor, "October 27, 1962: Transcripts of the Meetings of the ExComm," *International Security*, no. 3 (Winter 1987–1988), pp. 30–92.

25. Ibid., pp. 36–37.

26. Ibid., pp. 38–39.

27. Blight and Welch, *On the Brink*, pp. 170–171, 173.

28. McNamara, quoted in Blight and Welch, *On the Brink*, p. 187.

29. Ibid., p. 153.

30. Bundy and Blight, "October 27, 1962," pp. 72 ff.

31. Ibid., p. 75.

32. Numerous arguments to this effect by members of the ExComm appear in Bundy and Blight, "October 27, 1962," passim.

33. In his memoirs, Khrushchev noted, "In addition to protecting Cuba, our missiles would have equalized what the West likes to call 'the balance of power.' The Americans had surrounded our country with military bases and threatened us with nuclear weapons, and now they would learn just what it feels like to have enemy missiles pointing at you; we'd be doing nothing more than giving them a little of their own medicine." Strobe Talbott, ed. and trans., *Khrushchev Remembers* (Boston: Little, Brown, 1970), p. 494. A summary of ExComm deliberations on Khrushchev's possible motives for the deployment appears in Roger Hilsman, *The Cuban Missile Crisis: The Struggle over Policy* (Westport, Conn.: Praeger Publishers, 1996), pp. 79–81.

34. It will be important for U.S. and Soviet scholars to work together in order to establish more confidence in such arguments, admittedly tentative. Some Soviet scholars are now applying modeling and simulation techniques to the analysis of the Cuban missile crisis. See, for example, V. P. Akimov, V. B. Lukov, P. B. Parshin, and V. M. Sergeyev, "Karibskiy krizis: Opyt modelirovaniya" (The Caribbean crisis: Experience of modeling), *SShA: politika, ekonomika, ideologiya*, no. 5 (1989), pp. 36–49.

Chapter 2

Wilderness of Mirrors:
The 1983 "War Scare" and
U.S.–Soviet Relations

INTRODUCTION

The Cuban missile crisis was arguably the most dangerous single moment of the Cold War years. But 1962 may not have been the most dangerous year in the 45-year span from 1946 through 1991. Some evidence suggests that a series of apparently unrelated events from 1979 through 1983 may have culminated in a "war scare" that brought U.S. and Soviet political relations near to the point of violent conflict.

This study reviews some of the available evidence in support of the "war scare" thesis. In order to evaluate the war scare arguments, it is necessary but insufficient to consider the historical or anecdotal evidence. One must also ask: What difference would it have made, given the mutual deterrence that existed between the two nuclear superpowers for the decades of the Cold War? Accordingly, we also consider quantitative evidence on nuclear force structure and operations pertinent to the political atmosphere between Washington and Moscow in 1983. Together the anecdotal and quantitative evidence shed light on why a crisis might have turned to war in 1983 despite the apparent irrationality of any such conflict by any policy standard.

OPERATION RYAN

In May 1981 Soviet KGB chairman and future Communist Party chairman Yuri Andropov addressed a KGB conference in Moscow. He told his startled listeners that the new American administration of President Ronald Reagan was actively preparing for nuclear war. The possibility of a nuclear first strike by the United States was a real one. Andropov announced that, for the first time ever, the KGB and the GRU (Chief Intelligence Directorate of the Soviet General Staff) were ordered to work together in a global intelligence operation named Raketno Yadernoye Napadeniye (RYAN)—Nuclear Missile Attack.[1] During the next three years or so, the Soviet intelligence services were tasked to collect a variety of indicators, including political, military, and economic information, suggestive of any U.S. and NATO intent to launch a nuclear first strike. RYAN was, according to some sources, the largest intelligence operation conducted in time of peace in Soviet history.[2] The collection of indicators continued well into 1984 and was contributory to partial Soviet leadership paranoia that outran even the normal suspicions of intelligence professionals in Moscow Center.

In an attachment to a Center directive to KGB residents in NATO capitals in February 1983, it was stated that the threat of an immediate nuclear attack has acquired "an especial degree of urgency."[3] The KGB were tasked to detect and assess signs of preparation for RYAN in political, military, economic, and other sectors. The attachment noted that the United States maintained a large portion of its strategic retaliatory forces in a state of operational readiness. Soviet intelligence estimated that all American ICBMs, 70 percent of U.S. "naval nuclear facilities," and 30 percent of the American strategic bomber force were alerted and capable of rapid response. Thus, according to the instructions in the attachment, it was imperative to detect U.S. or NATO decisions or preparations for war as far ahead of D-day as possible. The authors go into considerable detail summarizing U.S. and NATO systems for military alert, including the aspects related to nuclear weapons.[4] Information about the U.S. Single Integrated Operational Plan (SIOP) for nuclear war, and about NATO's general defense and nuclear support plans, was specifically emphasized in the tasking from Center to the various residencies. Uncovering of the process leading to a decision for war by the United States and its NATO allies, and of the related measures by those countries to prepare for war, was imperative: It would enable Soviet leaders "to increase the so-called period of anticipation essential for the Soviet Union to take retaliatory measures."[5]

What had brought the Soviet Union to this brink of pessimism and near fatalism about U.S. intentions and, in the case of Andropov, nearly apocalyptic doomsaying? A series of events treated in isolation by political actors at the time apparently combined, in unexpected and potentially dysfunctional ways, to produce a mentality among some members of the Soviet high command that shifted policy expectations in Moscow tectonically from 1979 through 1984. If so, the sequence of events and their impact on Soviet decision makers fulfill the law of unanticipated consequences that often appears in social and political decision making.

This "law" is well known to social scientists and everyday practitioners of the arts of politics. It says that some of the effects of any decision or action will be unexpected and unpredicted and that some of these unexpected and unpredicted effects may be contrary to the policy intent of the original decision makers. This problem of unanticipated consequences certainly applies to the possibility of a U.S.–Soviet crisis slide in 1983, since the last thing that either intended was an actual outbreak of war.

THE INF DECISION

In December 1979, NATO took a decision to modernize its intermediate-range nuclear forces (INF) by deploying 572 new cruise and ballistic missiles in five European countries, beginning in November 1983. This "dual-track" decision also called for negotiations with the Soviet Union with the objective of limiting or eliminating its SS-20 intermediate-range mobile ballistic missiles, first deployed in 1977. The Soviets were strongly opposed to the NATO INF modernization: The connection between the Soviets' SS-20 deployments and NATO's theater nuclear force modernization was one of challenge and response from NATO's perspective, but not in the Soviet view.[6] Moscow mounted an aggressive active measures campaign through a variety of European peace movements and in other ways in order to stop the scheduled NATO deployments. The Soviet campaign failed to divide the Western alliance or to dissuade it from beginning its deployments on the original timetable. U.S. GLCMs first arrived in England in mid-November, and on November 23, Pershing II intermediate-range ballistic missiles were first deployed in West Germany.[7]

The Soviet military establishment was most concerned about the Pershings. Pershing IIs deployed in West Germany could be launched across trajectories that Soviet early-warning installations were poorly equipped to detect in good time. In addition, a Soviet intelligence appreciation in February 1983 estimated that the Pershings could strike at long-range targets in the Soviet Union within 4 to 6 minutes. This compared very unfavorably with the 20 minutes or so that Moscow assumed it would have to detect and react to missiles fired from the continental United States.[8] The Pershings reestablished for NATO a credible threat of escalation dominance below the threshold of general (global) nuclear war. Moscow could not initiate the use of theater nuclear weapons in Europe with any confidence that it could establish local or regional military superiority while American and Soviet strategic nuclear forces remained uninvolved and their respective homelands spared.

NATO and Soviet assessments of one another were complicated by the dual-purpose character of each side's modernized theater missiles. The missiles served to enhance deterrence, but they would also increase nuclear war fighting capabilities if deterrence failed. The missile deployments were a competition in political intimidation as much as they were an enhancement of deployed and usable military power. The competition in political intimidation was also an issue of alliance unity and management for the United States. NATO's steadfastness or weakening in the face of Soviet threats and blandishments would signal diminished U.S. influence within the Western alliance and a collapse of alliance unity on nuclear force modernization. Moscow's defeat, once NATO INF deployments began, was an affirmation of NATO solidarity and renewed U.S. leadership competency in alliance nuclear affairs. These political effects meant more to beleaguered Soviet military planners and political leaders than NATO's commitment to deploy additional firepower in Europe.

STAR WARS

On March 23, 1983, President Ronald Reagan surprised many of his own advisers as well as American listeners with his proposal for the Strategic Defense Initiative (SDI), rapidly dubbed "Star Wars" by media pundits and critics. Reagan also surprised allied NATO and Soviet audiences. The president shared with the U.S. public his vision of a peace shield that would protect the U.S. homeland from nuclear attack, even a large-scale attack of the kind that the Soviets could mount in the early 1980s. The reaction in Moscow was predictably negative but unpredictably hysterical.

The Soviet leadership might have denounced the U.S. initiative as a potential abrogation of the ABM Treaty and a complication of the U.S.–Soviet relationship of mutual deterrence, while at the same time pointing out that no feasible near-term technology could accomplish what the president demanded. Instead, the Kremlin reacted with public diplomacy filled with venomous denunciations of the Reagan administration and privately concluded that SDI was part of a U.S. plan to develop an effective nuclear war fighting strategy. Even if SDI were not a feasible technology within the present century, making sure that the United States could not deploy enough missile defense to neutralize Moscow's deterrent might cost a strapped Soviet economy more than it could bear. As Robert M. Gates has noted:

SDI was a Soviet nightmare come to life. America's industrial base, coupled with American technology, wealth, and managerial skill, all mobilized to build a wholly new and different military capability that might negate the Soviet offensive buildup of a quarter century. A radical new departure by the United States that would require an expensive Soviet response at a time of deep economic crisis.[9]

SDI therefore presented to the Soviet leadership a two-sided threat of military obsolescence and of economic stress. As in the case of INF, a Soviet propaganda campaign against SDI (in part by drawing upon well-informed U.S. critics who pointed to the gap between aspirations and available technology) failed to deter the Reagan administration from persisting in its research and development program on missile defense. This attempted great leap forward in defensive technology, combined with a U.S. strategic nuclear offensive force modernization and increased defense spending that began under President Jimmy Carter and continued under Reagan, faced the Kremlin leadership with depressing possibilities that haunted them far into Moscow nights. The Soviet economy would not permit matching of U.S. offensive and defensive force innovation and modernization. A future time of troubles might confront Soviet leaders by the end of the decade, faced with upgraded U.S. theater and intercontinental missile systems and early SDI technology for antimissile defenses. Even a first-generation SDI system might, according to Moscow pessimists, introduce enough uncertainty into the estimated effects of a Soviet *second* or retaliatory strike to weaken confidence in mutual deterrence and in strategic stability. A group of Soviet scientists issued a statement in May 1983 opposing the U.S. antimissile system in language that also reflected the views of top Soviet political and military leaders:

In reality, an attempt to create a so-called "defensive weapon" against the nuclear strategic weapons of the other side, which the U.S. president has announced, would inevitably result in the emergence of another element strengthening the American "first strike" potential. . . . Such a "defensive weapon" would leave no hope for a country subjected to massive surprise attack since it (the weapon) is obviously not capable of protecting the vast majority of the population. Antimissile weapons are best suited for use by the attacking side to seek to lessen the power of the retaliatory strike.[10]

KAL 007

Another factor contributory to exacerbating U.S.–Soviet tensions in 1983 was the shootdown of Korean Air Lines (KAL) flight 007 by Soviet air defenses on September 1, 1983. U.S. intelligence monitored and recorded the transmissions between the pilot of the Soviet fighter-interceptor that shot down the plane and his ground controllers. American policymakers, including President Reagan and Secretary of State George Shultz, referred to the contents of these intercepts as proof that the Soviet Union had deliberately and knowingly destroyed the civilian airliner in cold blood. UN Ambassador Jeane Kirkpatrick, playing selected excerpts from the pilot's transmissions for the benefit of UN and American media audiences, claimed that the Soviets "decided to shoot down a civilian airliner, shot it down, murdering the 269 people on board, and then lied about it."[11] However, some U.S. Air Force assessments of communications intelligence and other data available shortly after the shootdown disputed the claim that the Soviets must have known that KAL 007 was a civilian plane. It was quite possible that Soviet air defenses had inadvertently confused the track of KAL 007 with that of a U.S. Cobra Ball intelligence flight in the same general area on the evening of August 31.[12]

Moscow's reaction was anger and disbelief in U.S. characterizations of the Korean airliner's reason for straying over Russian territory dotted with secret military installations and noted on international aviation maps as a forbidden zone for civilian overflight. The Soviet leadership charged that the airliner had been on a U.S. intelligence mission. Besides the air force, other U.S. intelligence sources later concluded that Soviet air defenses might have confused the path of the Korean airliner with the nearby track of the American RC-135 reconnaissance plane on a Cobra Ball mission. The Central Intelligence Agency (CIA) reported in the president's daily intelligence briefing of September 2 that throughout most of the time interval when Soviet air defenses were attempting to track the "intruder" and deciding what to do about it, they may have thought they were tracking a U.S. RC-135 reconnaissance plane monitoring a Soviet ICBM test.[13] This supposition was not an unlikely hypothesis, given the well-known weaknesses of Soviet air defenses (painfully demonstrated several years later in the Gorbachev era when a German civilian flew a Cessna through Soviet air defenses and landed it in Red Square).

The Soviet leadership maintained the official position that KAL 007 was a deliberate intelligence provocation and that U.S. public denunciations of the Soviets for the shootdown were a deliberate escalation of East–West tension.[14] One consequence of KAL 007 was to add to the high priority already assigned to Operation RYAN. According to Christopher Andrew and Oleg Gordievsky, Party Chairman Andropov spent the last months of his life after the KAL 007 shootdown "as a morbidly suspicious invalid, brooding over the possible approach of a nuclear Armageddon."[15] After the collapse of the Soviet Union, the Russian government made public transcripts of the September 2, 1983, Politburo meeting to discuss the incident. Those high officials in attendance, especially Defense Minister Dmitri Ustinov, believed that Soviet actions the previous day had been appropriate and resented U.S. depiction of their actions as barbaric. Although the actual impact of the shootdown on day-to-day U.S.–Soviet foreign relations was slight, the Soviet perception of anti-Soviet rhetoric in Washington, together with Soviet concerns about SDI and INF modernization, raised the level of Kremlin anxiety about American intentions in the autumn of 1983 to levels not seen for many years.

THE SEPTEMBER SATELLITE WARNING INCIDENT

On September 26, 1983, a false alarm occurred in a Soviet early warning installation that could have, given the previously described mood of the Politburo in 1983 and the tense atmospherics of U.S.–Soviet political relations, become more than a footnote in history books. The incident took place in a closed military facility south of Moscow designed to monitor Soviet early warning satellites over the United States. On September 26 at this installation, designated Serpukhov-15, a false alarm went off, signaling a U.S. missile attack.[16]

According to Stanislav Petrov, a lieutenant colonel who observed and participated in the incident, one of the Soviet satellites sent a signal to his command bunker in the warning facility that a missile had been launched from the United States and was headed for Russia. Soon the satellite was reporting that five Minuteman ICBMs had been launched. The warning system was white hot with indicators of war. However, Colonel Petrov decided that the satellite alert was a false alarm less than five minutes after the first erroneous reports came into his warning center. He based this decision partly on the fact that Soviet ground-based radar installations showed no confirming evidence of enemy missiles headed for the Soviet Union. Petrov also recalled military briefings he had received, stressing that any enemy attack on Russia would involve many missiles instead of a few.[17]

Under the circumstances, Colonel Petrov's decision was a courageous one. He was in a singular position of importance and vulnerability in the command structure. He oversaw the staff at his installation that monitored satellite signals, and he reported to superiors at warning system headquarters, who, in turn, reported to the Soviet General Staff. The immediate circumstances were especially stressful for him because reported missile launches were coming in so quickly that General Staff headquarters had received direct, automatic notification. At the time, the Soviet version of the U.S. "football," or nuclear suitcase linking political leadership with nuclear commands, was still under development. This made prompt alert directly to the General Staff necessary.

Soviet investigators first praised and then tried to scapegoat Petrov for the system failures. The false alarm was actually caused when the satellite mistook the sun's reflection off the top of clouds for a missile launch. The computer program designed to prevent such confusion had to be rewritten.[18] The September warning incident took place weeks after the KAL 007 shootdown and shortly before the start of a NATO military exercise (see below) that may have been the single most dangerous incident contributing to the war scare atmosphere in 1983. The September satellite warning incident has another implication, carrying forward into post–Cold War Russia. The Russian satellite and early warning/

command-control network is undoubtedly less reliable now (in 2001) than it was in 1983 under more resourceful Soviet support.

ABLE ARCHER

According to several accounts, the most dangerous single incident in 1983 related to military stability between the superpowers was the Soviet reaction to NATO command post exercise Able Archer. The exercise took place from November 2 through 11 and was designed to practice the alliance's procedures for nuclear release and alert. Unfortunately, it took place within a context overshadowed by Soviet fears of U.S. and NATO plans for initiating a war in Europe and/or a nuclear war between the superpowers.[19]

As Able Archer got under way, Soviet and allied Warsaw Pact intelligence began routine monitoring of the exercise. NATO was, of course, observing and reacting to the Soviet monitoring of Able Archer. Soon the British and U.S. listening posts detected that "something was going badly wrong."[20] Intelligence traffic from the other side suggested that the Soviets might be interpreting Able Archer not as an exercise but as a real prelude to a decision for war. Soviet "paranoia" at Moscow Center during this time might have been fueled by the awareness that Moscow's own contingency plans for surprise attack against NATO used training exercises to conceal an actual offensive.[21]

According to Christopher Andrew and Oleg Gordievsky, there were two aspects of Able Archer that caused particular concern in Moscow. First, message formats and procedures used in previous exercises were different from the ones being used now. Second, the command post exercise simulated all phases of alert from normal day-to-day readiness to general alert.[22] Thus Able Archer seemed more realistic to Soviet monitors than earlier exercises had. In addition, thanks to Operation RYAN and the increasingly sensitive Soviet nose already out of joint and predisposed to find sinister meaning behind standard operating procedures, Able Archer rang unusual alarm bells in KGB and GRU intelligence channels. Thus KGB reports at one point during the exercise led the Center to believe that there was a real alert of NATO forces in progress, not just a training exercise.

Moscow Center on November 6 sent the London KGB residency a checklist of indicators of Western preparations for nuclear surprise attack. The checklist included requirements to observe key officials who might be involved in negotiations with the U.S. preparatory to a surprise attack, important military installations, NATO and other government offices, and communication and intelligence centers. Several days later, KGB and GRU residencies in Western Europe received "flash" (priority) telegrams that reported a nonexistent alert at U.S. bases. The telegrams suggested two probable reasons for the "alert": concerns about U.S. military base security following a terrorist attack against a U.S. Marine barracks in Lebanon; and U.S. Army maneuvers planned for later in the year. But the telegrams also implied that there might be another reason for the putative U.S. "alert" at these bases: the beginning of plans for a nuclear surprise first strike.[23]

Soviet reactions to Able Archer apparently had gone beyond warnings and communications within intelligence bureaucracies. During the NATO exercise, some important activity took place in Soviet and Warsaw Pact military forces. Elements of the air forces in the Group of Soviet Forces, Germany and in Poland, including nuclear capable aircraft, were placed on higher levels of alert on November 8–9.[24] Units of the Soviet Fourth Air Army went to increased levels of readiness, and all of its combat flight operations from November 4 through 10 were suspended. Soviet reactions may have been excessive and driven by selective perception, but they were not posturing. According to then (1983) Deputy Director of Intelligence Robert M. Gates, writing in reflection after the end of the Cold War:

After going through the experience at the time, then through the postmortems, and now through the documents, I don't think the Soviets were crying wolf. They may not have believed a NATO attack was imminent in November, 1983, but they did seem to believe that the situation was very dangerous. And U.S. intelligence had failed to grasp the true extent of their anxiety.[25]

EAST GERMAN INTELLIGENCE

The Soviets may not have been crying wolf, but they were crying Wolf. Even prior to Able Archer, the KGB enlisted allied intelligence services, especially the highly regarded East German foreign intelligence directorate (HVA—Hauptverwaltung Aufklärung) of Colonel-General Markus Wolf, in its Operation RYAN intelligence gathering and reporting. According to Ben B. Fischer of the CIA's History Staff, Wolf created an entire early warning system that included required reports keyed to a KGB catalog of indicators of U.S. or NATO preparations for war; a large situation center for monitoring global military operations with a special link to the KGB headquarters; an HVA headquarters staff dedicated to RYAN; special alert drills, annual exercises, and military training for HVA officers that simulated a surprise attack by NATO.[26]

Of special interest is that East German wariness about a possible nuclear attack continued after the war scare atmosphere had apparently calmed down in Moscow. Acting in his capacity as head of foreign intelligence and deputy director of the East German Ministry for State Security, Wolf tasked the entire ministry in June 1985 to conduct an aggressive search for indicators of planning for a nuclear missile attack. His Implementation Regulation of June 5 directed that the operational and operational-technical service units of the ministry engage in "goal oriented operational penetration of enemy decisionmaking centers." Top priority, he stated in the same message, are "signs of imminent preparations of a strategic nuclear-missile attack (KWA)" as well as other imperialist state plans for military surprise.[27] In addition, the East German political leadership had built a large complex of bunkers (*Führungskomplex*, or leadership complex) near Berlin designed to save the military, political, and intelligence elites from nuclear war.[28] (See Appendix 2 at the end of this chapter for the entire text of Wolf's directive.)

Markus Wolf was more skeptical than alarmists in Moscow about the urgency for RYAN. But he carried out orders to increase surveillance and collect indicators pertinent to a possible surprise attack for reasons of alliance solidarity, fraternal intelligence sharing, and bureaucratic self-protection. Although the foreign intelligence services of East Germany and the Soviet Union often cooperated for obvious reasons, their specific reactions to Cold War situations of threat were by no means always identical. Wolf's reputation as an intelligence icon (allegedly the model for John Le Carre's fictional spymaster, Karla, although Le Carre denies it) and his tenacious competency at intelligence (respected by friends and enemies alike) made him the least likely intelligence officer in the entire Soviet bloc to overreact to indicators of crisis or possible war. Wolf's reputation, to the contrary, was that of an intelligence supervisor who was careful, methodical, and politically astute in his judgments about allies and adversaries.[29] Wolf contends, in fact, that his service eventually provided a definitive estimate that no threat of war was imminent, based in part on NATO documents obtained by one of his agents who worked at the alliance's Brussels headquarters.[30] He was careful not to dispute any of Moscow Center's pessimistic assumptions about NATO intentions in real time, however.

THE SOVIET NUCLEAR DETERRENT

Nuclear forces have quantitative and qualitative attributes. Numbers of warheads and launchers matter, but so, too, do the operational characteristics of forces and the military-strategic assumptions on which they are deployed. By 1983, the Soviet Union had long since attained parity in numbers of deployed systems and the capability for assured retaliation after surviving a first strike. On the other hand, there were important qualitative differences between U.S. and Soviet force structures related to assumptions made by American and by Soviet political and military leaderships about the requirements for deterrence and for war if necessary.

Speaking broadly, the Soviet view of deterrence was different from the American one and involved some additional subtleties. Soviet military writers distinguished between deterrence as *sderzhivanie* (forestalling or avoiding) and deterrence as *ustrashenie* (intimidation).[31] Deterrence in the Soviet view was not a deterministic outcome of force balances. It was as dependent on political factors as it was on military factors.[32] Thus military-strategic parity, or an essential equivalence in deployed force structures, was not in itself a sufficient condition for military stability. The imperialist camp, led by the United States and NATO, was a political threat by virtue of its existence and regardless of particular fluctuations in its patterns of military spending. Therefore, Soviet survival in the nuclear age could not be trusted to force balances alone. How the forces would operate in time of crisis or threat of war had to be taken into account.

This stance on the part of many Soviet military thinkers was quite logical from their perspective. One must remember that, notwithstanding their disclaimers about the historical inevitability of socialist victory, some Soviet leaders by the 1980s recognized that their economy had failed. As dedicated Marxists they knew what might follow from that: If the economy could not be saved, then neither could national defense and the communist grip on Soviet power. Somehow resources had to be freed up for economic growth and renewal, but this required a favorable threat assessment. This combination of a reduced threat assessment and economic restructuring was not attempted seriously by the Kremlin leadership until Mikhail Gorbachev became party chairman in 1985.

In the early 1980s the Soviet leadership was in a bind. The need for reduced defense expenditures and for economic restructuring was obvious. But the perceived threat from the West was not judged to have been diminished compared to previous decades—quite the contrary. The Carter projected defense buildup, followed by Reagan's even larger increases and hostile rhetoric, convinced the Soviet leadership that there were no immediate prospects for U.S.–Soviet detente. The explicitness of Carter military doctrine (PD-59) on the requirement for protracted nuclear war fighting (for deterrence) had resonated in Moscow in the same way as the INF deployment decision a year earlier had. For present purposes, the point is not whether any of these U.S. or NATO decisions was correct or incorrect in itself. It is the cumulative effect of these decisions as seen from Moscow and in the context of Soviet threat perception that is pertinent to our discussion.

Soviet force structure in 1983 also affected its view of the requirements of deterrence and of nuclear crisis management. The makeweight of Soviet strategic retaliatory forces was its ICBM force: All of these in 1983 were deployed in underground silos. In order to guarantee their survival against a U.S. first strike (which might, in the view of Soviet military

planners, come as a "bolt from the blue" or from escalation after conventional war fighting in Europe), these land-based missiles would have
to be launched before U.S. warheads exploded against their assigned
targets.[33] This meant, in American military jargon, that Soviet ICBMs
would have to be launched "on warning" or "under attack."[34] Only
launch on warning could guarantee that sufficient numbers of Soviet
ICBMs would survive a well-orchestrated U.S. first strike. Soviet leaders
could not rely upon retaliation after ride-out to do so. According to some
expert analysts, neither did the United States plan to rely mainly on
retaliation after ride-out in order to fulfill the requirements of its retaliatory strike plans.[35]

According to Western experts, the Soviet armed forces were eventually
tasked to prepare for a continuum of retaliatory options from preemption
to retaliation after ride-out. However, leaders' decisions about a preferred option in actual crisis or wartime would have been constrained
by capabilities available at the time. During the latter 1960s and early
1970s, improved capabilities for rapid launch and better warning, communication, and control systems made it possible for Soviet leaders to
place more reliance upon launch on warning and to be less dependent
on preemption.[36] The option of preemption was not discarded. The variety of accidental or deliberate paths by which a nuclear war might be
initiated left the Soviet leadership no choice, in their view, but contingent
preparedness for a spectrum of possibilities.

Differences between U.S. and Soviet force structures would also have
implications for the willingness of either side to rely upon LOW as its
principal retaliatory option. U.S. retaliatory capabilities in 1983 were
spread more evenly among three components of a strategic triad: ICBMs;
submarine-launched ballistic missiles (SLBMs); and long-range bombers,
compared to Soviet forces. The most survivable part of the U.S. deterrent
was its fleet ballistic missile submarines (SSBNs) force, virtually invul-
nerable to first-strike preemption. The U.S. bomber-delivered weapons,
including air-launched cruise missiles (ALCMs), gravity bombs, and
short-range attack missiles (SRAMs), were slow flyers compared to the
fast-flying ICBMs and SLBMs. Nevertheless, the highly capable U.S.
bomber force, compared to its Soviet counterpart, forced the Soviets to
expend considerable resources on air defense and complicated their estimates of time-on-target arrivals for U.S. retaliatory forces.

The effects of force structure and doctrine combined created some significant pressures for Soviet reliance upon prompt launch to save the
ICBM component of their deterrent. Doctrine suggested that crises were
mainly political in their origin and were to be avoided, not managed.
The onset of a serious crisis was a threat of war. The U.S. view that
brinkmanship could be manipulated to unilateral advantage during a
crisis struck most Soviet leaders before and after Khrushchev as a high-

Table 2.1
1983 Force Outcomes

	Russia	United States
Surviving warheads	1,831	1,947
Surviving EMT	894	436
Reserve warheads	668	1,064
Reserve EMT	216	234

Note: EMT = Equivalent megatonnage.
Source: Author. Force structures are listed in Appendix 2.1.

risk acceptant strategy. The Soviet leadership, after Khrushchev's enforced retirement, did engage in rapid nuclear force building in order to eliminate American strategic nuclear superiority, but they also eschewed "adventurism" in the forward deployments of nuclear weapons and in the use of nuclear forces as backdrops Because they were pessimistic about "managing" a crisis once confrontation was forced upon them (in their view), Soviet leaders would have to include in crisis preparedness a capability for, and perhaps a bias toward, prompt launch to save the Strategic Rocket Forces. Pessimism about crisis management combined with an ICBM-heavy deterrent constrained Soviet leaders' choices once general deterrence (the basic Hobbesian condition of threat created by the international system of plural sovereignty and the security dilemma) turned to immediate deterrence (a situation in which one state has made an explicit military threat against another or others).

ANALYSIS

How might the strategic nuclear deterrent relationship between the Soviet Union and the United States in 1983 have been influenced by expected war outcomes if deterrence failed, given the factors discussed above? In order to answer this question, we first consider how stable the 1983 relationship was by comparing the outcomes that would have resulted from any breakdown of deterrence. Table 2.1 summarizes and compares the numbers of U.S. and Soviet retaliatory warheads and equivalent megatonnage expected to survive a first strike in 1983.

The results of Table 2.1 show that neither side could have launched a first strike without receiving a retaliatory blow that inflicted socially unacceptable and economically catastrophic damage. In addition, despite very different force structures, the two states' overall retaliatory capabilities are very similar. The degree of similarity is emphasized in the summary provided in Table 2.2.

Table 2.2
Ratio of U.S. to Soviet Survivors, 1983

Deliverable warheads	1.06
Deliverable EMT	.49
Reserve warheads	1.59
Reserve EMT	1.08

Notes: A ratio of unity (1.0) means the two sides are equal. Ratios higher or lower than 1.0 indicate results favorable to the United States or to the USSR, respectively.
EMT = Equivalent megatonnage.
Source: Author.

Table 2.3
Comparative First-Strike Advantages, 1983

Soviet first-strike advantage	9,507.25
U.S. first-strike advantage	8,134.89
Metastability index*	1.17

*The metastability index is the ratio of Soviet to U.S. first-strike advantage.

The ratio of U.S. to Soviet survivors is one possible measure of the stability of their nuclear deterrent relationship in 1983, but not the only one. Another possible measure compares the metastability of that relationship. A metastable relationship is one that simultaneously reduces the incentive for both sides to strike first. To measure this, we will calculate a Soviet first-strike advantage, a U.S. first-strike advantage, and the ratio between the two advantages. The "advantage" for each state is the difference between the number of warheads available for striking first, compared to the number available for retaliation after accepting a first strike (Table 2.3).

A metastability index of 1.0 is a best case: The two sides' first-strike advantages are equal and cancel one another out. The closer to 1.0 the metastability index, the greater the degree of first-strike stability. The more the index deviates from 1.0 (either higher or lower), the lesser the degree of stability. A metastability index of 1.17 says that, in 1983, the U.S. and Soviet first-strike advantages were very similar; therefore, there was little incentive to strike first in order to obtain a relatively preferred outcome. Of course, this is a very static measure and does not capture some of the true differences between the basic concept of *first-strike stability* and the more nuanced concept of *crisis stability*. Crisis stability involves issues that go beyond first-strike stability, including the perceptions and expectations of policymakers and their principal military advisers. The next section offers a proposal for comparing the 1983 war scare crisis with other possible "war scares" of the Cold War in order to develop some comparative historical perspective on the problem of crisis stability.

OTHER WAR SCARES?

Do the preceding conclusions apply only to the situation in 1983? Undoubtedly the situation at the top of the Soviet leadership was unsettled, feeding expectations that, if not paranoid, were certainly suspicious with regard to U.S. intentions. Comparison with other periods of tension and crisis might help to establish whether the analytic part of our methodology has applicability across different cases, before and after the Cold War. Let us, for example, take 1962, 1991, and 1995 as candidate benchmark "war scare" years.

The reasons for these choices are as follows. The Cuban missile crisis of 1962 is self-evidently the most dangerous single 13 days of the Cold War. The failed coup of August 1991 led to the demise of the Soviet Union and solidified the end of the Cold War. From August 19 through 21, the world waited nervously for the outcome of the power struggle between Boris Yeltsin and democratic forces and the "Emergency Committee for the State of Emergency" of usurpers in Moscow. During the crisis, the exact chain of command by which Kremlin leaders would authorize nuclear release was uncertain and fogged from outside observers, including the U.S. president and NATO. Gorbachev was a temporary prisoner in his dacha in Foros in the Crimea, and the other two nuclear briefcases or "footballs" used by leaders to authorize nuclear retaliatory launch were in the possession of the Defense Minister and the Chief of the General Staff. On August 19, Defense Minister Dmitri Yazov ordered the armed forces, including strategic nuclear forces, to Increased Combat Readiness. According to Peter Vincent Pry:

During the August 1991 coup, the United States was in grave danger without knowing it. A NATO or Strategic Air Command exercise, or the generation of U.S. forces to counter Moscow's escalation to Increased Combat Readiness, might have provoked the Committee (the coup plotters) to launch a preemptive nuclear strike.[37]

The situation in 1995 was somewhat different. There was no legitimacy crisis in Russia. But another kind of risk of accidental or inadvertent war presented itself. On January 25, 1995, a U.S.–Norwegian scientific experimental rocket launched from Andoya Island off the Norwegian coast was identified by Russian early warning as a possible threatening launch vehicle headed for Russia. The initial launching position and early trajectory of the meteorological rocket resembled, from the perspective of operators at the Russian missile attack warning system, a possible U.S. submarine-launched ballistic missile fired off the northern coast of Russia and arriving within ten minutes or so over Russian territory. Russia's General Staff had in fact anticipated that a likely form of any U.S. surprise nuclear strike would begin with submarine-launched ballistic missiles fired from the Norwegian and/or Barents Seas. The General Staff was especially concerned about the possibility of an SLBM electromagnetic pulse (EMP) precursor strike disabling radar warning systems, cutting off strategic communications, and disabling computers. Russian President Boris Yeltsin for the first time opened his "football" or briefcase with communications codes used to authorize a nuclear launch. After some minutes it was determined that the rocket's trajectory would not actually impact Russian territory, and a mistaken prompt launch by Russian rocket forces was avoided.[38]

Each of these cases offers anecdotally interesting, and somewhat disconcerting, evidence of a higher-than-normal risk of accidental or inadvertent nuclear war. But each case has unique political and military aspects. Some method permitting comparison across cases is called for. To accomplish this, we will use various measures of the "trigger happiness" or degree of dependency of the United States and the Soviet Union or Russia on launch on warning, or on force generation, in the four cases: the 1962 Cuban missile crisis; the 1983 war scare; the 1991 failed coup; and the 1995 mistaken scientific rocket. Each of these situations will be interrogated for the numbers of surviving and retaliating (arriving) warheads in each of four conditions: generated forces/launch on warning; generated forces/ride out attack; day-to-day alerted forces/launch on warning; day-to-day alerted forces/ride out attack. Both the numbers of surviving warheads and the relative percentages of dependency on (sensitivity to) force generation or launch on warning are computed in Table 2.4.

All Soviet and post-Soviet Russian forces were more dependent than their U.S. contemporary/counterparts on launch on warning, whether the Soviet or Russian forces were on generated or day-to-day alert. And Soviet or Russian forces riding out the attack were more dependent on generated alert during these crises than U.S. forces were. On the other hand, Soviet or Russian forces launched on warning were less dependent on generated alert than their U.S. counterparts in three of four crisis situations. Only in the Cuban missile crisis of 1962 were Soviet forces more dependent than those of the other side on generated alert.

The significance of these findings across various cases is as follows. The findings do *not* change the inescapable statistics of the Cold War nuclear balance. Neither the United States nor the Soviet Union (or later

Table 2.4
Surviving and Arriving Warheads: Four Scenarios and Four Time Periods

	U.S. 1962	USSR 1962	U.S. 1983	USSR 1983	U.S. 1991	USSR 1991	U.S. 1995	USSR 1995
Gen-LOW	2,630	412	8,011	9,504	9,375	9,228	6,726	5,786
Gen-ROA	2,517	344	6,273	4,425	7,390	4,373	5,511	3,329
Day-LOW	920	87	5,299	6,332	5,929	6,405	3,768	3,751
Day-ROA	807	13	3,561	909	3,944	822	2,553	536
% depend Gen Alert (LOW)	186	373	51	50	58	44	78	54
% depend Gen Alert (ROA)	212	2,471	76	387	87	432	116	521
% depend LOW (Gen)	4	20	28	115	27	111	22	74
% depend LOW (ROA)	14	552	49	597	50	679	48	600

Notes: Author's results table involves calculations from a model developed by Dr. James Scouras, Strategy Research Group. He is not responsible for its use here.

Gen = Generated forces; LOW = Launch on warning; ROA = Ride out attack; Day = Day-to-day alerted forces.

Sources: NIE 11-5-58, *Soviet Capabilities in Guided Missiles and Space Vehicles*, pp. 65–70; NIE 11-8/1-61, *Strength and Deployment of Soviet Long Range Ballistic Missile Forces*, pp. 121–138; and NIE 11-3/8-82, *Soviet Capabilities for Strategic Nuclear Conflict, 1981–1991*, pp. 483–490, all in Donald P. Steury, ed., *Intentions and Capabilities: Estimates on Soviet Strategic Forces, 1950–1983* (Washington, D.C.: CIA History Staff, Center for the Study of Intelligence, 1996). See also NIE 11-3/8-91, *Soviet Forces and Capabilities for Strategic Nuclear Conflict Through the Year 2000*, in Benjamin B. Fischer, ed., *At Cold War's End: U.S. Intelligence on the Soviet Union and Eastern Europe, 1989–1991* (Washington, D.C.: Central Intelligence Agency, 1999), pp. 359–368.

Russia) could launch a nuclear surprise attack without receiving historically unprecedented and socially unacceptable retaliation. But crisis behavior of leaders is conditioned not only by scientific facts but also by subjective expectations about the likely behavior of the other side. In each of these situations, strategic warning of a tense situation that might, with unknown probability, lead to an actual outbreak of war was already on the table. What mattered next was the expected reaction by each side to tactical warning of an actual attack in progress, or to indicators considered tantamount to confirmation of an attack.

The results summarized in Table 2.4 and in other information presented in this study suggest that, at the cusp of decision about how hard or how soft tactical warning would have to be, Soviet and Russian leaders were far too dependent on early alerted nuclear forces and, even more so, on launch on warning in order to guarantee retaliatory strikes against desired target sets. It deserves reemphasis that it is in the unknown, but potentially deadly, conjunction of images of the enemy and actual capabilities that the difference between a war and a crisis can be found. Neither theorists nor policymakers can derive any complacency from the fortuitous escape from disaster repeated four times.

Another issue raised by these findings is the operational propensity of the Russian nuclear command and control system. There is considerable evidence from Russians that the strategic nuclear command and control system may be tilted toward the prevention of decapitation and loss of control by enemy first strikes. Less emphasis, if any, is given to the avoidance of accidental/inadvertent nuclear war or escalation. We are not speaking here of technical use control devices such as Permissive Action Links (electronic locks that must be unlocked by codes before launch vehicles or warheads can be activated). Instead, we are now addressing the military ethos in the minds of principal commanders who control the use of, or have custody of, nuclear forces. According to Peter Vincent Pry, although the president of the Russian Federation is the only person who can legally order the launch of nuclear weapons, the General Staff "controls all of the electronic, mechanical, and operational means for waging nuclear war."[39]

This situation by itself is not necessarily disquieting. The United States, too, has arranged means by which retaliation will still take place in the event that the top political leadership and even the major military commands are destroyed in surprise nuclear attacks. These kinds of arrangements are called *delegation of authority and devolution of command.*[40] However, in the U.S. case, orderly political succession in peacetime or even during a crisis is ensured. In addition, the U.S. nuclear command and control system is designed to shift gradually from an emphasis on negative control (prevention of accidental or unauthorized nuclear release or launch) to positive control (guaranty that authorized alerting and launch commands will be readily obeyed).

The Russian nuclear command and control system apparently emphasizes positive compared to negative control even apart from times of crisis. Some Western experts believed that Russian officers charged with the day-to-day management of nuclear forces could, from the main General Staff underground command post at Chekov, have initiated a nuclear attack even in the absence of authorized commands from President Yeltsin or from senior officers.[41] Noted Russian analyst and nuclear arms control expert Alexei Arbatov warned in a 1992 article that the monopoly of the military in devising the control system and operational plan resulted "in a concept which guards not against an accidental strike due to a mistake, a nervous breakdown, or a technical problem, but against failure to respond to an attack promptly and on a massive scale. . . . This is a reflection of a typically militaristic mentality—the main goal is to crush the enemy; deterrence is just a sideline."[42]

The point of these citations is not to imply that Russians are, or ever were, war acceptant to an extent that Americans or others are not: Russians, above all others in this century, have paid the costs of war. The issue raised here is the possible consequences of system design combined with crisis stimulation to produce the equivalent of a "normal accident."[43] As in other large and complex organizations, standard operating procedures and organizational routines built into the nuclear command and control system, as well as the operational habits and expectations of operators, create biases and predispositions that could be dysfunctional in a crisis.[44] If, in addition, leading Russian military theorists expect that any Western attack might be preceded by strategic information warfare against computers and communication systems, cyberglitches could be mistaken for the first wave of enemy attacks during a period of tension. (See Chapter 5 for more on the problem of information warfare and its relationship to nuclear deterrence.)

CONCLUSION

Was the 1983 war scare real or imaginery, and how serious was it? These are important questions for students of Cold War history and of contemporary strategy and arms control. Not all aspects of the issue can be dealt with here. We can say this. Significant anecdotal evidence, combined with modeling of some aspects of U.S. and Soviet likely operational performance in 1983, supports the case that Soviet fears of an outbreak of war in 1983 were real and, in some cases, justified, given their political and military-strategic outlooks. U.S. intelligence needed to have done a better job of "seeing the other"—and not for the first time in 1983. A series of apparently discrete events between 1979 (NATO's

INF modernization decision) and November 1983 (Able Archer) cumulated unexpectedly into a "positive feedback loop" of negative expectations. Soviet foreign and military intelligence, tasked by their uptight political masters, reported back to Moscow Central those indicators and pessimistic appraisals that seemed to confirm initial suspicions that the West was up to something. And data analysis shows that this misperception by both sides could have been linked with a realistic concern on the part of Soviet military planners that their first strike might be their last. Nor are these patterns necessarily confined to 1983. Modeling of situations in 1962, 1991, and 1995 shows disturbingly similar Soviet and Russian dependencies on prompt launch and early force generation in a crisis.

The preceding discussion is not just a historical excursion: It offers some lessons for present and future arms control policy. The war scare episode does show the priority of politics over force balances in bringing nuclear armed states toward, or away from, the brink of war. But it also shows that the attributes of nuclear forces, including their launch readiness and firing doctrines, can contribute to an atmosphere of tension and mistrust. From a political standpoint, the relations between the United States and Russia are not now hostile, as they were between the Americans and the Soviets in the Cold War years. Every encouragement should be given to the Russians and the Americans, having decoupled the threat of war from their political relations, to reduce nuclear force sizes. Equally important, the two states should align their operational doctrines and crisis management expectations as far away from fast-trigger dependency as possible and toward relaxed expectations based on flexible and survivable, but nonprovocative, deployments and doctrines.

Appendix 2.1
U.S. and Soviet Strategic Nuclear Forces, 1983

	Launchers	Warheads	Total Warheads
Soviet Forces			
SS-11/3	550	1	550
SS-13/2	60	1	60
SS-17/3	150	4	600
SS-18/4/5	308	10	3,080
SS-19/3	330	6	1,980
SS-24 (fixed)	0	10	0
sub-total fixed land	1,398		6,270
SS-24 (rail)	0	10	0
SS-25 (road)	0	1	0
sub-total mobile land	0		0
sub-total land-based	1,398		6,270
SS-N-6/3	384	1	384
SS-N-8/2	292	1	292
SS-N-18/3	224	7	1,568
SS-N-20	200	10	2,000
SS-N-17	12	1	12
SS-N-5	9	1	9
sub-total sea-based	1,121		4,265
Bison	43	4	172
Tu-95 Bear B/G ALCM	100	2	200
Tu-95 Bear B/G Bomb	100	2	200
sub-total air-breathing	243		572
Total Soviet Forces	**2,762**		**11,107**

	Launchers	Warheads	Total Warheads
U.S. Forces			
Minuteman II	450	1	450
Minuteman III	250	3	750
Minuteman IIIA	300	3	900
Titan	45	1	45
sub-total land-based	1,045		2,145
Poseidon C-3	304	10	3,040
Poseidon C-4	192	8	1,536
Trident C-4	72	8	576
sub-total sea-based	568		5,152
B-52G gravity	41	4	164
SRAM		8	328
B-52G gravity	46	4	184
ALCM/SRAM		20	920
B-52H gravity	90	4	360
SRAM		8	720
B-52D	31	4	124
sub-total air-breathing	208		2,800
Total U.S. forces	**1,821**		**10,097**

Note: ALCM = Air-launched cruise missile; SRAM = Short-range attack missile.
Source: Author.

Appendix 2.2
East German Intelligence Support for "Operation RYAN"

Council of Ministers   Berlin, 5. 6. 1985
of the German Democratic Republic
Ministry for State Security
Deputy of the Minister

                                        Secret Document
                                        GVS—o008
                                        MfS-Nr. 12/85

                                        approved:
                                                (signed) Mielke
                                                General of the Army

1. Implementation Regulation to Order Nr. 1/85 of 15. 2. 1985,
   GVS MfS o008 –1/85

Comprehensive Use of Capabilities of the Service Units of the MfS for Early and
Reliable Acquisition of Evidence of Imminent Enemy Plans, Preparations, and Actions for Aggression

For implementation of the tasks assigned in Order Nr. 1/85 of the Minister of State
Security for early detection of acute threats of aggression and surprise military
activities of the imperialist states and alliance, in particular for prevention of a
surprise nuclear-missile attack against the states of the socialist community,
   I direct that:

1. The operational and operational-technical service units of the Ministry for State
   Security comprehensively use their specific capabilities and expand within the
   framework of their areas of responsibility in a planned and coordinated manner efforts to acquire and report, through goal-oriented operational penetration

of enemy decisionmaking centers and through recognition of special features (indicators) in the Operational Area, on the territory of the GDR and in the ether, early and reliable information that indicates imminent plans, preparations, and activities for aggression by the imperialist enemy.

Of top-priority importance in this regard are signs of imminent preparations of a strategic nuclear-missile attack (KWA) and of other surprise military plans of the imperialist states and alliance against the states of the socialist community.

2. For acquisition of information and recognition of indicators within the framework of early detection, the following main tasks in various areas of the adversary are to be accomplished as a matter of priority:

—Area of Political Leadership

- Discovery of measures for preparation and adoption of a political decision for a surprise attack, in particular for a surprise nuclear-missile attack (KWA);
- Discovery of mobilization measures for protecting the functions of the political leadership in conditions of a war/nuclear war;
- Confirmation of consultations of the NATO countries regarding surprise attack activities/nuclear-weapon strikes;
- Discovery of measures for maintaining the functioning of governments in conditions of war/nuclear war;
- Confirmation of orders, by signal, to military command authorities for preparation of nuclear attacks.

—Area of Military Command

- Intelligence on measures of direct preparation by US armed forces for surprise attack, in particular for a surprise nuclear-missile attack;
- Intelligence on measures for direct preparations of the armed forces of the other NATO countries for surprise attack, in particular for a surprise nuclear-missile attack;
- Confirmation of transmission by orders/signals for preparation of nuclear attacks to nuclear strike forces/troops/transport.

—Enemy Intelligence Services

- Confirmation of intelligence measures that would immediately precede a nuclear-missile attack;
- Conformation of counterintelligence measures that would immediately precede a nuclear-missile attack.

—Civil Defense

- Conformation of measures for increasing the state of readiness of civil defense organs;
- Confirmation of measures for preparation of secure accommodations for care of the population, for stockpiling of food and water supplies;
- Confirmation of measures for securing medical care for the population in case of a nuclear attack;

- Confirmation of preparations for evacuation measures (specialists, population);
- Confirmation of deviations in the behavior of prominent personalities and other persons in possession of classified information as well as their family members and persons close to them, which can be viewed as measures for protecting their own security (among other things, sudden moving into specially outfitted secure accommodations, unexpected departure from normal residential areas and from border zones at home and abroad);
- Confirmation of measures for protecting important material assets and cultural assets from the effects of a nuclear counterattack.

—Economic Area

- Confirmation of mobilization measures for protecting utilities and securing the property of large enterprises and banks;
- Confirmation of mobilization measures for protection of the activity of key industrial sites under nuclear-war conditions;
- Confirmation of measures for mobilizing means of transportation for nuclear-war conditions.

3. For implementation of the assigned tasks, the operational and operational-technical service units are to concentrate on the following list of key areas for early recognition of extraordinary activities and occurrences in accordance with Order Nr. 1/85:

Main Directorate A and Department XV of the regional administrations [BV or Bezirkverwaltungen]:

—Use and goal-oriented expansion of operational capabilities in the Operations Area, with concentration on political decisionmaking centers and military command centers.

Main Directorate I:

—Area of responsibility for border reconnaissance;

—Enemy activities against the armed forces and national defense installations.

Main Directorate II and Department II of the regional administrations:

—Activities of enemy intelligence services, especially against military targets on the territory of the GDR;

—Activities and behavior of select foreign representations in the GDR and of the Western military liaison missions and military inspection commissions.

Main Directorate III and Department III of the regional administrations, Department 26/MfS and Department 26 of the regional administrations:

—Priority tasks in accordance with directives for cooperation with HVA/Department VII/C.

Main Directorate VI and Department VI of the regional administrations:

—Persons and shipments of goods crossing the border;

—Activities of enemy services and organs against border-crossing points.

Main Directorate VII and Department VII of the regional administrations:

—Enemy activities against the organs, installations and forces of the Ministry of the Interior, Civil Defense and against battle groups;

—Information from resettled agents [illegals], members or former members of Western Armed Forces.

Main Directorate VIII and Department VIII of the regional administrations:

—Activity and behavior of Western liaison missions and military inspection commissions;

—Military forces of the West Berlin Garrison along GDR transportation routes;

—Anomalies in the situation along the transit routes of the GDR.

Main Department IX and Department IX of the regional administrations:

—Information from investigations.

Main Department XVIII and Department XVIII of the regional administrations:

—Enemy activity against key areas and installations of the national economy important for national defense of the GDR and of economic-technical areas.

—Warnings from traveling cadre.

Main Department XIX and Department XIX of the regional administrations:

—Enemy activity against militarily important areas of the GDR transportation system;

—Preparations for major changes in the schedules of the Bundesbahn [West German Railroad] in the FRG [Federal Republic of Germany];

—Assaults against the operations of the German Reichsbahn [East German Railroad] and of the Main Office of Waterways in West Berlin;

—Warnings from IMs [agents] involved in cross-border activities and from traveling cadre.

Main Department XX and Department XX of the regional administrations:

—Enemy activity against key and selected local state organs;

—Enemy activities against key installations of the post-and-communications systems and science and research [centers];

—Warnings from traveling cadre.

Department XXII and Working Group XXII of the regional administrations:

—Relevant information from targeting and control of terrorist and other potential extremists in the Operations Area and use of appropriate foreign contacts.

Central Operations Staff:

—Significant incidents and one-time occurrences.

Regional administration Rostock:

—Conduct of ships from capitalist countries in the ports and on the sovereign waters of the GDR:

—Anomalies in the refitting of GDR ships in the ports of the imperialist states and with passage through foreign sovereign waters;

—Enemy activity against port facilities and off the coasts of the GDR.

Regional administrations Berlin and Potsdam:

—Information related to political, military and intelligence-related operational cases in West Berlin;

—Anomalies in the political-security situation in the capital city (BV Berlin only).

Regional administrations bordering the FRG and West Berlin:

—Changes in the character of enemy activity against the national borders;

—Buildup of enemy intelligence activities and sabotage preparations in the GDR border areas.

The tasks associated with accomplishing these main tasks are to be summarized in detail and coordinated with Main Directorate A.

4. My deputy and chief of the Staff is responsible for summarizing the results of cooperation between the HV A and the other operational and operational-technical service units of the MfS, which are to fulfill the tasks for accomplishing Order Nr. 1/85 as well as execute them in the spirit of the Order. Confirmation in this regard is the responsibility of the chiefs of the main departments/independent departments. In the regional administrations, the chief of Department XV through the chief of the regional administration is to ensure corresponding cooperation with the departments of the BV and the county-level service units. Support for the work of selected IMs with equipment and facilities of the HV A in accordance with Point 2 of Order Nr. 1/85 is to be verified at the same level.

5. Reporting with regard to Order Nr. 1/85 is to be transmitted by the shortest route and without delay with the indicator "Order 1/85" to the Situation Center (LZ) of Department VII of the HV A (during business hours, to Department VII, telephone WTsoh 3332 [presumably a secure phone] or telephone 27358, after close of business to the ODH [Duty Officer]). The highest level of urgency is to be used in sending cables. Reports must always indicate who else was informed.

Other non-urgent information and reports with regard to the contents of the Order are to be sent to HV A, Department VII/C.

6. This Implementation Regulation enters into effect immediately.

(signed) Wolf
Colonel-General

Source: Courtesy Dr. Ben B. Fischer, Central Intelligence Agency.

NOTES

The author gratefully acknowledges Dr. Ben B. Fischer, Central Intelligence Agency, for sources pertinent to this study and for additional helpful suggestions; Dr. Raymond L. Garthoff, Brookings Institution, for important critical comments and corrections; and Dr. James Scouras, Strategy Research Group, for permission to adapt his analytical model for this study. None of these persons is responsible for any arguments or opinions herein.

1. Christopher Andrew and Oleg Gordievsky, *KGB: The Inside Story* (New York: HarperCollins, 1990), p. 583.

2. Christopher Andrew and Oleg Gordievsky, eds., *Comrade Kryuchkov's Instructions: Top Secret Files on KGB Foreign Operations, 1975–1985* (Stanford, Calif.: Stanford University Press, 1993), pp. 68–90, provides a full account of RYAN.

3. See Reference No. 373/PR/52, Attachment 2, *The Problem of Discovering Preparation for a Nuclear Missile Attack on the USSR*, in ibid., pp. 74–81, citation p. 74.

4. Ibid., pp. 77–81.

5. Ibid., p. 76.

6. My appreciation of the Soviet perspective here owes much to helpful comments from Raymond Garthoff. See also Raymond L. Garthoff, *Detente and Confrontation: American-Soviet Relations from Nixon to Reagan* (Washington, D.C.: Brookings Institution, 1985), pp. 864–872.

7. Robert M. Gates, *From the Shadows: The Ultimate Insider's Story of Five Presidents and How They Won the Cold War* (New York: Simon and Schuster, 1996), p. 262.

8. Andrew and Gordievsky, *Comrade Kryuchkov's Instructions*, p. 76. Soviet fears of the preemptive value of Pershing II seemed excessive from the U.S. and NATO perspective. The range of the Pershing II given by U.S. official sources would not have permitted prompt attacks against main military command bunkers in or near Moscow. However, Soviet military planners might have feared that, once in place, Pershing II missiles could be enhanced and given extended ranges, bringing Moscow and its environs within their reach.

9. Gates, *From the Shadows*, p. 264.

10. Statement of Soviet scientists on SDI quoted in Andrei A. Kokoshin, *Soviet Strategic Thought, 1917–91* (Cambridge, Mass.: MIT Press, 1998), p. 182.

11. Gates, *From the Shadows*, p. 268.

12. Seymour M. Hersh, *"The Target Is Destroyed": What Really Happened to Flight 007 and What America Knew About It* (New York: Vintage Books, 1987), esp. pp. 147–150 and 246–247.

13. Ibid., p. 267.

14. Andrew and Gordievsky, *KGB*, p. 597.

15. Ibid., p. 598.

16. My account of this episode is taken from David Hoffman, " 'I Had a Funny Feeling in My Gut': Soviet Officer Faced Nuclear Armageddon," *Washington Post*, February 10, 1999, p. A19.

17. Ibid.

18. Ibid.

19. Accounts of Able Archer appear in Andrew and Gordievsky, *KGB*, pp. 599–600; Gates, *From the Shadows*, pp. 270–273. See also Gordon Brook-Shepherd, *The Storm Birds: Soviet Postwar Defectors* (New York: Wiedenfeld and Nicolson, 1989), pp. 328–335.

20. Brook-Shepherd, *The Storm Birds*, p. 329.

21. Andrew and Gordievsky, *KGB*, p. 599.

22. Ibid.

23. Ibid., p. 600.

24. Peter Vincent Pry, *War Scare: Russia and America on the Nuclear Brink* (Westport, Conn.: Praeger Publishers, 1999), p. 41.

25. Gates, *From the Shadows*, p. 273.

26. Ben B. Fischer, "Intelligence and Disaster Avoidance: The Soviet War Scare and U.S.–Soviet Relations," ch. 5 in Stephen J. Cimbala, ed., *Mysteries of the Cold War* (Aldershot, United Kingdom: Ashgate Publishing Co., 1999), pp. 89–104, esp. p. 98. I gratefully acknowledge Ben Fischer for calling this important aspect of Operation RYAN to my attention.

27. Council of Ministers of the German Democratic Republic, Ministry for State Security, Deputy of the Minister, Implementation Regulation to Order Nr. 1/85 of 15.2.1985: *Comprehensive Use of Capabilities of the Service Units of the MfS for Early and Reliable Acquisition of Evidence of Imminent Enemy Plans, Preparations, and Actions for Aggression* (Berlin, June 5, 1985).

28. Fischer, "Intelligence and Disaster Avoidance," p. 98.

29. Markus Wolf's *Man without a Face: The Autobiography of Communism's Greatest Spymaster* (New York: Times Books, 1997) is a first-person account of his amazing career.

30. Markus Wolf, *Spionage Chef im geheimen Krieg: Erinnerungen* (Dusseldorf and Munich: List Verlag, 1997), p. 332, cited in Fischer, "Intelligence and Disaster Avoidance," p. 101.

31. Raymond L. Garthoff, *Deterrence and the Revolution in Soviet Military Doctrine* (Washington, D.C.: Brookings Institution, 1990), pp. 24–25.

32. William E. Odom, *The Collapse of the Soviet Military* (New Haven, Conn.: Yale University Press, 1998), pp. 1–15, is excellent on this point. See also Garthoff, *Deterrence and the Revolution in Soviet Military Doctrine*, pp. 16–22.

33. Ghulam Dastagir Wardak, comp. and Graham Hall Turbiville, Jr., gen. ed., *The Voroshilov Lectures: Materials from the Soviet General Staff Academy*, Vol. I (Washington, D.C.: National Defense University Press, 1989), pp. 69–75.

34. In theory according to some U.S. distinctions, launch "on warning" (LOW) would take place in response to multiple indicators that an attack had been launched but prior to the actual detonations of warheads on U.S. soil. Launch "under attack" (LUA) would be delayed until after actual detonations had occurred. Skeptics can be forgiven for assuming that launch "under attack" was a euphemism in declaratory policy for action policy that was likely to be launch "on warning." Launch on warning would be necessary to save the ICBM force from prompt destruction: The difference between LOW and LUA might, at most, affect some components of an already partly alerted U.S. bomber force.

35. Bruce G. Blair, *The Logic of Accidental Nuclear War* (Washington, D.C.: Brookings Institution, 1993), p. 177 and passim.

36. Garthoff, *Deterrence and the Revolution in Soviet Military Doctrine*, p. 78.

37. Pry, *War Scare*, p. 81.

38. The preceding summary of the January 1995 incident is taken from ibid., pp. 214–221.

39. Ibid., p. 152.

40. Paul Bracken, *The Command and Control of Nuclear Forces* (New Haven, Conn.: Yale University Press, 1983), passim.

41. Pry, *War Scare*, p. 152.

42. Alexei Arbatov, cited in ibid., p. 155.

43. Charles Perrow, *Normal Accidents: Living with High-Risk Technologies* (New York: Basic Books, 1984), develops this concept.

44. This case is argued with regard to U.S. systems in Scott D. Sagan, *The Limits of Safety: Organizations, Accidents and Nuclear Weapons* (Princeton, N.J.: Princeton University Press, 1993). See especially his discussion of the U-2 "stray" into Soviet air space during the Cuban missile crisis, pp. 135–146.

Chapter 3

Operation Desert Storm:
A Truncated Triumph

INTRODUCTION

The U.S. and allied coalition victory in Operation Desert Storm was not only a military triumph. It was also a presumed vindication for U.S. investment in high-technology, conventional military power and especially for the advocates of air power as a potentially strategic and decisive arm of service. By all appearances, the ghost of Vietnam had finally been laid to rest by American know-how, exceptional theater command, and decisive presidential leadership. The U.S. military certainly had reasons to feel reassured about its performance in the Gulf war of 1991.

But the triumph over Saddam Hussein's forces in the Kuwaiti theater of operations and in Iraq was marked by some disappointments in policy and in strategy. Some of these setbacks were unavoidable: They resulted from the limitations placed on strategy by policy, by the nature of available technology, and by the whims of chance. But other disappointments were not inevitable. Some gaps between expectations and prewar or wartime accomplishments resulted from the failure to apply correctly models of decision to the exigent situation in Iraq.

U.S. efforts to deter Iraq from attacking Kuwait, to compel Iraq to withdraw its forces from Kuwait without war, and to destroy Iraq's nuclear weapons complex and Scud missile launchers (among others) resulted in part from the use of flawed expectations about how deterrence, compellence, and other derivatives of U.S. and Western military thinking would apply to events in a non-Western cultural context. On the other hand, Iraq lost the war because Saddam Hussein failed to perceive that the United States was no longer hobbled by a Vietnam syndrome inhibiting large-scale military action. Iraq also failed to anticipate the newly designed but untested U.S. way of war based on long-range precision strikes, stealthy platforms, and other attributes of "third-wave" warfare.

MISPERCEPTIONS AND MISTAKEN ASSUMPTIONS

Was Saddam Hussein Irrational or Crazy Like a Fox?

Iraqi armed forces invaded Kuwait in the early morning of August 2 without provocation and rapidly subdued resisting Kuwaiti defenders within several hours. Within a week Iraq had moved forward into Kuwait some 100,000 troops, armed with modern equipment including surface-to-surface missiles. Iraqi President Saddam Hussein announced that the government of Kuwait had been deposed and that a new regime would be installed more consistent with Hussein's definition of Islamic polity. The emir of Kuwait and his retinue had fled ahead of Hussein's tanks.

Saddam Hussein calculated, as Kim Il Sung had in 1950, that he could bring about a fait accompli in the form of a complete and total military conquest of Kuwait and the replacement of its regime by an Iraqi puppet. The essential political and military objectives would be accomplished while the United States, its NATO allies, and the other states in the Persian Gulf/Southwest Asia cauldron dithered about what to do. It was a reasonable supposition on the part of the Iraqi ruler. NATO allies of the United States were preoccupied with the winding down of the Cold War in Europe and with the changes going on in the Soviet Union. The Soviet Union, which had for many years built up the Iraqi armed forces through military aid, equipment, and training, would at worst, according to Hussein's reckoning, turn a deaf ear to the entreaties of the Americans or the United Nations.

The assumption that Hussein's preattack reasoning was fatally flawed confuses what is now known about Iraq's losses in Desert Storm with what Hussein could have estimated prior to August 1990 about the military capabilities and political will of his likely opponents.[1] One could argue that the invasion was a "reasonable" decision given Iraq's economic constraints, Kuwait's heedless twisting of Hussein's tail on oil prices, and confused U.S. signals with regard to American vital interests.[2] It was also the case that Hussein's decisions *subsequent* to the invasion were not consistently off the mark. His expectation was that the United States would not be willing to wage war. If it were, it would not have much toleration for high casualties and protracted ground warfare. Therefore, his air forces could even lose and still leave him with an intact army capable of inflicting a political defeat on the United States and its allies by extracting unbearable domestic political costs for them. The chain of reasoning breaks down, as we now know, because the coalition's air campaign proved more destructive and more demoralizing to Iraqi *ground forces* than Hussein had expected.[3] Nevertheless, air power alone could not cause the departure of Iraqi forces from Kuwait: It required a ground offensive, the beginning of which caused the Iraqi leadership to recognize for the first time that its strategy had totally failed.

Even the United States had, within recent memory, shown more official and unofficial sympathy toward Iraq than Iran during the war that those two states fought for most of the decade in the 1980s.[4] U.S. public diplomacy during the period of Iraq's military buildup and diplomatic posturing against Kuwait was not, in the event, very deterring.[5] In addition to the much-disputed meeting between U.S. Ambassador April Glaspie and Saddam Hussein in late July 1990, higher officials also provided little reassurance that the United States would come to the defense of Kuwait if Kuwait were attacked by Iraq.[6]

Undoubtedly, Hussein also believed that the Arab states of the Gulf, Southwest Asia, and North Africa would live up to their well-deserved reputations for finding excuses not to oppose his version of Arab imperialism. An additional factor in Hussein's optimism against any U.S. military attack was his misperception of the influence of the Vietnam syndrome on the willingness of the United States to employ force under very different circumstances. Hussein's conjecture—that any prewar expectation of high casualties would deter an American military response—confused U.S. domestic politics in a conflict of uncertain political purpose with politics in a war of undoubted vital interest.[7]

The Iraqi leadership's reading of U.S. intentions may not have been illogical from Iraq's perspective. Iraq's invasion of Kuwait and the U.S. response surprised each other. Most astonishing to the Iraqis was the unequivocal U.S. reaction. President George Bush laid down the general thrust of U.S. policy in his address to the nation of August 8. The U.S. president outlined four policy objectives that must be met in order to resolve the crisis on terms that were judged satisfactory to American interests. First, the United States insisted upon the "immediate, unconditional and complete withdrawal" of all Iraqi forces from Kuwait.[8] Second, the legitimate government of Kuwait had to be restored. Third, the stability and security of the Persian Gulf were defined explicitly by the president, as by more than one of his predecessors, as vital U.S. interests. And fourth, President Bush indicated that he would be concerned about the lives of American citizens living abroad, including those in Kuwait and Iraq.[9]

Bush ordered an immediate embargo of all trade with Iraq and with allied cooperation froze all Iraqi and Kuwaiti financial assets in the United States and elsewhere. U.S. diplomacy sought to isolate Iraq as an aggressor state and to mobilize international opinion against it. Toward that end, U.S. leaders succeeded in getting the UN Security Council on August 6 to approve for the first time in 23 years mandatory sanctions under Chapter VII of the UN Charter. This gave international blessing to the U.S. effort to ostracize Iraq from other military, economic, and political support. Further to the discomfiture of Iraq, the Soviet Union under Gorbachev did not even make sympathetic noises in the direction of Baghdad. Instead, Gorbachev sided with Bush and with the United Nations in declaring the Iraqi aggression illegal and in calling for a restoration of the status quo ante. This was the first post–Cold War crisis in which the superpowers acted in diplomatic concert, and it gave to the Americans a virtual carte blanche for a military response of the most unambiguous sort.

The response was not long in coming. Bush immediately authorized the deployment of elements of the 82nd Airborne Division to Saudi Arabia; much more would follow. By the middle of September 1990, the United States had some 150,000 troops in the region, including air force and naval personnel. This expectation was realized along with the commitment of forces and support from a total of 26 countries, including forces from Egypt, Morocco, and Syria. Many more U.S. forces were to follow in October and November, with increasing controversy over the political objectives motivating the deployments.

Five major elements were unique to the conflict between Iraq and the U.S.-led military coalition, and these elements worked in U.S. favor. First, U.S. and coalition political objectives (expel Iraq from Kuwait and reduce the threat posed by Iraq to its neighbors) were easily translated into military objectives. Second, Desert Storm remained a conventional war, that is, without the use of weapons of mass destruction. Third, the United States and its allies were permitted to deploy and build up forces in Saudi Arabia without enemy interference or attack. Fourth, Saudi Arabia had modern infrastructure, including ports and airfields, that made possible both rapid deployment and high-intensity combat operations. Fifth, the geography and terrain in the region allowed U.S. and allied armored forces to maneuver to advantage against their opponents.[10]

U.S. Deterrence before Desert Storm

It is customary for analysts to define the problem of preventing Iraq's attack on Kuwait as one of *deterrence*, and the subsequent mission of getting Iraq to withdraw from Kuwait as *compellence*. Deterrence aims at prevention, and compellence at the undoing of an action already taken or in progress.[11] One can overstate the difference between deterrence and compellence, implying that deterrence is always passive, and compellence always active. This is far from the case. It is sometimes impossible to make a deterrent threat credible by words or military preparedness without an actual demonstration in battle. At this point, defense and deterrence may be commingled. One can respond to an attack with forcible defense per se, which is simply designed to defeat the attack and to destroy the attacking forces and eliminate their combat power. Or one can use defense as a way of making a statement relative to intrawar deterrence: Defense, once in progress, makes more apparent the willingness of the defender to pay actual costs in lives lost and resources expended in battle. What was previously a hypothetical possibility that the defender would resist is now a certainty.[12]

President Bush and his advisers assumed that the ability to exclude Iraq from meaningful allied support was a necessary condition for the establishment of escalation dominance in the crisis. The United States moved rapidly and successfully on the diplomatic front to obtain military and other support from NATO allies, and troop commitments were obtained from Egypt, Syria, and Morocco for deployments in support of U.S. forces in Saudi Arabia. The Soviet Union was also engaged in support of the U.S. aim to reverse the results of the attack on Kuwait. The United Nations Security Council supported the embargo of trade with Iraq in goods other than foodstuffs and medicine. As the diplomatic noose closed in on Hussein as a result of effective U.S. international politicking and a globally shared dependency on oil, Iraq's options became more limited. Divested of support for its war effort on the part of its former Soviet ally, Iraq, in desperation, turned to its former enemy, Iran. During September 1990, Saddam Hussein offered attractive terms to Iran for terminating their conflict, including the repatriation of Iranian prisoners of war. Further diplomatic isolation of Iraq was brought about by its own incompetence: Sacking of the French embassy in Kuwait resulted in a French decision in September to dispatch an additional 4,000 troops to the region.[13] France had previously declined to join in the active naval quarantine against Iraq on the grounds that doing so would make it a cobelligerent.

The diplomatic aspects of crisis management were supported by an extensive military buildup that would rise to more than half a million U.S. forces in the Persian Gulf region by the end of January 1991. Having inserted the trip-wire force to establish U.S. commitment, the Bush administration then built it into a formidable air-, ground-, and sea-based force supported by allied deployments that were more than ceremonial. The commitment of other Arab forces to the defense of Saudi Arabia testified to the isolation that Hussein's diplomacy had imposed on him. The difference between the U.S. ability to mobilize international support for its position and Iraq's inability to do so created military alternatives for the Americans and limited the military options available to Iraq. As the U.S. and allied military buildup proceeded, the window of opportunity for a blitzkrieg against Saudi Arabia, of the kind that Hussein had imposed on Kuwait, rapidly closed.

Therefore, the United States had succeeded by mid-September of 1990 in employing a variant of coercive diplomacy that prevented Iraq from accomplishing further aggressive aims in the region. This variant of coercive diplomacy is termed by Alexander George the "try-and-see" variation.[14] This is the more passive of the two basic forms of coercive diplomacy; the other form is an ultimatum with a time limit for compliance attached to it. The difference between the two variations can be illustrated by reference to the Cuban missile crisis of 1962. The try-and-see variation was the blockade imposed against further shipments of missiles into Cuba; the blockade could preclude additional shipments of medium- or intermediate-range ballistic missiles, but it could not by itself cause the Soviet Union to remove the missiles. Only the additional pressure of an ultimatum that the missiles had to be removed within 24 hours, with the warning that if the Soviets could not do so the United States would, finally forced Khrushchev's hand on October 28.[15]

After having deployed a blocking and deterring force into Saudi Arabia and the Gulf region, the United States was in a position analogous to that of President Kennedy after having imposed the quarantine against Soviet missile shipments into Cuba in October 1962. The United States had established a line that Hussein could not cross without raising the risks of escalation, as Khrushchev could not have repeatedly violated the quarantine without risking at least conventional war between the superpowers. The analogy is one of approach to decision making and of the character of the relationship between force and policy. Obviously the United States was in a superior military position relative to that of its antagonist, in 1962 as in 1990. The United States could have won a conventional war in the Caribbean in 1962; the Soviet Union would have been left with the option of nuclear escalation or conventional war in Europe with a very high probability of nuclear escalation. In similar fashion, the U.S. position of force superiority relative to that of Iraq was obviously a very important factor in calculations being made in Baghdad and in Washington. An all-out war in the Gulf would be costly, but the eventual expulsion of Iraq from Kuwait and the destruction of Hussein's regime seemed to be highly probable, if not inevitable, outcomes.

Compellence: Upping the Ante

The deterrent objectives of the U.S. deployments seemed easier to accomplish than the compellent ones, however. It did not suffice, according to U.S. policy, merely to deter Hussein from attack on Saudi Arabia. U.S. political objectives, as previously noted, included the withdrawal of Iraqi forces from Kuwait and the restoration of the emirate government in power prior to the invasion. This compellent mission was more complicated than the deterrent one, in both political and military terms. Politically, the allies and UN support that the United States had signed onto the deterrent mission now complicated the planning for any use of military force for the purpose of compellence. The Soviet Union was not eager to go beyond its commitment to the slow squeeze on Iraq by blockade and embargo. Tightening of the blockade by the interdiction of air traffic to and from Iraq was proposed by nine European states for consideration by the UN Security Council on September 18. This in itself, a further refinement of the try-and-see variant of coercive diplomacy, would be complicated to administer and posed the risk of inadvertently strafing or forcing down a civilian jetliner.

Compellence required the Iraqi leadership to reverse a course of action previously undertaken, as opposed to the simpler task of deterring further aggression perhaps being contemplated. An unprovoked attack on Iraq launched by U.S. forces without UN approval would not have broad international, allied NATO, or Gulf Cooperation Council support. The United States needed a compellent option that supported the diplomacy of slow squeeze and wasted away at the Iraqi military position. Instead, during September Iraq moved further toward the termination of its war with Iran, transferring its forces from that front into Kuwait. U.S. planners, who had anticipated in August an Iraqi force in Kuwait of some 250,000 troops, faced the prospect that by the end of December 1990 there might be as many as 600,000 Iraqi forces deployed in forward defensive positions or in operational reserves of high readiness stationed behind the covering forces. However inferior in professional competency to the crack U.S. divisions being deployed in Saudi Arabia when fighting on the *offensive*, the Iraqi forces in Kuwait presented a significant defensive capability against any ground invasion.

On November 8, 1990, Bush announced a virtual doubling of the U.S. military deployments to the Gulf. This was taken by many in Congress and in the news media as a shift from a defensive to an offensive strategy. Leaders in Congress, although it had gone into recess following the election two days earlier, indicated their concern and demanded to know whether the Bush administration had abandoned the blockade for a course of action leading to war. The official Bush explanation was that the addition of some 200,000 combat forces to the estimated 230,000 U.S. forces already deployed in Persian Gulf area did not constitute a transition from a defensive to an offensive military strategy. Instead, it amounted to a tightening of the screw, an increase in compellent pressure by a demonstrative show of force that might be used—or might not. As explained by a U.S. "senior official" in early November 1990, "What we are trying to do is tell Saddam Hussein, 'Look, we are serious.' "[16] The administration was not yet prepared to issue an ultimatum de-

manding Hussein's withdrawal, although the ground was being prepared for that next step as the compellent pressure on Iraq was being
tightened. U.S. Secretary of State James Baker sought and received the
approval of the Soviet leadership of a conditional use of force if other
options were to no avail. And U.S. officials worked with other UN del-
egations throughout November on candidate resolutions authorizing the
use of force against Iraq; American diplomats worked against the deadline of the expiration of U.S. chairmanship of the UN Security Council
on December 1.

The "senior official" cited above also noted, in contrast to some other
Bush administration policymakers, that the new U.S. military deployments were not related to any assumed failure of economic sanctions.
The official told reporters that it was too soon (early November) to draw
any conclusion about how well sanctions might ultimately work.[17] The
new deployments were designed to support the sanctions by conveying
to Hussein a sense that his time for compliance was not unlimited: They
represented an ultimatum of a sort, although with no specific time line
for compliance.[18] This relatively passive form of compellence failed to
move Iraq; in response, Saddam Hussein mobilized another 150,000 to
200,000 forces for deployment into or near Kuwait, raising his expected
total to over 600,000 by January 1991. It therefore became clear to U.S
officials that a stricter form of coercive diplomacy would be necessary,
one of the more active forms of compellence.

In the last week of November 1990, the United States worked at a
hectic pace to establish a consensus among the permanent members of
the UN Security Council in favor of dropping the last shoe. On November 29, the Security Council voted 12 to 2 (1 abstention) to authorize
the use of force against Iraq if Iraq did not withdraw from Kuwait by
January 15. During the 47-day period between passage of the resolution
authorizing members to use "all necessary means" to enforce UN resolutions on Kuwait, the Security Council announced a "pause of good
will" and a concentration on diplomatic approaches to resolve the crisis.[19] This made little immediate impression on Iraq, which vowed de-
fiance immediately prior to the expected Security Council resolution
authorizing force if necessary.

U.S. officials indicated that they sought the time limit not as a guarantee that American and allied forces would take the offensive after that
date but as an open door through which subsequent attacks could be
launched at any time. Although this seemed to allow the United States
the upper hand in the competition in coercive bargaining, the ultimatum
variant of the coercive strategy was not without risk. An ultimatum gave
Iraqi planners an outside date to use as a guideline for military preparedness. Possible first-strike moves by Iraq in the interim between the
authorization of force after a deadline and the arrival of the deadline

were not precluded. Iraq also had the option of coercive "reprisal" attacks in response to the UN-imposed deadline, attacks short of all-out war but stressing of the coalition supporting U.S. and UN objectives.

One obvious question to which the answer was not known at the time of the passage of the UN resolution authorizing force against Iraq was how the U.S. Congress would figure into the equation of U.S. compellence. A Congress strongly in support of the president would add to the credibility of compellent threats, but forcing Congress to stand up and be counted on this issue risked defeat for the administration, lacking a congressional majority. Both houses of Congress eventually voted to authorize U.S. use of force against Iraq in January; and armed with these resolutions together with that of the United Nations, Bush was legally and politically protected against charges of "Presidential war."[20] In the weeks ahead this would prove to be a considerable asset for him, with regard to the support of the international community, Congress, and the U.S. public.

By virtually doubling the size of the force deployed in the Persian Gulf immediately after the fall elections, Bush had circumvented a congressional and public debate over the shift from deterrence to compellence as the mission of U.S. forces. A force of roughly 200,000 could be maintained in Saudi Arabia almost indefinitely without significant strain on U.S. resources and patience: A force of 400,000 or more (ultimately more than 500,000 U.S. forces) was too large for such an extended, constabulary mission. Pressures would surely build within the armed forces and within the administration for a resolution of the crisis by war or by Iraq's voluntary withdrawal from Kuwait. While Bush administration officials publicly scorned the idea of "saving face" for Hussein and viewed his aggression against Kuwait as criminal and inadmissible, they understood that the avoidance of war would require some kind of bargaining over minor aspects of the crisis, if not major stakes. The other option was to fight, and the Bush coercive strategy could threaten to fight with more credibility following the UN resolution of late November authorizing force if necessary.

However, once the guns speak, military persuasion is not silent. The United States would still be fighting for political objectives, holding together a diverse multinational coalition, including Arab states of heterogeneous ideological persuasion and regime character. The "economy of violence" that Niccolò Machiavelli recommended would call for a rapid and decisive campaign against Iraqi forces in Kuwait, but it was less clear how much further the United States and its allies ought to go. Military forces find targets of opportunity hard to resist, and plenty of hints emitted from high places in Washington to suggest to Saddam Hussein that his regime's days, and perhaps his own, were numbered, should war begin.

THE BEST-LAID PLANS: ASSUMPTIONS

The uppermost question in the minds of U.S. and allied planners, with regard to planning for the outbreak of war should compellence fail, was the decision whether Saddam Hussein should be permitted to survive in power. Wartime operations might give the coalition the opportunity to depose him, but not necessarily at an acceptable cost in battlefield casualties and allied disunity. Hussein's strategy for the conduct of war could be assumed to include a postwar world in which he maintained effective control over Iraq's armed forces and security services, allowing for his later return to the Middle East and Persian Gulf stage of prime-time players. If Bush objectives for going to war against Iraq included dethronement of Hussein and the breaking of his political and military power over Iraq, then U.S. and allied military operations fell short of the commitment necessary to attain those objectives.

Variations of the Instant Thunder air war plan, first developed in the Pentagon and modified in Riyadh, called for a variety of strikes against military and other targets and posited ambitious battle damage objectives. The 84 targets are enumerated by target class in Table 3.1, together with expectations for target destruction conveyed in early Distant Thunder briefings.

The U.S. Joint Chiefs of Staff (JCS) had concluded that only massive uses of air power against a wide variety of targets could force Iraq out of Kuwait and bring the war to an acceptable conclusion.[21] Air force planners interviewed academics, journalists, "ex-military types," and Iraqi defectors to determine "what is unique about Iraqi culture that they put a very high value on? What is it that psychologically would make an impact on the population and regime of Iraq?"[22] Israeli sources allegedly advised that the best way to hurt Saddam Hussein was to target his family, his personal guard, and his mistress.[23] The expectation that the air war alone could either loosen Hussein's grip on Kuwait or cause the destruction and capitulation of Iraq's forces in the Kuwaiti theater of operations (KTO) was to be disappointed, despite one of history's most one-sided bombing campaigns over a period of 39 days preceding the outbreak of a 100-hour ground war.

Planners frequently approach the problem of targeting as a question of the destruction of so many physical things: bridges, air defenses, depots, and so forth. This is a legitimate concern, but from the point of the relationship between force and policy, it is not the most important issue. Targeting can also be treated as the effort to disrupt or to destroy the coherence of an enemy organization. The command system of an opponent is its "brain," without which the body is susceptible to paralysis or disintegration. Targeting the command and control system of an opponent, including the opponent's leadership, is thought by some analysts

Table 3.1
Instant Thunder Air War Plan: Early Target Categories and Damage
Expectancies

Category of Target	Number of Targets	Objectives
strategic air defense	10	destroyed
strategic chemical	8	long-term setback
national leadership	5	incapacitated
telecommunications	19	disrupt/degrade
electricity	10	destroy 60 percent in Baghdad, 35 percent of the country
oil (internal consumption)	6	destruction of 70 percent
railroads	3	disrupt/degrade
airfields	7	disrupt/degrade
ports	1	disrupt
military production and storage depots*	15	disrupt/degrade

*Presumably this includes known nuclear, biological, and chemical weapons production
    and storage facilities (NBC targets).
Source: Adapted from Michael R. Gordon and General Bernard E. Trainor, *The Generals'
    War: The Inside Story of the Conflict in the Gulf* (Boston: Little, Brown, 1995), pp. 86, 89.

to be an economical approach to victory, compared to a prolonged war
of attrition. The countercommand approach commends itself especially
when political power and enemy leadership are concentrated in one or
a few hands. Undoubtedly this was one reason why the headquarters of
dictator Muammar Qaddafi were specifically targeted during the U.S.
raids against Libya in 1986.

However, targeting for coercion, as opposed to targeting for destruction, is more complicated than the killing of one individual or the elimination of a few persons in a leadership group. Targeting for coercion is
an influence process directed at a reactive military organization.[24] Military organizations react and adapt to changed conditions, according to
repertoires of procedures and professional expectations. The U.S. and
allied bombing offensives against Germany in World War II proved to
be less effective than the most optimistic proponents of strategic air
power had assumed on account of the ability of German civil and military organization to adjust previously established routines and priorities.
As another example, the air-delivered knockout blows against the British
Isles, anticipated by prewar planners and futurists, did not materialize,
and those that did failed to coerce Britain into surrender in 1940.[25] In the

latter case, misjudgment about Luftwaffe targeting priorities shifted the thrust of their attacks away from potentially crippling strikes against British airdromes to terror raids against cities. The age of information warfare equips commanders with more numerous and more diverse media of observation, communication, and assessment. This may increase or decrease their vulnerabilities, as C. Kenneth Allard has argued with unusual emphasis:

The command structure is the one part of a military organization that, more than any other, must function as a weapon of war. It must either be a lethal, predatory weapon, capable of preying upon and killing other command structures—or else it runs the risk of becoming a bizarre, expensive techno-gaggle more likely to generate friction than to reduce it.[26]

There are two kinds of strategies for attacking an enemy command and control system. First, devastating attacks against a small but highly important target set may be indicated, especially if striking or destroying that target set might bring the entire system to a halt or render it confused and paralyzed. Or second, prompt and massive strikes against a variety of military and economic assets must convince the enemy that further destruction is both possible and potentially ruinous to him. Eliot A. Cohen has noted that "to use air power in penny packets is to disregard the importance of a menacing and even mysterious military reputation."[27] The two-faced potential of air power for coercion and for attrition may require a willingness on the part of policymakers for immediate and dramatic escalation now, in order to quicken the decision in the enemy's capital to avoid further punishment and denial later. The history of command and control systems shows that there is no one right way to organize a defense establishment or a fighting force. It follows that there is no all-purpose magician's trick that will destroy the cohesion of one.[28]

The original Instant Thunder plan was modified considerably by air force planners in the "Black Hole" planning cell under the direction of Lt. Gen. Charles Horner and Brigadier General "Buster" Glosson. The resulting plan retained from Instant Thunder the concept of working from the "inside out" in order to destroy or incapacitate highly valued target classes. But it rested on no single theory or approach to command and control disruption; and it called for attrition of Iraq capabilities in order to impair the Iraqi war machine *and* as a means of causing Iraq to rethink its continued occupation of Kuwait.

THE AIR CAMPAIGN: OBJECTIVES AND ASSESSMENT

The United States and its allies launched on January 16, 1991, a massive air campaign against Iraq. The objective of the campaign was to induce an Iraqi compliance with the demands of President Bush and the United Nations for a prompt withdrawal of his forces from Kuwait. The U.S. and allied air campaign was unprecedented in its scope. More than 2,000 U.S. and other coalition aircraft flew as many as 3,000 sorties per day. The setting for the application of air power was ideal. Bombing targets were not obscured by jungle, woods, or other natural interference and camouflage. Iraq's air force was no match for the combined air power of the allies. As former U.S. Air Force Chief of Staff Gen. Michael Dugan noted, "If there ever was a scenario where air power could be effective, this was it."[29]

From an operational standpoint, the U.S. air campaign against Iraq had a number of overlapping phases. The first phase involved attacks against Iraqi command and control targets; against nuclear, chemical, and biological warfare manufacturing facilities; and against other components of the Iraqi military infrastructure. In preparation for this, the suppression of Iraqi air defenses was emphasized in order to clear the skyways for the operation of coalition aircraft throughout Iraqi battle space. In the next phase, an interdiction campaign was designed to isolate Saddam Hussein's crack Republican Guard and other forces from reinforcement and resupply of forward deployed elements in the KTO. In the final phase, air support would be provided to the ground forces of the coalition as they moved against the Iraqi forces remaining in Kuwait.[30]

The Iraqi air force, including its air defenses, was caught by surprise on January 16. This might seem monumentally absurd, since President Bush had received UN authorization to use force against Iraq as of January 16. The expectation that the United States would attack eventually did not transfer into an accurate prediction by Iraqi intelligence about the specific timing of the attack. In a classical case of "signals to noise" confusion, the flurry of last-minute diplomatic exchanges and proposals in search of a peaceful resolution to the Gulf crisis by various world leaders probably obscured from Iraq the resolution and immediate preparation for war of the United States and allied air forces. The initial attacks on January 16 were devastating, clobbering Iraqi air defenses and command and control targets with such effectiveness that the Iraqi Air Force was essentially out of the picture of air superiority combat.

These initial successes in the strategic air war left the missions of interdiction and close air support for the ground phase of the war to be accomplished. The interdiction campaign against a "target-rich" environment included Iraq's entire military infrastructure, not omitting its stationary defensive forces in Kuwait and its mobile armored and mechanized forces in Kuwait and in Iraq. The objectives of the interdiction campaign were to weaken further the command and control of the Iraqi armed forces so that they would be forced to fight in disaggregated globules; to reduce the combat power of Hussein's crack Republican Guard forces so that they could not intervene decisively to rescue other Iraqi forces later cut off and destroyed in Kuwait; and to continue the destruction of other military and defense-related targets in order to increase the price that Iraq would have to pay to keep fighting.

The third point is most pertinent to the discussion here. The U.S. and allied air campaign was designed not only to destroy a complex of targets in Iraq for the purpose of *denying* those capabilities to Saddam Hussein but also to *punish* the Iraqi leadership by influencing their expectation of further damage to come. The air campaign was as much a war of coercion as it was a war of destruction. The hope in some compartments of the U.S. and allied governments was that the bombing campaign by itself might induce the Iraqis to withdraw from Kuwait without the necessity for a major ground offensive. It was also the case that a mainly coercive air campaign could not avoid inflicting significant numbers of enemy casualties and causing some unplanned collateral damage. As Eliot A. Cohen noted in his assessment of the U.S. and allied air war against Iraq, there is no getting around the point that force "works" by causing destruction or death or by presenting the enemy with the fear of destruction and death.[31] And making fear believable in the enemy's mind requires that you actually have both the capability and the will to carry out the necessary punishment and denial missions.

A distinction must be made between the operational-tactical and the strategic level of warfare, relative to the political objectives of President Bush and U.S. allies, in order to assess the limits of coercive air war in the Gulf.[32] Even under the most optimistic assumptions about the effectiveness of air power, ground operations would be necessary in order to "mop up" those Iraqi forces remaining in Kuwait, unless Iraq chose to withdraw them voluntarily. Air power can neither hold ground nor forcibly disarm soldiers in their defensive redoubts. These limitations of air power are acknowledged but incidental to the argument whether air power could accomplish the strategic objectives of the United States in Iraq by itself. The theory that it could rested on assumptions about the coercive effectiveness of air power in both punishment and denial roles.

Western strategists generally accept that the punishment capabilities of nuclear weapons are more meaningful for deterrence than their denial capabilities. Most U.S. strategists also generally assume that, for conventional forces, the reverse is true: Conventional denial capabilities are more important than conventional deterrence based on the threat of retaliatory punishment. Thus, it would be argued by many strategists that a coercive air campaign with conventional forces should be counterforce rather than countervalue. Its objective would be to destroy the instruments of military power of the opponent in order to induce the opponent to see the futility of further fighting.[33] In addition to avoiding gratuitous attacks on civilians, a counterforce-oriented campaign reduces the competency of the enemy force, thereby influencing the decision calculus of the enemy leadership against continued fighting.

Although these arguments are widely held in the U.S. defense community, they must be qualified in several ways. In conventional war, the decision calculus of an opponent may not be amenable to influence based on subjective estimates of future losses, until the point at which the back is broken of the opponent's entire war machine. Instead of gradually shifting his will to fight from the "yes" into the "no" column, air and other attacks may meet with stiff resistance until a "catastrophic fold" appears in his ability to fight back. Sudden collapse of an opponent's fighting power may shift his decision calculus overnight from extreme optimism to extreme pessimism. Hitler insisted that wonder weapons, including newer versions of V-2 rockets, would come to his rescue even as his leading generals saw their forces collapse on the Eastern and Western Fronts. During the last months and weeks of war, Hitler issued orders affecting imaginery or mostly destroyed forces. Only the virtual collapse of the city of Berlin on his head finally persuaded the fuhrer that all was lost.

A second qualification is that air power, especially in the massive doses administered by the allied coalition against Iraq in January and February 1991, is not a surgical instrument. The precision of bombing has improved dramatically since World War II—and even since Vietnam. Nonetheless, the collocation of civil and military installations and the inevitable bombing errors ensure that massive numbers of sorties against "military" targets will also include significant amounts of "collateral damage." There is no such thing as a purely counterforce air war, except on a very small, and therefore insignificant, scale. This argument, if correct, implies that not only the denial aspects of counterforce campaigns but also the inadvertent punishment that inevitably accompanies them are important in inducing the opponent to "cooperate" by negotiating for war termination.

Third, coercion of an enemy government that is losing a military campaign is more likely to be successful if that government is divided into various factions. The "outs" can exploit the losses already sustained by the armed forces and by the civilian population to bring policy judgments to bear against the prior decisions of the "ins." If, on the other hand, the enemy leadership is united in its pursuit of war aims, or if dissenters lack powerful and influential voices compared to those in favor of continued war, the potential for coercive influence is diminished.[34] One of the factors that limited the effectiveness of U.S. air power in Vietnam was the lack of any "peace party" within the political leadership of North Vietnam. Although they emphasized tactical flexibility in their use of diplomacy and fighting tempo, North Vietnam's strategic compass never deviated from the objective of taking over South Vietnam. In similar fashion, Hussein brooked no opposition to his decisions, reducing the opportunity for any dissident faction to organize in favor of early war termination. In cases such as these, the coercive influence of air power may be as dependent upon the expectations of an undivided enemy leadership about future punishment, including their own survival, as it is dependent upon the diminished future competency of their armed forces. Conventional deterrence, unlike nuclear deterrence, depends upon punishment and denial capabilities that are based in the same military forces.

The air war against Iraq was one of the most one-sided campaigns in modern military history. Nevertheless, it was characterized by partial success in the carrying out of air combat operations and by the failure to properly identify and destroy certain strategic target sets, including Iraq's nuclear manufacturing complex and mobile Scud ballistic missiles. With regard to air tactical operations, for example, pilots had to deal with the complications of equipment malfunctions, gaps in intelligence on enemy defenses and targets, adverse weather, lack of timely bomb damage assessment (BDA), and "minimal understanding of what higher headquarters was trying to accomplish from one day to the next."[35]

After three days of actual air operations from January 17 through 19, coalition air commanders, in order to reduce losses to Iraqi air defenses, started to shift low-altitude bombing missions to medium-altitude. This did not affect the accuracy of laser-guided bombs delivered from platforms like the F-117 (stealth) fighter-bomber, but it did reduce the accuracy of unguided bombs dropped by F-16s and FA-18s above 10,000 feet. The restriction in favor of medium-altitude bombing, which remained in place until the ground war began on February 24, limited the ability of F-16s and FA-18s to attack pinpoint targets, including dug-in Iraqi armor, fiber optic cable junctions, and bridges.[36]

Another U.S. disappointment was provided by the inability of the coalition to destroy Iraq's nuclear complex. This objective was not realized for a number of reasons, but two stand out. First, prewar intelligence was inadequate to provide a clear picture of either the scope or the character of Iraq's nuclear program. The Iraqi nuclear program was based on diversity and concealment. Three separate methods of uranium enrichment were being pursued simultaneously, and these were more easily concealed from foreign intelligence and from International Atomic Energy Agency (IAEA) inspectors than the large reactors needed for plutonium production. Post–Desert Storm inspections revealed 39 nuclear facilities at 19 different locations within Iraq.[37] Figure 3.1 depicts the locations of major facililties revealed in postwar inspections.

Another gap between decision theory and military practice was the effort to destroy Scud missiles, especially the difficulty encountered in

Figure 3.1
The Nuclear Program as a Target System

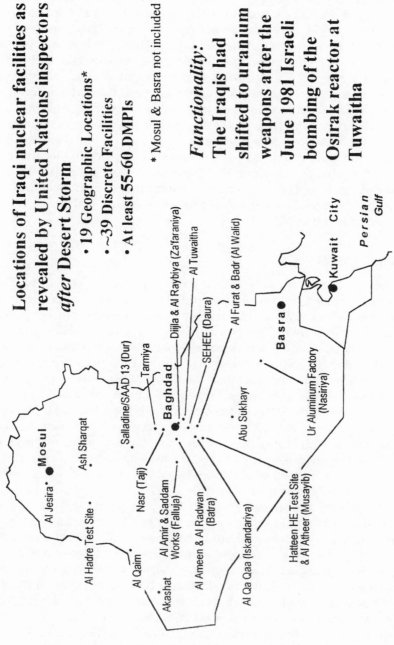

Locations of Iraqi nuclear facilities as revealed by United Nations inspectors *after* **Desert Storm**

- **19 Geographic Locations***
- **~39 Discrete Facilities**
- **At least 55-60 DMPIs**

* Mosul & Basra not included

Functionality:
The Iraqis had shifted to uranium weapons after the June 1981 Israeli bombing of the Osirak reactor at Tuwaitha

Mosul

Al Jesira

Ash Sharqat

Al Hadre Test Site

Nasr (Taji)

Salladine/SAAD 13 (Dur)

Tarmiya

Al Qaim

Al Amir & Saddam Works (Falluja)

Akashat

Al Ameen & Al Radwan (Batra)

Al Qa Qaa (Iskandariya)

Hatteen HE Test Site & Al Atheer (Musayib)

Diijla & Al Raybiya (Za'faraniya)

Al Tuwaitha

SEHEE (Daura)

Al Furat & Badr (Al Walid)

Baghdad

Abu Sukhayr

Ur Aluminum Factory (Nasiriya)

Basra

Kuwait City

Persian Gulf

Sources: Barry D. Watts; U.S. Air Force, *Gulf War Air Power Survey*, 1993.

destroying mobile Scuds. This problem is an interesting example of Carl von Clausewitz's "friction" generated by the overlap between political and military considerations.[38] The Scuds did not represent a significant *military* threat to U.S. and allied coalition operations in the air or on the ground. Instead, they were a *psychological* weapon. Iraq launched several at Israeli cities and threatened additional launches. Iraq was known to have the capability to equip its ballistic missiles with chemical and biological warheads: The warheads were premated to some ballistic missile delivery systems. A great many air strikes were diverted from other possible targets in order to increase the number of attacks against the elusive mobile Scuds, with little success. Nonetheless, there is, according to the Gulf War Air Power Survey Summary Report, "no indisputable proof that Scud mobile launchers—as opposed to high-fidelity decoys, trucks, or other objects with Scud-like signatures—were destroyed by fixed-wing aircraft."[39] The results of the air war for certain major categories of targets, compared to original objectives laid down by planners, are summarized in Table 3.2.

VIDEO WAR

A very significant aspect of Desert Storm was the way in which the media reported the war and the public perceived it. Video images of targets destroyed by precision air-delivered weapons created a virtual reality of their own. This virtual reality was that of a video game war in which the technological superiority of one side preordained the defeat of the other. In addition, the grunt war between opposed ground forces was so short and one-sided that the image of bloodless combat was reinforced. Low casualty levels for the United States and allied combatants also supported the image of push-button or holodeck war. This favorable impression was, as U.S. policymakers recognized, a wasting asset: A longer war with higher casualty levels might shatter the holodeck illusion. If this supposition is correct, it may help to explain why the war was ended before all of Hussein's Republican Guard was destroyed as an effective fighting force.

The rise of "virtual reality" to equal status with "reality" during Desert Storm may also have influenced the way in which the war was fought. The air war was prolonged until unopposed coalition airpower had exhausted its ability to destroy or damage important target sets. Only mobile Scud launchers and unknown facilities for weapons of mass destruction evaded significant attrition or destruction. Owning the skies, CENTCOM (Central Command) air war managers could stage repeated attacks against identified rearward target sets with plenty of munitions left over for massive dumps on demoralized front-line Iraqi troops. The pictures of these reluctant warriors promptly surrendering to U.S. and

Table 3.2

Summary of Air Campaign against Selected Target Sets, Desert Storm

Target Sets	Intended Objectives/Effects	Actual Results
IADS (SAD) and Airfields	Early air superiority —suppress medium- and high-altitude air defenses throughout Iraq —contain/destroy Iraqi Air Force	IADS blinded and suppressed, or in some cases intimidated —low-altitude AAA, IR SAMs remained; Iraqi Air Force bottled up on bases —possible two air-to-surface Iraqi sorties; 375 of 594 HABs destroyed/damaged —Iraqi Air Force flees to Iran beginning January 25
Naval	Attain sea control —Permit naval operations in northern Persian Gulf	All Iraqi naval combatants neutralized or sunk —other vessels sunk Silkworm missiles remain active throughout war
Leadership and Telecommunications/C3	Disrupt government, destroy key government control facilities Isolate Iraqi leadership from forces in KTO and weaken leadership control over people	Some disruption, to uncertain degree —Hussein remains in power — no decapitation of politicomilitary high command Telecommunications reduced substantially —links to KTO are never completely cut — international communications cut
Electricity	Shut down national grid —minimize long-term damage to civilian economy	Rapid shutdown of grid —electrical grid down 55 percent by January 17, 88 percent by February 9 —lights out in Baghdad; some unintended damage to generators
Oil	Cut flow of fuel and lubricants to Iraqi forces — avoid lasting damage to oil production	Refining capacity down 93 percent by Day 34 Destruction of about 20 percent of the fuel and lubricants at refineries and major depots — 43-day war precluded long-term effects

Table 3.2 (continued)

Target Sets	Intended Objectives/Effects	Actual Results
NBC	Destroy chemical/biological weapons — prevent use against coalition — destroy production capability Destroy nuclear program	Some chemical weapons destroyed — most survived — chemical use by Iraq deterred — no biological weapons found by United Nations (UN) Nuclear program "inconvenienced" (UN)
Scuds	Prevent/suppress use — Destroy production and infrastructure — Keep Israel out of war	Firings somewhat suppressed, not salvos —Scud operations pressured —aircraft destroy few (if any) MELs/TELs
Railroads/Bridges	Cut supply lines to KTO —prevent retreat of Iraqi forces	All important bridges destroyed —many workarounds by Iraqis Short duration of war limits effects
Republican Guard (RG) and Other Ground Forces in KTO	Destroy the RG Reduce combat effectiveness 50 percent (armor and artillery) by G-day (start of ground war)	RG immobilized —attrition by G-day is less than 50 percent —some RG units and 800+ tanks escape Front-line forces are destroyed in place or waiting to surrender —attrition by G-day is greater than 50 percent —morale destroyed by air bombardment

Notes: IADS = Integrated Air Defense System; SAD = Strategic Air Defense; AAA = Anti-Aircraft Artillery; IRA SAMS = infrared surface-to-air missiles; HABS = Hardened Air Bases; KTO = Kuwaiti Theater of Operations; MELs/TELs = mobile Scuds; NBC = Nuclear, biological, and chemical.

Military support (MS), Breaching targets (BR), and KTO SAMs are included within other categories above.

Source: Thomas A. Keaney and Eliot A. Cohen, directors, *Gulf War Air Power Survey* (Washington, D.C.: U.S. Government Printing Office, 1993), republished in 1995 as Thomas A. Keaney and Eliot A. Cohen, *Revolution in Warfare? Air Power in the Persian Gulf* (Annapolis, Md.: Naval Institute Press, 1995), pp. 102–103, as adapted by the author.

allied forces, or to a UAV (unmanned airborne vehicle) drone aircraft in one instance, added to the fictive image of war without uncertainty, chance, and danger.

The video digitization of warfare, as part of the fallout from Desert Storm, reasserted itself in the next major air campaign against Iraq in late December 1999. Satellite images of U.S. strikes against Iraqi military and command targets were rapidly made available via the Internet to a global network of military buffs and other curious onlookers. Part of the reason for making this imagery available was to convince the U.S. media and public that the strikes had been necessary and successfully carried out. Another intended audience, equally important to the American domestic one, was the Iraqi military and political establishment apart from Saddam Hussein. The digitized images on the Internet spoke loudly to possibly disaffected Special Republican Guards and others whose headquarters, communications, and other infrastructure had been destroyed without the loss of a single U.S. or British casualty. The message was: "We can do this at long range, with impunity, and if necessary, forever." Satellite reconnaissance, once so highly classified that the U.S. officially denied its existence, was now being plugged into a global infosphere in order to support U.S. military strategy and diplomacy. Military cyber-persuasion had arrived with the video digitization of warfare.

One might also argue that the Gulf war began the "celebritization" of news reporting, a trend that continued through media coverage of the O. J. Simpson trial, Princess Diana's death, and the Clinton sex scandals leading to the president's impeachment in 1998. The line between celebrity status and expertise in media reporting is now virtually nonexistent. Talking heads become "experts" by appearing a sufficient number of times on the most-watched programs. Anyone's opinion is as good as anyone else's. This situation might be mildly amusing in its consequences for U.S. domestic politics, but its implications for war reportage are not reassuring. If the United States gets into a future war that goes badly instead of well at the outset, putative experts aplenty will be found who pronounce the death of American military power in sonorous tones. Publics accustomed to video wars with low casualties will resist the reality of Clausewitz's battlefield and tune out the bad news or seek scapegoats. The day-to-day aspects of the media-military relationship in Desert Storm offered little controversy, but the longer-term potential for disequilibrium between war on reel and real war is a very serious problem.

CONCLUSION

The image of unalloyed triumph in Desert Storm contrasted with the reality of failed prewar deterrence and the inability to compel Iraq to withdraw its forces from Kuwait without war. On the other side of the hill, Saddam Hussein failed to anticipate the new U.S. operational art based on high technology, conventional weapons, and supporting C4ISR. He doubted that Bush would wage war even after a six-month deployment of U.S and allied forces to the Gulf and after Bush had obtained UN and U.S. congressional approval for the use of force to expel Iraq from Kuwait.

U.S. models of coercive air war succeeded in destroying targets highly valued by the Iraqi leadership and military. But the air campaign did not cause Saddam Hussein to withdraw his forces from Kuwait or to surrender his forces deployed in Kuwait and in southern Iraq. Only the onset of the ground war and its one-sided character compelled Husssein to offer peace terms acceptable to the allies. The air war did cause some useful attrition of Iraq's crack Republican Guard ground forces, but many others escaped to fight another day and to help keep Hussein in power in Baghdad for the remainder of the decade. U.S. expectations for the destruction of Iraq's nuclear weapons complex and its other weapons of mass destruction, including chemical and biological weapons stores and manufacturing facilities, fell below stated coalition war aims.

NOTES

1. I am grateful to Paul Davis for emphasizing this point in a critique of an earlier draft of this manuscript.

2. On Hussein's motives, see Richard Herrmann, "Coercive Diplomacy and the Crisis over Kuwait," ch. 10 in Alexander L. George and William E. Simons, eds., *The Limits of Coercive Diplomacy*, 2nd ed. (Boulder, Colo.: Westview Press, 1994), pp. 234–235.

3. Michael R. Gordon and General Bernard R. Trainor, *The Generals' War: The Inside Story of the Conflict in the Gulf* (Boston: Little, Brown, 1995), p. 331.

4. Bruce W. Jentleson, *With Friends Like These: Reagan, Bush, and Hussein, 1982–1990* (New York: W. W. Norton, 1994).

5. Bernard E. Trainor, "War by Miscalculation," ch. 8 in Joseph S. Nye, Jr., and Roger K. Smith, eds., *After the Storm: Lessons from the Gulf War* (New York: Madison Books/Aspen Institute, 1992), p. 198, notes that the U.S. track record for deterrence over the preceding four decades was successful against the main threat of Soviet aggression but less successful against lesser threats, as a number of regional and local wars attest.

6. Testimony of John Kelly, Assistant Secretary of State, July 31, 1990, to U.S. Congress, House Foreign Affairs Committee, cited in Paul K. Davis and John Arquilla, *Deterring or Coercing Opponents in Crisis: Lessons from the War with Saddam Hussein* (Santa Monica, Calif.: RAND, 1991), pp. 67–68.

7. John Keegan, "The Ground War," ch. 5 in L. Benjamin Ederington and Michael J. Mazarr, eds., *Turning Point: The Gulf War and U.S. Military Strategy* (Boulder, Colo.: Westview Press, 1994), p. 77.

8. The White House, Office of the Press Secretary, Address by the President to the Nation, August 8, 1990.

9. Ibid.

10. Jeffrey D. McCausland, "Governments, Societies and Armed Forces: What the Gulf War Portends," *Parameters*, no. 2 (Summer 1999), pp. 2–21.

11. Thomas C. Schelling, *Arms and Influence* (New Haven, Conn.: Yale University Press, 1966), pp. 69–73.

12. Ibid., p. 78.

13. *Time*, September 24, 1990, pp. 31–35. This raised the total of French forces committed to the immediate theater of operations to 7,800.

14. Alexander L. George, "The Development of Doctrine and Strategy," ch. 1 in Alexander L. George, David K. Hall, and William E. Simons, *The Limits of Coercive Diplomacy* (Boston: Little, Brown, 1971), pp. 1–35.

15. This has become a somewhat contentious point, among historians of the Cuban missile crisis, as to whether Robert Kennedy did or did not issue an ultimatum through Soviet ambassador Anatoly Dobrynin on October 27. In his report to the Supreme Soviet on the Cuban crisis, Soviet Premier Nikita S. Khrushchev noted, "We received information from Cuban comrades and from other sources on the morning of October 27th *directly stating* that this attack (a U.S. air strike and/or invasion of Cuba) would be carried out in the next two or three days. We interpreted these cables as an *extremely alarming warning signal.*" Quoted in Graham T. Allison, *Essence of Decision: Explaining the Cuban Missile Crisis* (Boston: Little, Brown, 1971), pp. 64–65 (italics in original).

16. Dan Balz and R. Jeffrey Smith, "Bush Ordered Escalation to Show Resolve, Aide Says," *Washington Post* News Service, *Philadelphia Inquirer*, November 11, 1990, p. 16A.

17. By Christmas, however, Vice President Dan Quayle was stating in public that sanctions had failed to dislodge Hussein from Kuwait. It now seems apparent that President Bush had determined to expel Iraq from Kuwait by means of force, if necessary, by mid-November at the latest. According to Jeffrey Record, in the fall of 1990 it was an open secret in Washington that "the Bush administration's worst nightmare was a voluntary Iraqi withdrawal from most or all of Kuwait, which would have effectively eliminated war as an administration option." Jeffrey Record, *Hollow Victory: A Contrary View of the Gulf War* (Washington, D.C.: Brassey's, 1992), p. 40.

18. Ibid.

19. *New York Times*, November 30, 1990, p. A1.

20. However, the vote was very close, supporting the point made earlier that Hussein's apparent hardheadedness in not being compelled to withdraw from Kuwait voluntarily was not as irrational or unreasonable as some now depict it to have been. See Davis and Arquilla, *Deterring or Coercing Opponents in Crisis*, p. 54. The Senate vote to authorize force, for example, was 52 to 47 in favor.

21. Rick Atkinson, *Washington Post* News Service, "Hussein, Baghdad Would Be Air Force's Top Targets," *Philadelphia Inquirer*, September 17, 1990, p. 10A.

22. Ibid.

23. Ibid.

24. Paul Bracken, *The Command and Control of Nuclear Forces* (New Haven, Conn.: Yale University Press, 1983), pp. 92–93.

25. See George H. Quester, *Deterrence before Hiroshima: The Airpower Background to Modern Strategy* (New York: John Wiley and Sons, 1966).

26. C. Kenneth Allard, "The Future of Command and Control: Toward a Paradigm of Information Warfare," ch. 10 in Ederington and Mazarr, *Turning Point*, p. 188. This passage has the virtue of benign overstatement but of a nevertheless valid point. Command systems are not literally weapons of destruction, but a bad command system can be the medium for self-destruction through ossified command channels, poor situation awareness, confused intelligence assessment, and so on.

27. Eliot A. Cohen, "The Mystique of U.S. Airpower," ch. 4 in Ederington and Mazarr, *Turning Point*, p. 63.

28. A generalization aptly documented in Martin van Creveld, *Command in War* (Cambridge, Mass.: Harvard University Press, 1985).

29. Gen. Michael Dugan, "The Air War," *U.S. News and World Report*, February 11, 1991, p. 26.

30. Gordon and Trainor, *The Generals' War*, passim, esp. p. 212, and Dugan, "The Air War." General Dugan's description of the phased air campaign notes that the phases are overlapping and not altogether sequential.

31. Cohen, "The Mystique of U.S. Airpower," p. 61.

32. For comparison, see the analysis of U.S. air power in Robert A. Pape, Jr., "Coercive Air Power in the Vietnam War," *International Security*, no. 2 (Fall 1990), pp. 103–146.

33. An argument to this effect appears in ibid., passim.

34. Fred Charles Ikle, *Every War Must End*, rev. ed. (New York: Columbia University Press, 1991), pp. 60–83.

35. Barry D. Watts, *Clausewitzian Friction and Future War* (Washington, D.C.: Institute for National Strategic Studies, National Defense University, October 1996), p. 22.

36. Ibid.

37. Ibid., p. 26.

38. The concept of friction is applied to the Gulf war in ibid., pp. 37–58.

39. Thomas A. Keaney and Eliot A. Cohen, *Revolution in Warfare? Air Power in the Persian Gulf* (Annapolis, Md.: Naval Institute Press, 1995), p. 78. Originally published as *Gulf War Air Power Survey Summary Report* in 1993.

Part II

Present and Future Cases

Chapter 4

Information Warfare and Nuclear Weapons: Back to the Future?

American military history reveals a consistent pattern of optimism that technology can suspend the need for strategy or for war. Military analysts and academic experts in security studies have described a post–Cold War world dominated by a "Revolution in Military Affairs," (RMA) based on high-technology, conventional weapons and nearly complete knowledge of the wartime environment.[1] Other experts have suggested that nuclear and other weapons of mass destruction are the past tense of military art. Information-based nonnuclear weapons, in this vision, are the future of war.[2] The assumption of entirely separate paths for nuclear weapons and for information warfare may be correct in general but incorrect for some kinds of situations, including crises between nuclear armed states. In nuclear crises or arms races, nuclear power and information strategies may come together to create a new, and potentially terrifying, synthesis.

The assumption that deterrence based on nuclear weapons will be superseded by a postnuclear dominion of information-based weapons is more hopeful than it is assured. It plays to the already apparent advantages of the United States in automated communications, control, and decision systems. But this "feel good" scenario may be jarred by uncooperative opponents who choose to play to American weakness instead of strength. This possibility, that malefactors would try to negate U.S. advantages in postnuclear weapons by threatening nuclear or other WMD use against U.S. bases or allies, or against the American homeland, has been explored by concerned government officials and by academic experts.[3]

Less attention has been devoted to the possibility of inadvertent escalation or warfare as a result of *unanticipated* or *unplanned* interactions between nuclear deterrence and the information revolution. The coexistence of the old war form of mass destruction with the newer war form of information dominance may not always be a peaceful one. In fact, the waging of information conflict against a nuclear-capable opponent may corrupt its decision-making process in ways that lead to deterrence failure, to escalation instead of intended deescalation of a crisis, or to both. The following discussion highlights three possible paths to a dysfunctional collision course between nuclear deterrence and information conflict: These examples by no means exhaust the logical possibilities, but they do serve to offer pertinent illustrations of the nontriviality and complexity of the infowar-deterrence relationship.

INFORMATION WARFARE: WHAT IT IS AND WHY IT MATTERS

For present purposes, *information warfare* can be defined as activities by a state or nonstate actor to exploit the content or processing of information to its advantage in time of peace, crisis, and war and to deny potential or actual foes the ability to exploit the same means against itself.[4] This is intended as an expansive, and permissive, definition, although it has an inescapable bias toward military and security-related issues. Information warfare can include both *cyberwar* and *netwar*. Cyberwar, according to John Arquilla and David Ronfeldt, is a comprehensive, information-based approach to battle, normally discussed in terms of high-intensity or mid-intensity conflicts.[5] *Netwar* is defined by the same authors as a comprehensive, information-based approach to societal conflict.[6] Cyberwar is more the province of states and conventional wars; netwar, more characteristic of nonstate actors and unconventional wars.[7]

There are at least three reasons why the issues of information warfare and its potential impact upon nuclear deterrence are important. First, there is the growing significance of information warfare as a speculative construct for military-strategic thinking, especially in countries with high-technology militaries. Along with this trend is the emergence of technologies that have made policymakers and planners more sensitive to the significance of communications, computers, and networks of information in time of peace, crisis, and war.

Second, there is some appreciation on the part of the U.S. defense community, at least, that infowar may have *strategic* potential. This means that infowar could, by itself, bring about fundamental or decisive changes in the peacetime balance of power—*or* in friendly or enemy *perceptions* of the balance. In addition, in time of war, infowar could be a major, if not decisive, factor in determining the outcome of a military conflict. The Gulf war of 1991 has been called, not without reason, the first information war.[8] However, compared to what is conceivable or potentially available for future info-warriors, Desert Storm was an early-generation dress rehearsal.[9] The United States and its allies must assume that other states will be able to acquire and to use infowar technologies: Leadership in present-day infowar is no assurance of future preeminence. This warning against infowar complacency is especially timely now, when direct military challenges to U.S. security are seemingly nonexistent. Military-strategic surprise is, by definition, almost never anticipated by the victim.[10]

The assertion that information warfare is an issue of potentially strategic significance for U.S. planners and policymakers is not an endorsement of the idea that the United States is vulnerable to an imminent info-driven Pearl Harbor. The U.S. national information infrastructure (NII) "has yet to suffer a major attack or anything close to it despite numerous smaller attacks."[11] Although some military functions are vulnerable to attacks against part of the NII, a "strategic" disruption of the entire U.S. computer and communications system by hackers would require fictional capabilities not yet available. The more realistic aspect is that partial attacks could distort policymakers' and commanders' perceptual universes or information flows in crises or wartime situations, leading to faulty decisions.[12] Even the carrying out of successful attacks is not easy. As Martin C. Libicki has noted:

Can communications be sufficiently disrupted to retard or confound the nation's ability to respond to a crisis overseas? An enemy with precise and accurate knowledge of how decisions are made and how information is passed within the U.S. military might get inside the cycle and do real damage—but the enemy must understand the cycle very well. Even insiders can rarely count on knowing how information is routed into a decision; in an age in which hierarchical information flow is giving way to networked information flow the importance of any one predesignated route is doubtful.[13]

A third reason for the significance of the infowar/deterrence relationship is the continuing reality of nuclear deterrence in the world after the Cold War. Contrary to some expectations, nuclear weapons and arms control issues have not vanished over the horizon in a post–Desert Storm euphoria. There are at least four reasons for this.

First, Russia still has many thousands of nuclear weapons, including those of intercontinental range. U.S. officials anxiously await the ratification by the Russian State Duma (lower house of the Russian legislature) of the Strategic Arms Reduction Treaty (START) II agreement that would reduce permitted strategic nuclear warheads for each side to between 3,000 and 3,500 force loadings.[14] U.S. Department of Defense funds have been authorized by congressional Nunn-Lugar legislation for the destruction, dismantlement, and secure storage of much of the Cold War Soviet nuclear arsenal. Russia's willingness to ratify START II and to proceed to a Clinton-sought START III is related to two other important security issues: NATO enlargement and continued adherence to the ABM Treaty of 1972.[15]

A second reason why nuclear deterrence remains important in the post–Cold War world is that the other acknowledged nuclear powers, in addition to the United States and Russia, show no inclination to abandon nuclear weapons as ultimate deterrents. China is, in fact, by all accounts engaged in a significant modernization of its military technology base, including the base that supports improved delivery systems for nuclear weapons. France maintains the *force de dissuasion* as its ultima ratio and, despite increased cordiality with NATO of late, continues its Cold War tradition of reserving only to French decision the right to launch nuclear weapons in retaliation. British modernization of nuclear strategic delivery systems for ballistic missile submarines continued into the 1990s, with U.S. assistance. With regard to declaratory strategy for nuclear use, while NATO has pushed nuclear weapons into the background as weapons of last resort, Russia's conventional military weakness has propelled its nuclear weapons into the forecourt.

A third reason for the continued importance of nuclear deterrence is the spread of nuclear weapons among "opaque" proliferators and the potential for additional nonnuclear states to acquire these and other weapons of mass destruction. The "opaque" proliferators, whom virtually everyone now includes in the category of nuclear-competent actors, are India, Israel, and Pakistan. Experts disagree about the sizes of their weapons inventories or deployment capabilities on short notice; more significant, even their military and scientific experts have stopped denying the all but certain nuclear-acquired status of these three countries. In addition to these opaque proliferators, other candidate nonnuclear states thought to be pursuing nuclear capability include Libya, Iran, Iraq and (until 1994) North Korea. The potential for regional destabilization once any of these currently nonnuclear states acquires nuclear weapons is enhanced given their apparent interest in other weapons of mass destruction and in delivery systems for nuclear, chemical, and/or biological weapons.[16]

Fourth, nuclear deterrence remains important because nonstate actors, including terrorists, interstate criminal organizations (ICOs), and revolutionary actors of various sorts, may acquire nuclear or other weapons of mass destruction. Although for some of their purposes nuclear weapons would be superfluous, for other objectives they would, even in small numbers and puny yields, be quite appropriate. Terrorists who could present a plausible threat to detonate even a small nuclear device within a target state could raise the potential risk of hostage rescue operations, for hostages and for armed forces of the target state.[17] Terrorists allied with a state actor and equipped with nuclear weapons could gain from their ally valuable intelligence, sanctuary, and diplomatic cover. Criminal cartels could replenish their coffers by trafficking in nuclear weapons or weapons-grade materials as middlemen, even if they were not the end users themselves. Consider the increased degree of freedom for U.S. opponents in Panama (Just Cause) or in Iraq (Desert Shield and Desert Storm) if Noriega's agents in the Canal Zone or Saddam's operatives in Kuwait had had available even a small nuclear device, well timed and strategically located.

A fifth reason for the continuing significance of nuclear deterrence in the post–Cold War system is, somewhat paradoxically, Russia's military and economic weakness for at least the remainder of this century. There are two aspects of this weakness that might contribute to nuclear deterrence failure based on failed crisis management, mistaken preemption, or accidental/inadvertent war. First, Russia's conventional military weakness makes it more reliant on nuclear weapons as weapons of first choice or first use, instead of last resort. Second, Russia's economic problems mean that it will have difficulty maintaining personnel morale and reliability. In addition, Russia's military will also be lacking in funds to modernize and properly equip its early warning and nuclear command, control, and communciations systems. Russia's military and economic weaknesses may encourage, at least in the near term, reliance on prompt launch doctrines for nuclear retaliation and emphasis on nuclear first use in situations where conventional forces are in jeopardy. In addition, at least some Russian thinkers have noted the potentially strategic significance of information warfare and have connected the consequences of information attacks to potentially nuclear responses:

From a military point of view, the use of information warfare means against Russia or its armed forces will categorically not be considered a non-military phase of a conflict, whether there were casualties or not . . . considering the possible catastrophic consequences of the use of strategic information warfare means by an enemy, whether on economic or state command and control systems, or on the combat potential of the armed forces. . . . Russia retains the right to use nuclear weapons first against the means and forces of information warfare, and then against the aggressor state itself.[18]

The preceding argues the significance of the relationship between infowar and deterrence in general. The sections that follow offer three more specific perspectives on the relationship between infowar and nuclear deterrence. We consider the implications of the nuclear deterrence–information warfare nexus in situations of (1) crisis management, (2) preemption, and (3) accidental/inadvertent nuclear war or escalation. These are not mutually exclusive categories, and some illustrative material could be just as easily provided under one heading as under another. Since no nuclear weapons have been fired in anger since Nagasaki, placement of illustrations or cases is more like a moving finger of historical analogy than a scientific experiment. For example, it is quite reasonable that the same incident could illustrate pertinent points about crisis management or the risk of accidental/inadvertent war, or both.

INFORMATION WARFARE AND NUCLEAR CRISIS MANAGEMENT

Crisis management, including nuclear crisis management, is both a competitive and cooperative endeavor between military adversaries. A crisis is, by definition, a time of great tension and uncertainty.[19] Threats are in the air, and time pressure on policymakers seems intense. Each side has objectives that it wants to attain and values that it deems important to protect. During crisis, state behaviors are especially interactive and interdependent with those of another state. It would not be too far-fetched to refer to this interdependent stream of interstate crisis behaviors as a system, provided the term *system* is not reified out of proportion. The system aspect implies reciprocal causation of the crisis time behaviors of "A" by "B," and vice versa.

One aspect of crisis management is the deceptively simple question, What defines a crisis as such? When does the latent capacity of the international order for violence or hostile threat assessment cross over into the terrain of actual crisis behavior? It may be useful to separate traffic jams from head-on collisions. A traffic jam creates the potential for collisions but leaves individual drivers with some steering capacity for the avoidance of damage to their particular vehicles. A breakdown of general deterrence in the system raises generalized threat perceptions among salient actors, but it does not guarantee that any particular state-to-state relationship will deteriorate into specific deterrent or compellent threats. Therefore Patrick Morgan's concept of "immediate" deterrence failure is useful in defining the onset of a crisis: Specific sources of hostile intent have been identified by one state with reference to another, threats have been exchanged, and responses must now be decided upon.[20] The passage into a crisis is equivalent to the shift from Hobbes's world of omnipresent potential for violence to the actual movement of troops and exchanges of diplomatic demarches.

The first requisite of successful crisis management is clear signaling. Each side must send its estimate of the situation to the other in a way that the other correctly interprets. It is not necessary for the two sides to have identical or even initially complementary interests. But a sufficient number of correctly sent and received signals are prerequisite to effective transfer of enemy goals and objectives from one side to the other. If signals are poorly sent or misunderstood, steps taken by the sender or receiver may lead to unintended consequences, including miscalculated escalation.

The first requirement for effective crisis management includes high-fidelity communication between adversaries and within the respective decision-making structures of each side. High-fidelity communication in a crisis can be distorted by everything that might interfere physically, mechanically, or behaviorally with accurate transmission. Electromagnetic pulses that disrupt communication circuitry or physical destruction of communication networks are obvious examples of impediments to high-fidelity communication. Cultural differences that prevent accurate understanding of shared meanings between states can confound deterrence as practiced according to one side's theory. As Keith B. Payne notes, with regard to the potential for deterrence failure in the post–Cold War period:

Unfortunately, our expectations of opponents' behavior frequently are unmet, not because our opponents necessarily are irrational but because we do not understand them—their individual values, goals, determination and commitments—in the context of the engagement, and therefore we are surprised when their "unreasonable" behavior differs from our expectations.[21]

A second requirement of successful crisis management is the reduction of time pressure on policymakers and commanders so that no untoward steps are taken toward escalation mainly or solely as a result of a misperception that "time is up." Policymakers and military planners are capable of inventing fictive worlds of perception and evaluation in which "h hour" becomes more than a useful benchmark for decision closure. In decision pathologies possible under crisis conditions, deadlines may be confused with policy objectives themselves: Ends become means, and means, ends. For example: The war plans of the great powers in July 1914 contributed to a shared self-fulfilling prophecy among leaders in Berlin, St. Petersburg, and Vienna that only by prompt mobilization and attack could decisive losses be avoided in war. Plans so predicated, on the inflexibility of mobilization timetables, proved insufficiently flexible for policymakers who wanted to slow down the momentum of late July/ early August toward conciliation and away from irrevocable decision in favor of war.

A third attribute of successful crisis management is that each side should be able to offer the other a safety valve or a "face-saving" exit from a predicament that has escalated beyond its original expectations. The search for options should back neither crisis participant into a corner from which there is no graceful retreat. For example, President John F. Kennedy was able, during the Cuban missile crisis of 1962, to offer Soviet Premier Khrushchev a face-saving exit from his overextended missile deployments. Kennedy publicly committed the United States to refrain from future military aggression against Cuba and privately agreed to remove and dismantle Jupiter medium-range ballistic missiles previously deployed among U.S. NATO allies.[22] Kennedy and his ExComm advisers recognized, after some days of deliberation and clearer focus on the Soviet view of events, that the United States would lose, not gain, by public humiliation of Khrushchev that might, in turn, diminish Khrushchev's interest in any mutually agreed-upon solution to the crisis.

A fourth attribute of successful crisis management is that each side maintains an accurate perception of the other side's intentions and military capabilities. This becomes difficult during a crisis because, in the heat of a partly competitive relationship and a threat-intensive environment, intentions and capabilities can change. Robert Jervis has explained the process by which beliefs that war was inevitable might have created a self-fulfilling Cold War prophecy:

[T]he superpowers' beliefs about whether or not war between them is inevitable create reality as much as they reflect it. Because preemption could be the only rational reason to launch an all-out war, beliefs about what the other side is about to do are of major importance and depend in large part on an estimate of the other's beliefs about what the first side will do.[23]

Intentions can change during a crisis if policymakers become more optimistic about gains or more pessimistic about potential losses during the crisis. Capabilities can change due to the management of military alerts and the deployment or other movement of military forces. Heightened states of military readiness on each side are intended to send a two-sided signal: of readiness for the worst if the other side attacks and of a nonthreatening steadiness of purpose in the face of enemy passivity. This mixed message is hard to send under the best of crisis management conditions, since each state's behaviors and communications, as observed by its opponent, may not seem consistent. Under the stress of time pressure and of military threat, different parts of complex security organizations may be taking decisions from the perspective of their narrowly defined bureaucratic interests. These bureaucratically chosen decisions and actions may not coincide with policymakers' intent nor with the decisions and actions of other parts of the government.

If the foregoing is accepted as a summary of some of the attributes of successful crisis management, information warfare has the potential to attack or to disrupt crisis management on each of the preceding attributes.

First, information warfare can muddy the signals being sent from one side to the other in a crisis. It can do this deliberately or inadvertently. Suppose one side plants a virus or worm in the other's communications networks.[24] The virus or worm becomes activated during the crisis and destroys or alters information. The missing or altered information may make it more difficult for the cybervictim to arrange a military attack. But destroyed or altered information may mislead either side into thinking that its signal has been correctly interpreted when it has not. Thus, side A may be intending to signal "resolve" instead of "yield" to its opponent on a particular issue. Side B, misperceiving a "yield" message, decides to continue its aggression, meeting unexpected resistance and causing a much more dangerous situation to develop.

Infowar can also destroy or disrupt communication channels that impede successful crisis management. One way infowar can do this is to disrupt communication links between policymakers and force commanders during a period of high threat and severe time pressure. Two kinds of unanticipated problems, from the standpoint of civil-military relations, are possible under these conditions. First, political leaders may have predelegated limited authority for nuclear release or launch under restrictive conditions: Only when these few conditions obtain, according to the protocols of predelegation, would force commanders be authorized to employ nuclear weapons distributed within their command. (See the discussion of conflict termination, below, for related points about predelegation.) Clogged, destroyed, or disrupted communications could prevent top leaders from knowing that force commanders perceived a situation to be far more desperate, and thus permissive of nuclear initiative, than it really was. For example, during the Cold War, disrupted communications between U.S. National Command Authority and ballistic missile submarines, once the latter came under attack, could have resulted in a joint decision by submarine officers and crew to launch in the absence of contrary instructions.

Second, information warfare during a crisis will almost certainly increase time pressure under which political leaders operate. It may do this actually, or it may affect the perceived time lines within which the policymaking process can take its decisions. Once either side sees parts of its command, control, and communications (C3I) system being subverted by phony information or extraneous cybernoise, its sense of panic at the possible loss of military options will be enormous. In the case of U.S. Cold War nuclear war plans, for example, disruption of even portions of the strategic command, control, and communications system could have prevented competent execution of parts of the SIOP (the Single Integrated Operational Plan—the strategic nuclear war plan). The SIOP depended upon finely orchestrated time-on-target estimates and precise damage expectancies against various classes of targets. Partially misinformed or disinformed networks and communications centers would have led to redundant attacks against the same target sets and, quite possibly, unplanned attacks on friendly military or civil ground zeros.

A third potentially disruptive impact of infowar on nuclear crisis management is that infowar may reduce the search for available alternatives to the few and desperate. Policymakers searching for escapes from crisis denouements need flexible options and creative problem solving. Victims of information warfare may have diminished ability to solve problems routinely, let alone creatively, once information networks are filled with flotsam and jetsam. Questions to operators will be poorly posed, and responses will (if available at all) be driven toward the least common denominator of previously programmed standard operating procedures.

The propensity to search for the first available alternative that meets minimum satisfactory conditions of goal attainment ("satisficing") is strong enough under normal conditions in nonmilitary bureaucratic organizations.[25] In civil-military command and control systems under the stress of nuclear crisis decision making, the first available alternative may quite literally be the last—or so policymakers and their military advisers may persuade themselves. Accordingly, the bias toward prompt and adequate solutions is strong. During the Cuban missile crisis, for example, a number of members of the ExComm presidential advisory group favored an air strike and invasion of Cuba during the entire 13 days of crisis deliberation. Had less time been available for debate and had President Kennedy not deliberately structured the discussion in a way that forced alternatives to the surface, the air strike and invasion might well have been the chosen alternative.[26]

Fourth, and finally on the issue of crisis management, infowar can cause flawed images of each side's intentions and capabilities to be conveyed to the other, with potentially disastrous results. This problem is not limited to crisis management, as we shall see. A good example of the possible side effects of simple misunderstanding and noncommunication on U.S. crisis management will suffice for now. At the most tense period of the Cuban missile crisis, a U-2 reconnaissance aircraft got off course and strayed into Soviet airspace. U.S. and Soviet fighters scrambled and a possible Arctic confrontation of air forces loomed. Khrushchev later told Kennedy that Soviet air defenses might have interpreted the U-2 flight as a prestrike reconnaissance mission or bomber, calling for a compensatory response by Moscow.[27] Fortunately Moscow chose to give the United States the benefit of the doubt in this instance and to permit U.S. fighters to escort the wayward U-2 back to Alaska. The question why this scheduled U-2 mission had not been scrubbed once the crisis began has never been fully answered: The answer may be as simple as bureaucratic inertia compounded by noncommunication down the chain of command by policymakers who failed to appreciate the risk of "normal" reconnaissance under these extraordinary conditions.

All crises are characterized to some extent by a high degree of threat, short time for decision, and a "fog of crisis" reminiscent of Clausewitz's "fog of war" that confuses crisis participants about what is happening. Before the discipline of "crisis management" was ever invented by modern scholarship, historians had captured the rush-to-judgment character of much crisis time decision making among great powers.[28] The influence of nuclear weapons on crisis decision making is therefore not so dramatic as has been sometimes supposed. The presence of nuclear forces obviously influences the degree of destruction that can be done should crisis management fail. Short of that catastrophe, the greater interest of scholars is in how the presence of nuclear weapons might affect the decision-making process in a crisis. The problem is conceptually overdetermined: There are so many potentially important causal factors relevant to a decision with regard to war or peace.

Despite the risk of explanatory overkill for successful cases of crisis management, including nuclear ones, the firebreak between crises under the shadow of potential nuclear destruction and those not so overshadowed remains important. Infowar can be unleashed like a pit bull against the C4ISR of a potential opponent in conventional conflicts with fewer risks compared to the case of a nuclear-armed foe. The objective of infowar in conventional warfare is to deny enemy forces battlespace awareness and to obtain dominant awareness for oneself, as the United States largely was able to do in the Gulf war of 1991.[29] In a crisis with nuclear weapons available to the side against which infowar is used, crippling the intelligence and command and control systems of the potential foe is at best a necessary, and certainly far from a sufficient, condition for successful crisis management or deterrence. And under some conditions of nuclear crisis management, crippling the C4ISR of the foe may be simply unwise. What do we think the Russians will do when their bunkers go bonkers? The answer lies only partly in hardware: The mind-sets of people, their training, and their military-strategic culture must also be factored in.[30]

With or without nuclear weapons, it bears repeating that states are not simply seeking to avoid war once they have entered into a crisis: They are trying to accomplish their objectives without war, if possible, or to position themselves during the crisis so that if war occurs they will be favorably disposed to fight it. These two objectives are in tension at the margin. Nuclear weapons and the complexity of modern command and control systems make this tension more acute. Other aspects of these systems are noted below, but especially pertinent to crisis management are several attributes of nuclear weapons and delivery systems in addition to their high lethality. First, once launched, they cannot be recalled. Second, no defenses against large nuclear attacks are presently feasible. Third, governments and their command/control apparatuses are more fragile than forces. Governments and military commanders steering through a nuclear crisis are aware as never before that they are plausible specific and prompt targets of enemy war plans and that these attacks, once launched, cannot be blunted. This concentrates the mind wonderfully, but how effectively?[31]

PREEMPTION AND INFORMATION WARFARE

Preemption is the taking of a decision for nuclear first strike in the expectation that the opponent has already ordered its forces into attack. Preemption thus differs from preventive, or premeditated, war to forestall a possible attack at a future time.[32] Although preventive war was occasionally advocated by high U.S. officials during the Cold War, no American president ever approved a war plan based on that assumption. Preemption was, for the United States and for the Soviet Union, a more serious and continuing concern.[33]

The first requirement for the avoidance of nuclear preemption is that neither side conclude that war is "inevitable" or that the opponent has already begun it. The "war is inevitable" conclusion and the decision that the opponent has already begun a war are related but not necessarily the same. Leaders with a fatalistic bent might conclude that war was inevitable well before actual troop movements or shooting started. Something of this sort seems to have gripped the Austro-Hungarians and the Germans in the weeks immediately preceding the outbreak of World War I. The judgment that one's possible adversaries have already begun to fight, correct or not, can also lead to a decision for war. In late July 1914, Germany judged Russian mobilization on the basis of Germany's own mobilization planning: Mobilization for Germany was tantamount to war.[34] Russia's mobilization envisioned a concentration of forces near the frontiers in order to hold a defensive position but not necessarily a decision to attack into enemy territory. Understanding Russia's mobilization through its own conceptual lenses, the kaiser and his advisers judged that war had, in fact, begun, although Russia's tsar was still vacillating.[35]

A second requirement for the avoidance of nuclear preemption is that each side's forces and strategic command, control, and communications be survivable against any conceivable surprise attack. This is a tall order, and only the U.S. and Soviet systems in the Cold War years could aspire to meet the requirement against a large and diverse arsenal. The second part of the requirement, survivable command and control systems, is much harder to attain. Much depends upon the standard of survivability

Table 4.1
U.S. Cold War Views of Nuclear Deterrence

	Image of Soviets	Weapons/C3 Requirements	Character of U.S.– Soviet Deterrence
Assured destruction	Aggressive but cautious	Destroy USSR as a modern society	Basically strong, but shaky at the margin
War fighting	Bold, potentially undeterrable	Match or exceed Soviet counterforce capabilities across conflict spectrum	Precarious, at risk from Soviet counterforce advantage
Finite deterrence	Fearful of nuclear war	Several hundred warheads on Soviet cities	Overdetermined by excessive numbers of U.S. and Soviet weapons

Source: Based on, and adapted from, Richard Ned Lebow and Janice Gross Stein, *We All Lost the Cold War* (Princeton, N.J.: Princeton University Press, 1994), pp. 348–368. See also David W. Tarr, *Nuclear Deterrence and International Security* (London: Longman, 1991), chs. 5–7.

expected of the components of any command and control system: physical infrastructure (bunkers, computers, landlines); organizational hierarchy (chain of command); communications networks (vertical and horizontal or lateral); and not least, people (personal reliability, professional ethos).[36] One of these components could fail while others performed up to the expected standard, whatever that was. For example, the destruction of physical infrastructure would not necessarily disrupt the entire chain of command nor change the personal reliability of individuals.

The standard of survivability for forces and command systems can be set high or low. At one extreme, the simple requirement to strike back with a minimum retaliatory force against the cities of the opponent might satisfy the requirements of policymakers. At another extreme, policymakers might demand nuclear forces and command systems sufficient to fight an extended nuclear war through many stages. Richard Ned Lebow and Janice Gross Stein, among others, classify U.S. schools of thought about the military requirements of nuclear deterrence into three groups: (1) mutual assured destruction, (2) nuclear war fighting, and (3) finite deterrence.[37] Table 4.1 summarizes the tenets of the various schools of thought in terms of each school's (1) images of Soviet foreign and security policy objectives, (2) weapons and C3 requirements; and (3) presumed character of U.S.–Soviet nuclear deterrence.

The model of minimum deterrence never appealed to U.S. presidents once nuclear weapons and delivery systems became plentiful in number: They wanted options in addition to several hundred retaliatory strikes against cities.[38] On the other hand, despite considerable hubris in declaratory policy, no U.S. forces and command systems ever met the standard of being able to conduct an "extended" large-scale nuclear war.[39] For the most part, strategists and government officials judged that this was neither necessary nor advisable for deterrence. Most U.S. strategists and policymakers agreed, notwithstanding other differences of opinion, that forces and command systems had to be survivable enough to guarantee "unacceptable" retaliation against a variety of enemy target sets. Arguments about degrees of damage that would meet the standard of "unacceptable" continued throughout the Cold War.[40]

A third requirement for the avoidance of preemption is that the management of nuclear alerts must be competent. This means that the alerting process itself must allow for gradations of military activity and that such activities must take place according to the guidance previously established by political leaders for the operation of nuclear forces.[41] Alerts also send to the other side, intentionally or not, signals about intent: Is the alert of side A a precautionary measure because of its fears of side B, or is it an ominous sign that side A is preparing to attack? Alerts are open to ambiguous interpretation. For example, as German forces massed on the western borders of the Soviet Union in the spring of 1941, Soviet and foreign intelligence sources warned the Kremlin of Hitler's plans to attack. Stalin chose to ignore those warnings, and the launch of Operation Barbarossa on June 22, 1941 caught Soviet border forces premobilized and unprepared.[42] Owing to security, nuclear alerts may be more opaque than prenuclear ones, with equal possibilities of ambiguity in intelligence assessment of their significance.

A fourth requirement for the avoidance of preemption is the timely and accurate communication of the activities and status of military forces at the sharp end of the spear to higher political and military authorities. Political leaders are, on the evidence, often ignorant of the operational details and standard operating procedures by which their own militaries alert, move, feed, transport, and hide.[43] Two problems here are breadth versus narrowness of vision, and time lines. At the strategic level of command, one is concerned with the "big picture" of fleets, armies, and air wings moving in combined arms formations. At the tactical level, things are more immediately dangerous and personal. The term *GI* may have survived as slang because it expressed succinctly the worldview of the grunt. Differences in time horizon also matter in ascertaining the status of one's own forces during times of peace, crisis, or war. The time lines of the high command are extended; those of tactical commanders, dominated by the imminent likelihood of being under fire.

The operation of U.S. maritime forces during the Cuban missile crisis offers one illustration of this difference in time and perspective between center and periphery. President Kennedy and his advisers were concerned to avoid, if possible, a direct confrontation at sea between Soviet and American forces. To that end, they exercised a degree of close supervision over U.S. Navy forces in the theater of operations that some in the navy chain of command, including the Chief of Naval Operations, found objectionable. From the perspective of Admiral Anderson and some of his tactical commanders, operating a blockade was a dangerous exercise that had to be left to military experts if it was to be carried out successfully. The standpoint of Kennedy and McNamara was that this was no ordinary tactical operation: Shooting between Soviet and American naval forces in the Caribbean could have strategic consequences.[44]

A fifth requirement for the avoidance of nuclear preemption is that flexible options be available to policymakers and to force commanders. This requirement has two parts. First, policymakers and their military advisers must be aware of flexible options and believe that they can be carried out under the exigent conditions. Second, those actually holding custody of nuclear weapons or operating nuclear forces must understand the options and be prepared actually to carry them out once told to do so. Each of these requirements is not necessarily easy to meet. Policymakers may not know the availability of options or may be reluctant to order the military into unpreferred choices under duress. For example, Kaiser Wilhelm II, in the late stage of the crisis preceding the outbreak of World War I, ordered his Chief of the General Staff, General Helmuth von Moltke, to reverse the direction of the main German mobilization from west to east (against Russia instead of France). The astonished von Moltke responded that "it cannot be done." Moltke meant that it could not be done without disrupting the intricate railway timetables for moving forces and supplies that had been painfully worked out according to the prewar Schlieffen plan, based on an assumed prompt offensive westward against France through Belgium.

A second aspect of this requirement is that those holding custody of nuclear weapons, including nuclear force commanders once weapons have been released to them, understand those flexible options of interest to policymakers and are prepared to implement them. Policymakers have sometimes engaged in wishful thinking about available military options: Because flexibility is deemed necessary, it is therefore assumed to be possible. An example of misbegotten assumptions of this sort is provided by the behavior of Russia's high command in the last week of the July 1914 crisis. Foreign Minister Sergei Sazonov sought a partial mobilization, including only Russia's western military districts, directed against Austria-Hungary but not against Germany. The intent was to send a message to Austria of Russia's determination not to permit further

Austrian aggression against Serbia. Sazonov was unaware that the Russian General Staff had in fact done no serious planning for a partial mobilization under these or similar circumstances of possible multifront war against Germany and Austria. Neither Russia's War Minister nor the Chief of the General Staff warned Sazonov to this effect. When the tsar at Sazonov's urging ordered into effect a partial mobilization, the General Staff and the rest of the military chain of command sat on their hands, hoping it would be superseded by an order for general mobilization that they were prepared to implement.[45]

The nuclear war plans of the Cold War were as elaborate as the Schlieffen plan, and policymakers' lack of familiarity with them is well documented. Few presidents received more than a once-and-done briefing on the SIOP.[46] Faced with a serious nuclear crisis or actual war, presidents would have been presented with a short menu of options and advised that other options could not be improvised on the spot. U.S. presidents and Soviet premiers of the Cold War years thus had political control only over the actual decision to start a nuclear war but little effective control over the military execution of that command once given.

Information warfare might contribute to a failure on the part of policymakers or the command system to meet each of these requirements for the avoidance of preemption.

First, infowar might raise first-strike fears based on the mistaken assumption by one side that the other had concluded that "war is inevitable." It might do this in one of two ways. First, deliberate attack on the information systems of the other side in a crisis might lead the victim to conclude mistakenly that war had already begun. The United States has had some experience with infowar against itself of this sort. In 1979 and in 1980, misplayed tapes or failed computer chips resulted in false warnings of attack at the North American Aerospace Defense Command (NORAD). In the June 3, 1980 incident, indicators of attack from Soviet land- and sea-based missiles spread from NORAD to other key nuclear command posts. U.S. military commands prepared for retaliation in case of valid attack warning: Minuteman launch control officers were alerted to be ready for possible launch orders, and bomber crews on bases throughout the United States ran to alert aircraft and started their engines.[47] Fortunately, no crisis was in progress at the time, and operators were quickly able to calm fears throughout the nuclear chain of command.

A second way in which infowar might raise first-strike fears is by confusion of the enemy's intelligence and warning systems (see also below for the discussion of this factor in relation to accidental/inadvertent war) but in unexpected ways. If warning systems and the fusion/analysis centers to which they are connected overreact to confusion in their shared information nets, interpreters might conclude that the other side has already launched a first strike or an "infoattack" preparatory to pre-emptive attack. And this logic might not, in the abstract, be totally flawed. From the perspective of traditional military strategy, it makes sense to attack the enemy's command and control system, including warning systems, in the early stages of a war. A blinded and misinformed opponent can be defeated in battle faster and at lower cost, as U.S. air strikes in the Gulf war of 1991 demonstrated.

Weaknesses in the contemporary Russian warning and information systems for nuclear conflict suggest that the danger of feared attacks against Russia's command and control system is not hypothetical. Russia's military leadership has acknowledged slippage in the reliability of personnel in the Strategic Nuclear Forces, including the Strategic Rocket Forces responsible for land-based, long-range missiles. Inadequate pay and impoverished living conditions for the troops are compounded by insufficient funding for replacements and upgrades to computers and electronics that tie together warning systems, communications, and commanders. Cleavage of Ukraine and the Baltics from Russia's western perimeter cost Moscow important warning radar sites, and key satellite tracking stations formerly under Moscow's control now reside in the newly independent states of Georgia, Kazakhstan, and Ukraine. These technical and personnel problems in Russia's warning and response system are compounded by Russia's proclivities in military strategy related to nuclear weapons. Russia's approved military doctrine expressly permits nuclear first use under some conditions, and Russia's Strategic Rocket Forces remain on a hair-trigger, launch-on-warning posture capable of nuclear preemption.[48]

Third, infowar might contribute to preemption by complicating the management of alerting operations. Even the alerting of conventional forces on the part of major powers requires many complex interactions among force components. Nuclear forces must be alerted under separate protocols that ensure safety and security of those weapons and also guarantee that alerted nuclear forces do not invite attack on themselves. Ground-launched and most air-delivered weapons must be moved from storage sites and mated with launch vehicles. Submarines will be surged from port en route to their holding stations or probable launch positions. As one side's forces and command systems surge to higher levels of activity, the other side's intelligence sensors will be taking in more and more raw information. With strategic nuclear forces and command systems as complicated as those of the Cold War Americans and Soviets, the potential for mischievous misconstruction of alerting operations existed even without present and foreseeable potential for infowar.

What, for example, were the Soviets to make of the massive U.S. military alert of U.S. conventional air, ground, and naval forces during the Cuban missile crisis, poised for an invasion of Cuba if the president so

decided? U.S. leaders at the time viewed the preparations as precautionary, should the Soviets refuse to remove the missiles and the crisis turn
uglier. Soviet leaders understandably saw things differently. They concluded by October 27 that the United States was definitely preparing for
an invasion of Cuba. U.S. participants in Cuban missile crisis decision
making aver that there were preparations for invasion but no plan for
invasion, as such, had been approved. This distinction, from the Soviet
and Cuban standpoint, might have been distinction without a difference.[49]

Now imagine a rerun of this crisis with more up-to-date information
warfare techniques: a "holodeck" version with the same political setting
but with the technology of the year 2010. In the holodeck version, U.S.
planners might insert corruptions into Soviet information networks that
simulated an overwhelming attack force about to strike at Cuba, when
in fact such a force was far from being fully prepared. And Khrushchev,
aided by manipulation of U.S. information systems, might have simulated a full-scale nuclear alert of Soviet forces in order to intimidate
Washington. We know now that if the United States had actually invaded Cuba or if the Soviets had actually gone to full nuclear alert in
the Cuban missile crisis, the probability of a mutually acceptable outcome short of war would have been reduced. U.S. planners were unaware for much of the crisis period of certain tactical nuclear weapons
deployed with Soviet ground forces and authorized for use in case of an
American invasion of Cuba.[50] And it was helpful to the avoidance of fear
of preemption that the U.S. alerting of its nuclear forces, including at
least one alert broadcast *en clair*, was not matched by as boisterous a
military statement from Moscow.[51]

Related to the third factor in avoiding preemption, careful alert management, is the fourth: timely and accurate communication of force
status. Leaders must know the status of their own forces and must correctly communicate this to the adversary (unless, of course, they are deliberately attempting to conceal force status because they are actually
planning to attack). For example, during the Soviet-orchestrated invasion
of Czechoslovakia in 1968 by forces of the Warsaw Pact, NATO was
careful to avoid provocative overflights or troop movements that could
be misunderstood as a responsive military intervention. A disquieting
example during the Cuban missile crisis was the apparent firing of a test
ICBM from Vandenberg Air Force Base over the Pacific. Although this
missile was not weaponized, Soviet observers could be forgiven if they
had assumed otherwise in the middle of the worst crisis of the Cold
War. Fortunately, Soviet air defense or other watchers never detected the
launch or, if they did, chose not to make an issue of it.[52] One can, on the
other hand, overdo the issue of making clear to the opponent the preparedness of one's forces. The U.S. Strategic Air Command (SAC) com-

mander who broadcast alerting orders in the clear during the Cuban missile crisis, doubtless to impress his Soviet interlocuters, was trying too hard. Such braggadocio was unintended by his superiors and, under more trying circumstances, could only have contributed to Soviet fears of attack (or of an out-of-control U.S. commander with nuclear weapons, thus overlapping with the problem of accidental/inadvertent war).

A fifth requirement for the avoidance of preemption, the availability of flexible options, might also be put at risk by information warfare. Logic bombs, worms, or viruses that attack information might also deny policymakers and high commanders of the other side an accurate reading on their own command system and forces. It was hard enough to convince Cold War U.S. leaders, on the evidence, that they had options other than those of massive nuclear retaliation. SIOP planners, convinced that nuclear flexibility was the road to defeat in war by overcomplicating the command system, had little or no interest in preparing mini-nuclear strike packages. As a result, in an actual crisis, the president might have wanted smaller or more selective options than actually existed on the available menu. Former Secretary of Defense Robert McNamara recalled, with reference to the Cuban missile crisis, that he considered the SIOP options then available irrelevant to the crisis.[53] This is quite a statement, considering that McNamara had just overseen a major overhaul of nuclear war plans with the very object of introducing selective nuclear options.

The issue of flexibility can be misconstrued, and that is to be avoided in this context. Flexibility is a two-edged sword. Nuclear flexibility does not imply that any nuclear war would or could be waged at an acceptable cost. It means, to the contrary, that however terrible a smaller nuclear war would be, a larger one would be that much worse. This issue should not sidetrack us. The present point is that an infowarrior could "persuade" his opponent that the opponent's information system is full of electronic junk or that his command/control system for nuclear response is about to die off. So persuaded, preemption for fear of death could appeal to leaders even before the other side had made its own irrevocable decision for war.

Preemption for want of information owing to cyberdistortion, intended by the other side as intimidation, is a possible path to war in an age-of-information complexity. Even the Cuban missile crisis, taking place in an environment of comparative information simplicity, was dangerous enough in this regard. For example, U.S. leaders at one stage wondered whether Khrushchev was still in control in Moscow.[54] Fear existed that he had been overruled by a more hard-line faction within the Politburo after a relatively conciliatory message from Khrushchev on Friday, October 26, was followed by another message from the Soviet premier the next day, harsher in tone and more demanding in substance.

In Moscow, some Soviet leaders feared that Kennedy was a virtual prisoner of hawkish forces that might overthrow his regime unless he acquiesced to an air strike or invasion of Cuba. Fortunately, these mistaken images were not compounded by infowarriors using perceptions management to make them more convincing.

ACCIDENTAL/INADVERTENT WARFARE AND INFORMATION CONFLICT

Preemption, however mistaken, is a deliberate choice made by desperate policymakers. Accidental/inadvertent nuclear war is the result of a process that nobody intended. Since war grows out of a process, it may erupt in ways that were not anticipated by policymakers or planners. The following discussion outlines some of the requirements of avoiding accidental/inadvertent war and explains how infowar might lead actors to fall short of meeting those requirements. There is, admittedly, some overlap between issues and factors that relate to preemption and crisis management, on one hand, and those involved in a discussion of accidental/inadvertent war. The overlap is only partly the result of the approach taken by this investigator: Nuclear weapons and the speed with which they can inflict unprecedented destruction create overlap among the "real-world" causes of nuclear-related policy dysfunction.

The first requirement for the avoidance of accidental/inadvertent war is the ability to balance the requirements for positive and negative control. This can be discussed as two separate requirements, although they are intimately related. Negative control is the prevention of any nuclear release or launch except by duly authorized command. Positive control means that forces are promptly and reliably responsive to authorized commands. In some discussions, this is characterized as the "always–never" problem: always ensuring that forces are responsive when required but never permitting actions that are unintended by political and/or military leaders.[55] Confusion can be introduced into the discussion by the term *positive control launch*, which is actually a form of negative control, as described here. Positive control launch, as in SAC Cold War "fail safe" procedures, restrains an attack from taking place unless a specific coded message authorizes the attack even after bomber aircraft have been loaded with weapons and routed to preliminary airborne destinations.

There is inherent tension between the requirements for negative and positive control at the margin, especially during the alerting of military forces.[56] Nuclear weapons make this tension acute. Steps taken to make forces ready for prompt retaliation after enemy attack can remove some of the controls against accidental or unauthorized use. More significant than changes in hardware are changes in the expectations of the people who operate forces and their associated command and control systems. As a confrontation between two states looms, military operators will shift their expectations from latent to manifest awareness of the worst possible performance of the system for which they are responsible. Forces will be exercised to guard against worst-case possibilities. However, too much alerting can wear out forces and reduce their actual readiness for war. Forces and command systems can only be maintained at high alert levels for a very short time before performance degradation sets in.

If alerts are extended beyond the "knee of the curve" for ready forces, then deteriorated performance, including performance capable of causing accidents, is a possible outcome. People get tired, machinery wears, and nerves are frayed. Stress levels rise. Interpretations of events are influenced by the strained condition of physical and human systems. Introduce the additional complexity of an attack by one side on the information bytes of the other, exacerbating stress and tension. One possible result of stress compounded by misinformation is the tendency to rationalize or falsely explain whatever action was recently taken. Another possible result is cognitive or motivational bias in assessments of the status of forces and command/control systems, including information networks.[57] A cognitive bias is a bias in the logical explanation for an event or forecast of a future event. Motivational bias is based on emotional needs of the observer that distort his or her perception of what is being observed.

First-strike fears compounded by information malaise and motivational or cognitive bias can also contribute to an outbreak of accidental/inadvertent war. If leaders believe that the opponent will attack at their weakest moment of preparedness, and if they are further persuaded by infowar that their command system is becoming a sewer pipe of enemy disinformation, they may shut down channels or networks that maintain negative control under stressful conditions. Consider, for example, the problem of crisis time communication with ballistic missile submarines. The possible disruption of these communications in time of war, and the equally strong possibility of prompt enemy attacks against the other side's SSBN force, led Cold War U.S. policymakers to enable submarines to launch their weapons under approved "fail deadly" procedures. This meant that faced with disrupted communications and under presumed attack from enemy attack submarines, U.S. ballistic missile submarines (under certain restrictive guidelines) might fire at predesignated targets. PALs (permissive action links, essentially electronic locks that could only be bypassed by encoded messages from the U.S. National Command Authority) were not installed on U.S. SSBNs during the Cold War, although they were in place on land-based and air-delivered weapons.[58]

The U.S. Navy argued that the environment in which maritime operations were carried out precluded PALs or other devices that depended upon the fidelity of shore-to-ship communications in wartime. In addition, the navy contended that procedural safeguards against accidental/inadvertent war were more important than mechanical or electronic locks. Navy training and tradition were the guarantors against nuclear usurpation.[59] This argument was not entirely self-serving. In the largest sense, the entire U.S. government depends upon the training and tradition of its military as the fundamental guarantees of civil supremacy in time of peace or war. The modern military has always had the physical power or capability to overthrow the government (or, at least, to overthrow the civilian leadership in Washington, D.C. temporarily) but never the inclination since the end of the Civil War.

The problem of accidental/inadvertent escalation or war is more complicated than simple military overthrow of civil power. Slippage of negative control in the direction of accidental or inadvertent war or escalation can occur in stages and without any lapse of military loyalty to civil authority. Disjunction between the intent of political leaders and military operators can take place when commanders are carrying out logical procedures under unusual, but possible, conditions.[60] Consider the management of U.S. naval forces during the Cuban missile crisis. Standard operating procedure called for the U.S. Navy to force any Soviet submarines within the quarantine line to the surface. Commanders proceeded quite logically from this standpoint to do exactly that. It was not fully appreciated by policymakers or by navy commanders that this could lead to inadvertent escalation and war.[61] Soviet submarines signaled by depth charges might respond not by surfacing, as required, but by attacking U.S. vessels. At one point in the crisis this was perceived by President Kennedy, who reportedly exclaimed "almost anything but that" when the possibility of military clashes between U.S. forces and Soviet submarines was mentioned.[62]

A second requirement for the avoidance of accidental/inadvertent war is the validity of warning and attack assessment. Leaders must have confidence that they can distinguish between false and true warning of attack. They must also expect, once having received valid warning of attack, that they will have time to respond appropriately. U.S. nuclear warning and attack assessment evolved during the Cold War into a tightly coupled system of warning sensors, analysis and fusion centers, communications links, commanders, and command posts. The nerve center of U.S. Cold War warning and assessment was NORAD, located in an underground and hardened shelter complex at Cheyenne Mountain, Colorado. NORAD even after the Cold War is the chef d'oeuvre of the elaborate U.S. warning system for surprise attack.

The problem of warning is related to the timing and character of response. Although warning and response can be separated for purposes of analysis, operational warning and response are closely related. The development of long-range, nuclear-tipped missiles required rethinking of many of the basic premises of warning and response on the part of U.S. officials. The time between launch of Soviet ICBMs and their detonations on North American soil would be 20 minutes or less; submarine-launched missiles might arrive even sooner, depending upon their assigned targets and launch positions. Warning therefore had to be automated to some extent, but the "person in the loop" could not be extracted without control passing to a machine. In addition, with such short time lines for warning and response, the initial warning decision and the responsive forces should be assigned to different commands. Thus, for example, the United States assigned to NORAD the strategic warning function, and to SAC and the navy the responsive forces and weapons. The function of NORAD was to establish the plausibility of warning within certain parameters and to initiate a series of conferences among political and military leaders.

The problem of mistaken warning and retaliation based on that mistake was taken very seriously by U.S., and presumably by Soviet, Cold War military and political leaders. The compensatory approach to possibly mistaken warning chosen by the United States was phenomenal redundancy, or "dual phenomenology." This locution meant that indicators of a possible attack would have to be confirmed from more than a single source of input data. For example, U.S. early warning Defense Support Program (DSP) satellites would first detect the exhaust plume of land- or sea-based missiles rising from their Soviet points of origin. Minutes later, ballistic missile early warning system (BMEWS) radars at Fylingdales Moor, England, Thule, Greenland, and Clear, Alaska, would confirm the initial observations by satellite and provide additional details about the size and character of the attack. The United States also deployed specialized radars for the detection of submarine-launched ballistic missiles, presumably off the Atlantic and Pacific coasts of the continental United States. The presumption of phenomenal redundancy was that even if a single part of system gave wrong indications or was out of operation at a particular time, the remainder of the system could effectively confirm, or disconfirm, that an attack was under way. (See Table 4.2 for a summary of kinds of sensors and their targets for warning of attack.)

Warning having been confirmed by more than one source, the problem of assessment remained. What kind of attack was in progress? Was it a massive surprise strike against a comprehensive target set? Or was it a "limited" strike intended for coercive purposes with follow-up attacks held in reserve? U.S. and Soviet leaders in the Cold War also would have been concerned about two possible kinds of errors in attack assessment. A Type I error results in delayed or flawed launch in response to actual attack. A Type II error results in premature or mistaken launch although

Table 4.2
Targets and Sensors for Attack Warning

Target Detected	Sensor	Signature Detected
Missiles	Ground-, air-, or space-based radar	Reentry vehicles, postboost vehicles, decoys, chaff, tanks
	Short-wave infrared detectors	Hot rocket exhaust against warm earth
	Long-wave infrared detectors	Warm reentry and postboost vehicles and tanks against cold space
Aircraft	Ground-, air-, or space-based radar	Body and contours of bombers and cruise missiles; inverse synthetic aperture images
	Over-the-horizon backscatter (OTH-B) radar	Moving planes against unmoving surface of earth
	Medium-wave infrared detectors	Warm bodies of bombers and cruise missiles against warm earth
Nuclear detonation	Ground-, air-, and space-based multispectral detectors	Visible flash, electromagnetic pulse, x-rays

Source: Adapted from John C. Toomay, "Warning and Assessment Centers," ch. 8 in Ashton B. Carter, John D. Steinbruner, and Charles A. Zraket, eds., *Managing Nuclear Operations* (Washington, D.C.: Brookings Institution, 1987), p. 313.

no actual attack is in progress.[63] The significant thing about Type I and Type II error probabilities is that they are relational. Steps taken to minimize the likelihood of one kind of error often increase the probability of the other type of mistaken decision. For example, building in more elaborate and redundant checks against false warning of attack (Type I) may slow down the decision-making process, thereby increasing the chance of a reaction too late for retaliatory forces to carry out their assigned missions.

The problem of valid warning and appropriate response is complicated by the tight coupling of sensors, assessment centers, and response systems. Certain high-technology organizations are especially prone, according to sociologist Charles Perrow, to "normal accidents."[64] So-called normal accidents occur in these kinds of organizations when individual component failures cause other components also to fail—but in unexpected ways. The result is a systemic dysfunction not anticipated by the designers of the system. Accident-prone high-technology organizations, according to Perrow, share two attributes: interactive complexity and tight coupling. Interactive complexity of these organizations increases the frequency of unexpected or seemingly anomalous interactions among the parts, including the human parts. Tight coupling implies: (1) parts of the system interact quickly; (2) sequences of activity are invariant—there is only one right way to do things; (3) little organizational "slack" is available to compensate for error; and (4) safety devices, including redundant checks and balances against failure, are limited to those planned for, and designed into, the system.[65] The Three Mile Island nuclear power disaster, airline crashes, space shuttle malfunctions, electric power grid brownouts, and other "normal accidents" may be inevitable in organizations dependent upon advanced technology and highly interactive parts. The Cold War U.S. nuclear warning, assessment, and response systems are also examples of high-risk, high-technology systems prone to normal accidents. Yet despite this documented failure propensity for these kinds of organizations, normal accidents in the U.S. nuclear command and control system were apparently rare, and obviously none were catastrophic.[66]

Three possible explanations exist for the avoidance of catastrophic failure in nuclear warning and attack assessment during the Cold War. First, the situation was overdetermined. Even the most dullard national political leadership would search for any way out before authorizing a nuclear attack, or a retaliation based on warning of attack. Second, redundancy built into the system ensured against any retaliation based on mistaken warning. Indeed, numerous false warnings became routine business during the Cold War for both U.S. and Soviet organizations charged with warning. Some might argue that the two sides became so habituated to false warning and the low likelihood of actual attack that they dropped their guards. This charge was laid by Gorbachev against the Soviet military after an intrepid West German pilot flew his Cessna aircraft into Red Square, through and under Soviet radar nets and interceptor squadrons. U.S. military leaders were not lulled into complacency about the possibility of accidental nuclear war. But evidence suggests that their confidence in the ability of the decision-making process to compensate for errors in warning and attack assessment, possibly contributory to accidental nuclear war, was excessive.[67]

A third possible explanation is that the United States and the Soviets got lucky. No lethal combination of mistaken warning *and* a nuclear crisis occurred simultaneously. The interactive complexity of both sides' warning systems was never fully road tested under Gran Prix conditions. The interaction between the U.S. warning and assessment system *and* its Soviet counterpart became a separate and dangerous part of the Cold War nuclear complex. That is: The cat watched the rat, and the rat watched the cat. All of this took place in very quick time. The potential for the two sides' interactively complex systems to set one another off, like new-wave smoke detectors that reacted not only to smoke but also to the alarm of another detector, was considerable.

Thus far we have established two requirements for the avoidance of accidental or inadvertent nuclear war or escalation: managing the trade-off between positive and negative control, and coping with the complexity of nuclear warning and attack assessment. A third attribute necessary for the avoidance of accidental/inadvertent war is solution of the problem of delegation of authority and, related to that, the issue of devolution of command.

The president, as head of the executive branch of the U.S. government, may delegate any of his or her responsibilities almost without limit. The U.S. Constitution and the Presidential Succession Act of 1947 have established a constitutional order of succession in case of presidential death, disability, or removal from office. The vice president stands at the head of this order of succession, followed by the Speaker of the House of Representatives and the President Pro Tempore of the Senate. After that, the heads of cabinet departments are enumerated from the oldest department to the youngest: State, Treasury, Defense (War originally), and so forth. The president is the only lawful person who can authorize nuclear release to force commanders and retaliatory attacks using nuclear weapons. However, the president is not a singular actor in this regard: He or she requires the cooperation of various other levels of command and responsibility. This need for more than a singular center of competency for nuclear decision, in case of presidential death or disability, overlaps the military chain of *command* with the civilian chain of *succession* in nuclear matters.

The death of a president or even the entire civilian political leadership in a surprise strike on Washington, D.C. cannot be permitted to paralyze U.S. retaliation, for the obvious reason that such vulnerability might invite attack. Therefore, predelegated or devolved command arrangements for nuclear *authorization* (or authentication) and *enablement* must be possible from other sources in extremis. "Authorization" means that the person or office conveying a command to a subordinate unit is lawfully entitled to do so. Enablement provides the necessary release mechanisms that allow operators to circumvent mechanical or electronic locks assigned to weapons in peacetime to prevent accidental or unauthorized use.[68] For example, an authorization code from the "football" or suitcase carried by a presidential aide tells the receiver that the president has, indeed, sent the indicated command. Enabling commands include the "unlock" codes to bypass electronic locks such as PALs or other use-control devices.

Devolution is a complicated matter because, at least in the U.S. Cold War case, authorization and enablement codes were usually not held by the same persons or at the same levels of command. The president and the secretary of defense, for example, can authorize nuclear release, but they have neither physical possession nor effective custody of nuclear weapons. Possession is related to custody but not necessarily identical to it. Custody implies control over the weapon, whether in one's possession or not. For example, tactical nuclear weapons may be deployed in storage sites guarded by personnel other than those who would actually use those weapons once authorized and enabled to do so. In theory, authorization and enablement commands would be unambiguous, and those lower on the chain of command should automatically carry out orders from higher echelons. The matter is not so simple in practice: Human operators, not automatons, are in the chain of command. And actual custody or physical possession of the weapons is the responsibility of lower echelons who are, in any military situation, capable of resistance of various kinds in response to orders. Even nuclear-age Willie and Joe have some discretion and may decide, mutatis mutandis, to think for themselves, once nuclear charges begin to move from storage sites to launch platforms.[69]

As orders cascade downward and outward through bureaucratic organizations, honest misconstructions and organizational self-interest are inevitable concomitants of crisis time mobilization. Organizations will do what they have been prepared to do: This normative model dictates that nuclear force commanders will follow orders to retaliate, once given, without even thinking about what they are doing. This model works for a situation of unambiguous clarity: Warheads have begun detonating on U.S. soil, the president has identified the transgressor and authorized retaliation, and public support for nuclear response can be assumed. Prior to the actual arrival of nuclear destruction on American targets, the expectations become more confused within and among bureaucratic compartments. One can imagine some elements taking the "wait and see" position, given the Cold War history of false alarms. Other elements might delay response and demand additional authentication for so significant an order. Psychological paralysis on the part of some persons in the face of orders to unleash nuclear death and destruction, knowing that their own kith and kin were at risk from enemy strikes of a similar kind, would be almost predictable and entirely human. (Table 4.3 depicts various loci in the U.S. nuclear command and control system by function and tabulates their respective kinds of influence.)

The U.S. nuclear command system works, according to one expert analyst, like a revolver. The function of the presidential center is "not to act as *a trigger to launch nuclear weapons*, but as a *safety catch preventing other triggers from firing*."[70] In time of peace and relaxed tension, the trigger safety is "on" so that the weapon cannot be fired: Negative control reigns supreme. As a crisis develops, the controls are progressively re-

Table 4.3
U.S. Nuclear Weapons: Command Functions and Capabilities

	Authority (lawful source of command for nuclear release)	Veto (effective ability to nullify orders from authorities)	Physical Capability (effective ability to use weapons and/ or launch vehicles)
President and Secretary of Defense	Yes	No	No
Enabling code holders (e.g., PALs)[1]	No, unless authority is predelegated	Yes	No
Authorizing code holders (e.g., Emergency Action Message (EAM) codes)[2]	No, unless authority is predelegated	No	Possible, if they also hold enabling codes and can transmit an apparently authentic order down the chain of command
Weapons holders	No, unless authority is predelegated	Yes	Possible, if weapons lack use-control devices or if codes have already been given out

[1]Some levels of command may hold authorization codes as well; for example, commanders in chief of unified and specified commands.
[2]Some levels of command may hold enablement codes as well; for example, commanders in chief of unified and specified commands.
Source: Adapted from Peter Douglas Feaver, *Guarding the Guardians: Civilian Control of Nuclear Weapons in the United States* (Ithaca, N.Y.: Cornell University Press, 1992), p. 40.

laxed to permit faster reaction to emergency: Positive control becomes more important. This process becomes apparent in the U.S. DefCon gradations for management of alerts: from level five (lowest, peacetime conditions) to level one (highest, ready for imminent war). As policymakers authorize the military to proceed from lower to higher levels of alert, restraints on force movement and preparedness are "unwrapped," and the criterion of readiness for combat takes precedence relative to peacetime safety and security. Alert management is a tricky business, and the United States, with as much experience as anybody, had its own share of snafus despite high levels of military personnel reliability and numerous checks and balances in the system.

Each of the requirements for the avoidance of accidental/inadvertent war (balancing positive and negative control, making and action upon valid warning and attack assessment, and maintaining authoritative and responsive delegation of authority and/or devolution of command) is potentially at risk from information warfare.

First, the balance between positive and negative control becomes a more complicated juggling act as alert levels are raised. Some components of the force, say ICBMs, are permanently at high levels of readiness for prompt launch. Others, such as the bomber force, require a great deal of care and feeding under stressful conditions before they are launch ready. Nuclear-armed sea-based cruise and ballistic missiles can be readied to fire in a short time, provided that the submarine is on station, but some submarines may need to proceed from port to station and others may be moved in connection with targeting requirements or possible threats to their survivability. Elements of the command system also require synchronized movement across disparate services and civilian departments. If NATO alerts are involved in addition to U.S. forces, as they would have been during any Cold War confrontation with the Soviets, the management of alert phasing and timing becomes even more complicated.

Info weapons introduced into this alerting process have the potential to disestablish the desirable balance between positive and negative control as forces are gradually empowered to go to war. From an enemy perspective, this might be considered a good thing: Confuse the American alerting process and make the wartime command system only partly ready for battle. That is conventional, not nuclear, logic. In a nuclear crisis, the two sides have a shared interest in avoiding nuclear war as well as a competitive desire to prevent one another's gains. Accordingly, each will want the other to maintain assured control over the balance between unlocking the cocked pistol for retaliation and preserving control over the military movements and actions that might trigger inadvertent war. And those military movements and actions are dangerous precisely because their inherent danger might not be so obvious. As Thomas Schelling has noted, war can begin not as a deliberate decision by policymakers but as the result of a process over which neither side has full control. The possible loss of control to be feared here is not military usurpation of civil authority or military disregard of authorized commands. Instead, it is a lack of correct foresight that results in a *sequence of events* foreseen by neither side, creating a new and more adverse climate of expectations about future behavior.[71]

If the two sides in a nuclear crisis get into a sequence of events not correctly foreseen by either and seek to interpret those events correctly, information warfare will be harmful, not helpful, to correct interpretation. An example is perceptions management by one side designed to suggest to the media, public, and legislature of the other side that the first side's intentions are only honorable.[72] The second side, according to this carefully orchestrated set of perceptions fed from one side to another, is really the "aggressor" or the "uncooperative" partner. And the media and political elites of the second side might believe the image created by enemy perceptions management, calling upon leaders to stand down forces and accept the demands of the opponent. Or leaders of the second side might be outraged at the cyberpropaganda of the first side, escalate their demands, and become more intransigent. As Robert Jervis has noted:

A state tends to see the behavior of others as more planned, coordinated, and centralized than it is. Actions that are accidental or the product of different parts of the bureaucracy following their own policies are likely to be perceived as part of a coherent, and often devious, plan. In a nuclear crisis, the propensity to see all of the other side's behavior as part of a plan would be especially likely to yield incorrect and dangerous conclusions.[73]

Messages may be received as intended, but their political effect is not necessarily predictable. Hitler's propaganda efforts to dissuade British and French military reactions to his occupation of Czechoslovakia worked as intended in the short run but established in the Nazi dictator's mind misleading impressions of the two states' weakness in resisting any further tearing up of the map of Europe. Boomeranged perceptions management appeared in Soviet Cold War forgeries of diplomatic and military communications between the United States and its allies. Most of these were transparent and, once found out, gave additional evidence of Soviet diplomatic perfidy to hawkish U.S. politicians and commentators.

Forces poised for immediate retaliation to possible surprise attack also interact with warning systems looking outward for indications of such an attack. False indicators planted by the other side's infowarriors to bring down air defense systems and missile attack warning radars are harbingers of disaster once forces and command systems have been alerted to war-expectant levels. Under those conditions, the vanishing of information from radar screens or fusion centers could be assumed as the first infowave of a nuclear attack, calling forth a preemptive response. Blank screens and obstructed communications leaving personnel in the dark for orders helped the United States in Desert Storm to clear the way for its air strikes against targets in Baghdad and at other locations within Iraqi state territory. The same phenomena might create unacceptable panic if the stakes were vulnerability to nuclear instead of conventional attack. Terrible pressures would rise from lower to higher command levels to "use them or lose them" before communications between and among National Command Authority (NCA), CINCs, and geographically dispersed force commanders were completely severed. The U.S.

president might be loath to order into effect any retaliation under these or similar circumstances, but this legal consolation might not make much practical difference.

High-altitude detonation of a small nuclear weapon by an enemy over its *own* territory and causing no prompt fatalities to U.S. or allied military personnel could nevertheless destabilize U.S. ground and space assets and confuse decisions based on those assets. For example, a nuclear explosion of about 50 kilotons above 100 kilometers in altitude would disrupt space assets by prompt radiation effects and by creating atmospheric disturbances. Unhardened satellites in low earth orbit (LEO), even after they survived the initial radiation, would be vulnerable to total dose destruction as they passed through aggravated radiation belts. Within weeks to months, all unhardened LEO satellites within a theater of operations could be degraded or inoperative. For example, the electromagnetic pulse from a single nuclear burst at an altitude as low as 40 kilometers has the potential to weaken electronics across the entire Persian Gulf region, or throughout the Korean peninsula. Ironically, today's more sophisticated microelectronic systems are more vulnerable to radiation than the cruder and simpler (less integration density, slower operating speed) electronic systems of yesteryear.[74]

In theory, no president would authorize the firing of nuclear forces on the basis of ambiguous warning information. But in the exigent circumstances, while clarification of the status of schizoid information systems was sought, force commanders would not be idle. At DefCon 3 or higher they would be taking appropriate measures to protect their divisions, fleets, and air wings from enemy surprise. These moves would almost certainly be noticed by the other side's intelligence and warning, *even if* no U.S. or allied nuclear weapons were released, moved, or loaded. Few, if any, military experts ever thought that a war would begin with a nuclear "bolt from the blue," absent preceding events: By definition, "bolt from the blue" is not accidental or inadvertent. Any accidental/inadvertent nuclear war in the years between 1946 and 1990 would have almost certainly begun at the level of foot patrols wandering off the map into restricted areas, maritime collisions on the heels of U.S.–Soviet "dodge-em" games at sea, or inadvertent strays by one side into restricted airspace of the other.[75] Confrontations at the tip of the lance have an entirely different meaning higher up the chain of command if links in the chain have been deliberately confused, or their interlink communications distorted, by cyberpathological strikes. As Bruce G. Blair has noted:

Central authorities cannot reasonably expect military organizations simply to carry out orders, however rational the orders may be. Organizations are not that pliant. Any attempt to assert positive or negative control in a way that requires major abrupt changes in operating procedures, a situation more likely to occur if operating routines escape attention in peacetime, would invite confusion and disorder.[76]

Consider, for example, the impression created by President Bill Clinton and Boris Yeltsin, pursuant to their agreement of 1994, that U.S. and Russian strategic nuclear missiles are no longer aimed at targets on one another's state territory. The agreement may have symbolic value, but it did little to change essential procedures for missile targeting. Although Russian missiles are supposedly set on "zero flight plan," the missiles' memory banks still store wartime targets. The Russian General Staff can, from command posts in Moscow and elsewhere, override the detargeting by means of a Signal-A computer network, reaiming silo-based missiles at U.S. targets within 10 seconds.[77] U.S. missiles can be retargeted against Russia just as rapidly.

In addition, Russian operational practice permits its command system about three or four minutes for detection of an attack and another three or four minutes for high-level decision making. Russia's command system and early warning network have obviously deteriorated since the end of the Cold War, along with the rest of Russia's military, raising the potential for accidents or inadvertency. For example, in January 1995, the firing of a Norwegian scientific rocket triggered the first-ever Russian strategic alert of their prompt launch forces, an emergency conference including the Russian president and other principal leaders, and activation of the Russian equivalent to the U.S. nuclear "football" or suitcases assigned to national command authorities.[78] According to U.S. press reports in April 1997, Russia's present-day nuclear command and control system was in danger of breaking down. A retired Strategic Rocket Forces officer charged that at least one recent system malfunction caused parts of the nuclear arsenal to go spontaneously into "combat mode."[79]

Finally on the problem of infowar and the avoidance of accidental or inadvertent war or escalation, the problem of delegation of authority or devolution of command is exacerbated by information distortion in the command system of either side. In the case of the U.S. nuclear command system, for example, the "cocked pistol" analogy implies that the pistol will fire back at the highest levels of alert unless authorized commands hold back retaliation.[80] An enemy seeking to paralyze U.S. retaliation by confusing the information networks for nuclear command would, instead, have an equal chance of cutting the command and control system into pieces. Each piece and the forces with which it could connect would then be a sovereign, postattack entity, firing back with whatever resources remained to it at targets of opportunity. Commanders unable to communicate with one another might assume that their counterparts were already dead or hopelessly cut off from proper orders. A dumb, blinded, and disaggregated nuclear response system would then take over from what had been a singular chain of nuclear command and control.

The preceding point applies both to accidental/inadvertent war or escalation and to conflict termination, explored in the next section. Stylized descriptions of nuclear warfare in the Cold War literature followed predictable scripts. One side's first strike subtracted weapons from the second side's inventory; the second strike fired back with its survivors; the first side struck again with its remaining forces; and so forth. These stylistic descriptions of force exchanges overlooked the differences among peacetime, crisis, and wartime assessments. Assessment is a qualitative process, dependent upon accurate and timely flow of information. It demands both central coordination, so that all arms of the military machine are operating according to a shared concept of alertness or battle, and decentralized operation or execution of orders. The loss of information necessary for crisis or wartime assessment may not take place in discrete and measurable stages but in weird, nonlinear ways. Accordingly, leaders in a crisis or early wartime situation literally *may not know what it is that they do not know.*[81]

An important aspect of the difference between conventional and nuclear deterrence is that the strategic problematique is so much more linear in the conventional case. The object of the military in a conventional war is to obtain dominant battlespace awareness and to deny the opponent the opportunity to use cyberspace effectively.[82] On the other hand, the problem of avoiding accidental/inadvertent nuclear war is more nonlinear, perhaps even chaotic, with regard to the information spectrum.[83] Exploitation of information, including electronic, is both a cooperative and a competitive activity when the avoidance of nuclear war is equally as significant as the accomplishment of one's military objective, should war occur. One side does not necessarily want to drive the other side's information regime off the field—or to corrupt it into a Mad Hatter's Tea Party of misinformation. Further, the distinction between "offensive" and "defensive" infowar may be more muddled in the case of nuclear deterrence and the avoidance of accidental war or escalation compared to the more straightforward task of prevailing in war, should it occur.

CONCLUSION

Nuclear weapons are still out there, stalking proponents of a post-nuclear world in which information dominance pushes weapons of mass destruction onto the ash heap of military history. Probable opponents of the United States in the twenty-first century, or regional aggressors against U.S. allies, either have, or are trying hard to get, nuclear weapons and ballistic missiles of theater or intercontinental range. Russia remains locked in an arms control relationship with the United States in which a process of denuclearization is hostage to the rundown state of Russia's economy and its conventional forces. Russia has therefore moved nuclear weapons to the front end of its deterrence strategy, and the 1999 version of its military doctrine leaves no doubt that Russia reserves the right to first use of nuclear weapons against an attack on its vital interests by a state armed with nuclear weapons or, in some instances, without them.

Nuclear deterrence depends upon the ability of both sides in a relationship to combine the selective use of threats with the equally selective offering of reassurances, in order to send and receive clear messages and to appraise accurately the intentions and capabilities of the other side. On the other hand, information warfare depends for its success upon the denial to the other side of accurate information, in order to confuse the opponent's decision-making process and thus to prevent timely decisions and actions. Where nuclear deterrence for its success requires clarity and transparency in the shared information environment between opponents, information warfare may push either or both sides into the fog of war. Deterrence succeeds on the basis of simple decision rules and the ability to present to policymakers a highly structured set of alternatives for prompt decision. Information conflict fuzzes the distinction among alternatives and denies the luxury of nuanced thinking. It is, in short, a shotgun marriage.

NOTES

1. A superior overview of this issue is Dorothy E. Denning, *Information Warfare and Security* (Reading, Mass.: Addison-Wesley, 1999), esp. pp. 21–42. Information has, of course, always been an important part of war and crisis management. But as Steven Metz and James Kievit have explained, the informational aspect of RMA may "alter the traditional relationship between operational complexity and effective control" as new means of acquiring, analyzing, and distributing information allow for added complexity in military action without sacrificing control or timing. See Metz and Kievit, *Strategy and the Revolution in Military Affairs: From Theory to Policy* (Carlisle Barracks, Pa.: U.S. Army War College, June 27, 1995), p. 4 and passim. See also Metz, *Armed Conflict in the 21st Century: The Information Revolution and Post-Modern Warfare* (Carlisle Barracks, Pa.: U.S. Army War College, Strategic Studies Institute, April 2000), pp. 59–64.

2. Alvin Toffler and Heidi Toffler, *War and Anti-War: Making Sense of Today's Global Chaos* (New York: Warner Books, 1993), passim.

3. Paul Bracken, *Fire in the East* (New York: HarperCollins, 1999), passim. See also Colin S. Gray, *The Second Nuclear Age* (Boulder, Colo.: Lynne Rienner Publishers, 1999).

4. For an introduction to this topic, see John Arquilla and David Ronfeldt,

"A New Epoch—and Spectrum—of Conflict," ch. 1 in John Arquilla and David Ronfeldt, eds., *In Athena's Camp: Preparing for Conflict in the Information Age* (Santa Monica, Calif.: RAND, 1997), pp. 1–22. See also, on definitions and concepts of information warfare: Martin Libicki, *What Is Information Warfare?* (Washington, D.C.: National Defense University, ACIS Paper 3, August 1995); Martin Libicki, *Defending Cyberspace and Other Metaphors* (Washington, D.C.: National Defense University, Directorate of Advanced Concepts, Technologies and Information Strategies, February 1997); Toffler and Toffler, *War and Anti-War*, pp. 163–207; John Arquilla and David Ronfeldt, *Cyberwar Is Coming!* (Santa Monica, Calif.: RAND, 1992); David S. Alberts, *The Unintended Consequences of Information Age Technologies: Avoiding the Pitfalls, Seizing the Initiative* (Washington, D.C.: National Defense University, Institute for National Strategic Studies, Center for Advanced Concepts and Technology, April 1996); and Gordon R. Sullivan and Anthony M. Coroalles, *Seeing the Elephant: Leading America's Army into the Twenty-first Century* (Cambridge, Mass.: Institute for Foreign Policy Analysis, 1995). A roadmap to information resources related to strategy and other military topics appears in James Kievit and Steven Metz, *The Strategist and the Web Revisited: An Updated Guide to Internet Resources* (Carlisle Barracks, Pa.: U.S. Army War College, Strategic Studies Institute, Army After Next Project, October 17, 1996).

5. Arquilla and Ronfeldt, "A New Epoch—and Spectrum—of Conflict," p. 6.

6. Arquilla and Ronfeldt, "The Advent of Netwar," ch. 12 in Arquilla and Ronfeldt, *In Athena's Camp*, pp. 275–294.

7. Ibid., passim.

8. Thomas A. Keaney and Eliot A Cohen, *Revolution in Warfare? Air Power in the Persian Gulf* (Annapolis, Md.: Naval Institute Press, 1995), pp. 188–212. See also Kenneth Allard, *Command, Control and the Common Defense*, rev. ed. (Washington, D.C.: National Defense University Press, 1996), pp. 273–303. For appropriate cautions, see Jeffrey Cooper, *Another View of the Revolution in Military Affairs* (Carlisle Barracks, Pa.: U.S. Army War College, Strategic Studies Institute, July 15, 1994), esp. pp. 8 and 36.

9. Martin C. Libicki, "DBK and Its Consequences," in Stuart E. Johnson and Martin C. Libicki, eds., *Dominant Battlespace Knowledge: The Winning Edge* (Washington, D.C.: National Defense University Press, 1995), pp. 27–58.

10. Richard K. Betts, *Surprise Attack: Lessons for Defense Planning* (Washington, D.C.: Brookings Institution, 1982).

11. Libicki, *Defending Cyberspace and Other Metaphors*, p. 10.

12. David S. Alberts, *Defensive Information Warfare* (Washington, D.C.: National Defense University, Directorate of Advanced Concepts, Technologies and Information Strategies, August 1996), p. 12.

13. Libicki, *Defending Cyberspace and Other Metaphors*, p. 30.

14. The White House, *Joint Statement on Parameters on Future Reductions in Nuclear Forces*, Office of the Press Secretary, Helsinki, Finland, March 21, 1997.

15. Jack Mendelsohn, "START II and Beyond," *Arms Control Today*, October 1996, pp. 3–9.

16. William C. Martel and William T. Pendley, *Nuclear Coexistence: Rethinking U.S. Policy to Promote Stability in an Era of Proliferation* (Montgomery, Ala.: Air War College, April 1994), pp. 3–5, 10–11, and passim.

17. Gen. Aleksandr Lebed, former national security adviser to Russian Presi-

dent Boris Yeltsin, claimed in a U.S. network television interview in September 1997 that many portable "suitcase" nuclear weapons (atomic demolition munitions, or ADMs) created during the Cold War for use with Soviet special operations forces could not be accounted for by the Russian military now. The U.S. *60 Minutes* program of September 6 raised the possibility that missing weapons could have been sold to terrorists or states like Iraq with nuclear ambitions. Russian defense officials denied that any nuclear weapons were unaccounted for.

18. V. I. Tsymbal, "Kontseptsiya 'Informatsionnoy voiny' " (Concept of information warfare), speech given at the Russian–U.S. conference on "Evolving Post–Cold War National Security Issues," Moscow, September 12–14 1995, p. 7, cited in Timothy L. Thomas, "Deterring Information Warfare: A New Strategic Challenge," *Parameters*, no. 4 (Winter 1996–1997), p. 82.

19. Alexander L. George, ed., *Avoiding War: Problems of Crisis Management* (Boulder, Colo.: Westview Press, 1991).

20. See Patrick M. Morgan, *Deterrence: A Conceptual Analysis* (Beverly Hills, Calif.: Sage Publications, 1983), and Richard Ned Lebow and Janice Gross Stein, *We All Lost the Cold War* (Princeton, N.J.: Princeton University Press, 1994), pp. 351–355.

21. Keith B. Payne, *Deterrence in the Second Nuclear Age* (Lexington: University Press of Kentucky, 1996), p. 57. See also Col. David Jablonsky, *Strategic Rationality Is Not Enough: Hitler and the Concept of Crazy States* (Carlisle Barracks, Pa.: Strategic Studies Institute, U.S. Army War College, August 8, 1991), esp. pp. 5–8 and 31–37.

22. Lebow and Stein, *We All Lost the Cold War*, pp. 122–123.

23. Robert Jervis, *The Meaning of the Nuclear Revolution: Statecraft and the Prospect of Armageddon* (Ithaca, N.Y.: Cornell University Press, 1989), p. 183.

24. A virus is a self-replicating piece of software intended to destroy or alter the contents of other software stored on floppy disks or hard drives. Worms corrupt the integrity of software and information systems from the "inside out" in ways that create weaknesses exploitable by an enemy.

25. James G. March and Herbert A. Simon, *Organizations* (New York: John Wiley and Sons, 1958), pp. 140, 146.

26. Lebow and Stein, *We All Lost the Cold War*, pp. 335–336.

27. Graham T. Allison, *Essence of Decision: Explaining the Cuban Missile Crisis* (Boston, Mass.: Little, Brown, 1971), p. 141. See also Scott D. Sagan, *Moving Targets: Nuclear Strategy and National Security* (Princeton, N.J.: Princeton University Press, 1989), p. 147, and Lebow and Stein, *We All Lost the Cold War*, p. 342.

28. For example, see Richard Ned Lebow, *Between Peace and War: The Nature of International Crisis* (Baltimore, Md.: Johns Hopkins University Press, 1981); Michael Howard, *Studies in War and Peace* (New York: Viking Press, 1971), pp. 99–109; Gerhard Ritter, *The Schlieffen Plan: Critique of a Myth* (London: Oswald Wolff, 1958); and D.C.B. Lieven, *Russia and the Origins of the First World War* (New York: St. Martin's Press, 1983).

29. As David Alberts notes, "Information dominance would be of only academic interest, if we could not turn this information dominance into battlefield dominance." See Alberts, "The Future of Command and Control with DBK," in Johnson and Libicki, *Dominant Battlespace Knowledge*, pp. 77–102, citation p. 80.

30. As Colin S. Gray has noted, "Because deterrence flows from a relationship, it cannot reside in unilateral capabilities, behavior or intentions. Anyone who

refers to *the* deterrent policy plainly does not understand the subject." Gray, *Explorations in Strategy* (Westport, Conn.: Greenwood Press, 1996), p. 33 (italics in original).

31. Ashton B. Carter, "Assessing Command System Vulnerability," ch. 17 in Ashton B. Carter, John D. Steinbruner, and Charles A. Zraket, eds., *Managing Nuclear Operations* (Washington, D.C.: Brookings Institution, 1987), pp. 555–610.

32. Richard Ned Lebow, *Nuclear Crisis Management: A Dangerous Illusion* (Ithaca, N.Y.: Cornell University Press, 1987), p. 25.

33. Ibid., pp. 31–74. See also David Alan Rosenberg, "The Origins of Overkill: Nuclear Weapons and American Strategy, 1945–1960," *International Security*, no. 4 (Spring 1983), in Steven E. Miller, ed., *Strategy and Nuclear Deterrence* (Princeton, N.J.: Princeton University Press, 1984), pp. 113–182, esp. p. 135 and pp. 143–144.

34. Donald Kagan, *On the Origins of War and the Preservation of Peace* (New York: Doubleday, 1995), p. 197.

35. L.C.F. Turner, "The Significance of the Schlieffen Plan," ch. 9 in Paul M. Kennedy, ed., *The War Plans of the Great Powers* (London: Allen and Unwin, 1979), pp. 199–221; and Holger M. Herwig, "The Dynamics of Necessity: German Military Policy during the First World War," ch. 3 in Allan R. Millett and Williamson Murray, eds., *Military Effectiveness*, vol. I (London: Unwin Hyman, 1988), pp. 80–115. See also Kennedy's note that German planning was unique and tantamount to war in his introduction to *The War Plans of the Great Powers*, pp. 15–16.

36. See Martin van Creveld, *Command in War* (Cambridge, Mass.: Harvard University Press, 1985), passim.

37. Lebow and Stein, *We All Lost the Cold War*, pp. 349–351.

38. Desmond Ball, "The Development of the SIOP, 1960–1983," ch. 3 in Desmond Ball and Jeffrey Richelson, eds., *Strategic Nuclear Targeting* (Ithaca, N.Y.: Cornell University Press, 1986), pp. 57–83.

39. Colin S. Gray, "Targeting Problems for Central War," ch. 8 in Ball and Richelson, *Strategic Nuclear Targeting*, pp. 171–193.

40. Lawrence Freedman, *The Evolution of Nuclear Strategy* (New York: St. Martin's Press, 1981), pp. 245–256.

41. Bruce G. Blair, "Alerting in Crisis and Conventional War," ch. 3 in Carter, Steinbruner, and Zraket, *Managing Nuclear Operations*, pp. 75–120; Sagan, *Moving Targets*, pp. 148–149.

42. Col. David M. Glantz, ed., *The Initial Period of War on the Eastern Front, 22 June–August 1941* (London: Frank Cass, 1993), esp. pp. 28–37 and 40–50.

43. Martin van Creveld, *Technology and War: From 2000 B.C. to the Present* (New York: Free Press, 1989), p. 247.

44. Lebow and Stein, *We All Lost the Cold War*, p. 341; Allison, *Essence of Decision*, pp. 138–139.

45. L.C.F. Turner, "The Russian Mobilization in 1914," ch. 2 in Kennedy, *The War Plans of the Great Powers*, pp. 252–268, argues that the distinction between Russian partial and general mobilization was essentially meaningless in terms of Germany's understanding of Russia's actions. See also Marc Trachtenberg, *History and Strategy* (Princeton, N.J.: Princeton University Press, 1991), pp. 80–87 and 94–95. Luigi Albertini refers to the plan for partial mobilization as "this bright idea of Sazonov's" and argues that the Russian General Staff had never worked up a plan for mobilization only against Austria-Hungary. See Albertini,

The Origins of the War of 1914, vol. 2, trans. and ed. Isabella M. Massey (London: Oxford University Press, 1953), pp. 292–293.

46. Lebow, *Nuclear Crisis Management*, p. 150.

47. Scott D. Sagan, *The Limits of Safety: Organizations, Accidents and Nuclear Weapons* (Princeton, N.J.: Princeton University Press, 1993), pp. 228–231.

48. Bruce W. Nelan, "Nuclear Disarray," *Time*, May 19, 1997, pp. 46–48.

49. Lebow and Stein, *We All Lost the Cold War*, p. 132. Raymond L. Garthoff, who participated in U.S. Cuban missile crisis decision making as a State Department official, contends that "no U.S. plan for an invasion of Cuba was under way" but acknowledges that "previously laid-down U.S. contingency plans for military action against Cuba were being refined, updated, and rehearsed. Garthoff, *Reflections on the Cuban Missile Crisis*, rev. ed. (Washington, D.C.: Brookings Institution, 1989), pp. 50–51. See, in particular, his discussion of the memorandum from McNamara on contingencies for military action against Cuba, referred by the Joint Chiefs to CINCLANT (Commander in Chief, Atlantic).

50. General Anatoli I. Gribkov and General William Y. Smith, *Operation ANADYR: U.S. and Soviet Generals Recount the Cuban Missile Crisis* (Chicago: Edition q Publishers, 1994), pp. 62–63, and appendix 1, Documents 1–3. See also Mark Kramer, "Tactical Nuclear Weapons, Soviet Command Authority, and the Cuban Missile Crisis," *Cold War International History Project Bulletin*, no. 3 (Fall 1993), pp. 40, 42–46, and James G. Blight, Bruce J. Allyn, and David A. Welch, "Kramer vs. Kramer: Or, How Can You Have Revisionism in the Absence of Orthodoxy?" *Cold War International History Project Bulletin*, no. 3 (Fall 1993), pp. 41, 47–50. The best evidence now suggests that prior to October 22 Moscow had given to the commander of Soviet forces in Cuba, Gen. Pliyev, predelegated authority to use nuclear-armed tactical missiles in the event of an American invasion.

51. On Soviet alerts during the Cuban missile crisis, see Richard K. Betts, *Nuclear Blackmail and Nuclear Balance* (Washington, D.C.: Brookings Institution, 1987), p. 120, and Bruce G. Blair, *The Logic of Accidental Nuclear War* (Washington, D.C.: Brookings Institution, 1993), pp. 23–24. On the worldwide military alert broadcast in the clear contrary to regulations, see Lebow and Stein, *We All Lost the Cold War*, p. 341.

52. Scott D. Sagan, *Moving Targets: Nuclear Strategy and National Security* (Priceton, N.J.: Princeton University Press, 1989), p. 146.

53. McNamara, in Blight and Welch, *On the Brink*, pp. 52 and 195.

54. Allison, *Essence of Decision*, p. 224.

55. Peter Douglas Feaver, *Guarding the Guardians: Civilian Control of Nuclear Weapons in the United States* (Ithaca, N.Y.: Cornell University Press, 1992), p. 12.

56. John D. Steinbruner, "Choices and Trade-offs," ch. 16 in Carter, Steinbruner, and Zraket, *Managing Nuclear Operations*, pp. 535–554, esp. pp. 539–541.

57. On the relationship between deterrence and stress, see Lebow and Stein, *We All Lost the Cold War*, pp. 331–338.

58. Sagan, *Moving Targets*, pp. 164–165.

59. Ibid.

60. Blair, *The Logic of Accidental Nuclear War*, passim; Bruce G. Blair, *Strategic Command and Control: Redefining the Nuclear Threat* (Washington, D.C.: Brookings Institution, 1985), pp. 65–78.

61. Steinbruner, "Choices and Trade-offs," pp. 542–543.

62. Allison, *Essence of Decision*, p. 137.

63. Ashton B. Carter, "Sources of Error and Uncertainty," ch. 18 in Carter, Steinbruner, and Zraket, *Managing Nuclear Operations*, p. 628.

64. Charles Perrow, *Normal Accidents: Living with High-Risk Technologies* (New York: Basic Books, 1984). Perrow's concept is further developed and applied to nuclear accident theory in Sagan, *The Limits of Safety*, pp. 31–36.

65. Sagan, *The Limits of Safety*, p. 34; Perrow, *Normal Accidents*, pp. 93–96.

66. But see Sagan, *The Limits of Safety*, pp. 228–246.

67. Ibid., p. 248.

68. Feaver, *Guarding the Guardians*, p. 38.

69. I suspect that Russian nuclear force commanders are worried about Ivan and Boris in this regard; if not, they ought to be, given the current morale of the Russian military. Russian Defense Minister Igor Rodionov declared in January 1997 that the possibility of a breakdown in the nuclear command and control system was very real.

70. Paul Bracken, *The Command and Control of Nuclear Forces* (New Haven, Conn.: Yale University Press, 1983), p. 196 (italics in original).

71. The most original thinking about this problem has been contributed by Thomas C. Schelling. See Schelling, *Arms and Influence* (New Haven, Conn.: Yale University Press, 1966), esp. pp. 99–111.

72. See Brian D. Dailey, "Deception, Perceptions Management, and Self-Deception in Arms Control: An Examination of the ABM Treaty," ch. 11 in Brian D. Dailey and Patrick J. Parker, eds., *Soviet Strategic Deception* (Lexington, Mass.: D. C. Heath, 1987), pp. 225–260, esp. pp. 230–231. The author overstates the degree of Soviet deception involved in their approach to ABM Treaty negotiation, but the discussion of the concept of perceptions management remains useful.

73. Jervis, *The Meaning of the Nuclear Revolution*, p. 155.

74. R. C. Webb, Defense Special Weapons Agency, *Implications of Low-Yield High Altitude Nuclear Detonations*, briefing to Nuclear Weapons and the Revolution in Military Affairs Workshop, September 16–17, 1997.

75. None of these illustrations are hypothetical. The first happened to U.S. forces in East Germany acting as authorized military observers; the second, to U.S. and Soviet naval forces in Cold War encounters too numerous to mention; the third, to KAL 007 in 1983, suspected by the Soviets (so they claimed) of espionage for the Korean CIA and for the United States.

76. Blair, *Strategic Command and Control*, p. 69.

77. Testimony of Dr. Bruce G. Blair, Senior Fellow in Foreign Policy Studies, Brookings Institution, before House National Security Committee, March 13, 1997, from Committee on Nuclear Policy, *Policy Brief*, vol. 1, no. 3, p. 1.

78. Ibid., pp. 1–2. See also Nelan, "Nuclear Disarray," p. 46.

79. James T. Hackett in *Wall Street Journal*, March 28, 1997, cited in *Russian Reform Monitor*, no. 251 (Washington, D.C.: American Foreign Policy Council, April 4, 1997). The term *combat mode* does not necessarily reveal very much about the actual operational status of Russian forces. Soviet forces of the Cold War years used the term *combat readiness* (*boevaya gotovnost'*) to include at least three different levels of preparedness for troops: routine, increased, and full combat readiness.

80. Bracken, *The Command and Control of Nuclear Forces*, pp. 196–197.

81. Ibid., esp. pp. 114–116, is especially good on this point.

82. Jeffrey Cooper, "Dominant Battlespace Awareness and Future Warfare," in Johnson and Libicki, *Dominant Battlespace Knowledge*, pp. 103–119, esp. pp. 115–116. See also Toffler and Toffler, *War and Anti-War*, p. 166, and Arquilla and Ronfeldt, *Cyberwar Is Coming!*, p. 6.

83. On the issue of nonlinear relationships and their potential relationship to deterrence, see Robert Jervis, "Systems and Interaction Effects," ch. 2 in Jack Snyder and Robert Jervis, eds., *Coping with Complexity in the International System* (Boulder, Colo.: Westview Press, 1993), pp. 25–46, esp. pp. 32–33.

Chapter 5

Armageddon by Osmosis: Must Nuclear Weapons Spread?

INTRODUCTION

In the 1960s experts predicted that within several decades nuclear weapons would be as abundant as mosquitoes and that the likelihood of nuclear war was, therefore, inevitably rising. Things did not turn out that way. Many explained the absence of major war in Europe for 45 years as the result of political realism and nuclear deterrence. Some theorists and policymakers now predict that the slow spread of nuclear weapons can be made compatible with future international peace and stability by mixing the same ingredients: realism and deterrence.[1] These optimistic expectations about the role of nuclear weapons in the post–Cold War world are likely to be disappointed.

Post–Cold War confidence in the perpetual success of nuclear deterrence in avoiding war is even more misplaced. The reasons why are both theoretical and practical. The theories on which the case for peaceful coexistence between stability and nuclear proliferation rest, once examined with care, provide an inadequate platform to support optimism. Practice also cautions against optimism. The nonnuclear states that seek to acquire nuclear weapons, other weapons of mass destruction, and ballistic missile delivery systems include an unrepresentative sample of antisystemic rogues, including some with regional scores to settle. Nuclear optimists assume that these states will reason as past nuclear powers have about the costs and risks of nuclear brinkmanship or war.

NUCLEAR WEAPONS AND DETERRENCE IN THE COLD WAR

The Cold War emphasis on deterring a major war in Europe and/or a conflict between the Americans and Soviets created a certain bias, not to say laziness, in analysis. As the numbers of survivable weapons in American and Soviet arsenals grew into many thousands, it became clear that there would be no winners or even Phyrric victors in a nuclear war. The task was war avoidance by means of nuclear threat. This nuclear bargaining could become quite sinister and dangerous at times, as in major superpower crises. But most of the time nuclear weapons just stood there in their silos or in bomb racks, silent sentinels reminding their purveyors of the imminent Armageddon that would almost certainly follow the first detonations in anger.

The U.S.–Soviet duopoly over large and survivable nuclear forces was one very important unique aspect of nuclear deterrence as it was practiced during Cold War. Another unique aspect was the absence of any countervailing defenses for nuclear offenses. For most of history the introduction of new offensive weapons had been followed by eventual breakthroughs in defensive countermeasures that might nullify those more threatening offenses. But the predominance of nuclear rocket missiles in the Cold War seemed to nullify this law of historical yin and yang between offensive and defensive technologies. The gap between offensive and defensive technologies was so wide as to invite ridicule, at least in the United States, of efforts to deploy national missile defenses (Reagan's program was dubbed "Star Wars" by critics and the media) or to develop a national civil defense plan to cope with the effects of nuclear war. It seemed to Cold War strategists that, as far as the technological eye could see ahead, defenses against nuclear attack were either wasteful or counterproductive to stability.[2]

Stability, in fact, became a new term of art in strategy, at least insofar as strategy coupled with nuclear arms control. Stability was thought by most American analysts and policymakers to rest on a U.S.–Soviet mutual hostage relationship based on offensive retaliation. A stable deterrent was one that could guarantee assured destruction of the opponent's society in revenge, regardless of the size or scale of the attack made upon it, and also regardless of the reason for the attack: for example, from fear of being attacked as opposed to a cold-blooded decision to launch a preventive war. The Great Deterrent was thus automated politically as well as technically.

Of course, as the numbers of American and Soviet nuclear weapons grew apace during the Cold War, the option presented itself to exceed minimum speed limits based on "assured destruction" of the opponent's society. The Soviet leadership looked at matters military and strategic through a different prism compared to the American one. The Soviet Union had had a different historical experience, of invasion and of temporary conquest, and operated from a different set of premises about the sources of global conflict. Conflict, in the Soviet view, was based on ideological incompatibility between capitalist and socialist systems. Weapons were symptoms of conflict, not causes of it. The possibility that the alliance of capitalist states embodied in NATO might initiate a war at any time could not be excluded. The Soviet Union therefore had to be prepared for another conflict, including a possibly nuclear one.

Thus, although the Soviet leadership of the Cold War years acknowledged the significance of nuclear weapons (after Stalin) and the reality of nuclear deterrence, deterrence was never the experiment in applied psychology or the substitute for war preparedness for Moscow that it appeared to be in Washington. Actually, nuclear deterrence in Washington was influenced from two sides: the technological, driven by the air force, and the social-scientific, originating in government-supported think tanks studying military problems out from under the control of the military brass. The newly independent air force was anxious to demonstrate that while the army and navy might have some roles in future warfare, air power had become the premier arm of service and it would be air power that would deliver the Sunday punch in the Great Deterrent. So pervasive was the air force hold on military thinking in the early years of the Cold War that the army and navy competed to outdo air power for strategic, that is, long-range and massive destruction, missions. The navy finally attained its own nuclear retaliation force in Polaris and successor generations of ballistic missile submarines; the army acquired property rights to ballistic missile defense, at least on the ground. Missiles were divided among all three arms of service, depending on mission and range.

The other source of influence on the American concepts of nuclear strategy and deterrence was social scientific thinking from universities, laboratories, and think tanks. The "good news" about this infusion of ideas and expertise from outside the military was that it provided fresh thinking that guarded against military command-mindedness and standpatism. On the other hand, the ideas of social scientists like Bernard Brodie, Henry Kissinger, and Herman Kahn drew a line between prenuclear and nuclear strategic thinking that bred distrust among military professionals. Many serving officers exposed to the new thinking were wary because the new concepts seemed to take insufficient cognizance of military history. Others objected to the apparent disparagement of combat experience on the part of some of the new nuclear strategists. Still other military traditionalists were offended by the analytical methods and cult mentality of some of the more quantitative, social-scientific strategists, including those who clustered around Secretary of Defense Robert S. McNamara.

There were, until the advent of Mikhail Gorbachev at the top of the Soviet leadership in 1985, no similar coteries of academic social-science thinkers with pervasive influence on the making of military strategy in Moscow. The formulation of military strategy in Moscow, including possible strategy for the use of nuclear weapons in combat, was the responsibility of a very circumscribed political and military elite. Their experience in World War II drove their thinking about military strategy, and their experience in Soviet bureaucracy was not one that encouraged innovation (unless approved by higher echelons) or the importation of thinking about military science or military art from the civilian world.

The preceding statements should not be interpreted to disparage the Soviet approach to military thinking or their writings about strategy during the Cold War. To the contrary, Soviet thinking about the relationship between war and politics and about the historical relationship between weapons and warfare was at least on a par with, if not superior to, its American and allied Western counterparts. The point here is not the subtlety or sophistication of Soviet compared to American military thinking but, rather, the difference in sociological origins and the resulting disparities in emphasis and in conceptual framework.[3] From the Soviet perspective, history showed that war was a normal feature of international life, and their nuclear armed adversaries could not be trusted not to wage war against them if the conditions seemed propitious. The American view of nuclear weapons, on the other hand, was more absolutist: They would not be employed unless and until the bad guys attacked the good guys, and then a righteous fist of Armageddon would be used to annihilate the bad guys.

The U.S. problem in this regard was not so much in convincing Moscow that its deterrent threats were meaningful in regard to an attack on American soil but in extending that nuclear deterrent threat to protect U.S. allies in NATO Europe. The deployment of U.S. nuclear weapons in Western Europe was intended to convince the Soviet leadership that no war started there could remain small or nonnuclear. Therefore, it was too risky for them to undertake. On the other hand, this required that the U.S. president offer an unconditional guarantee in peacetime that in the event of crisis or of war the president might prefer to emphasize in degrees. Nuclear weapons, as the French emphasized in creating their own independent nuclear force, did not lend themselves to subdivision or partialing out of effects. And if the Soviet Union really believed that a conventional military attack across the Fulda Gap automatically led to a series of nuclear exchanges between Montana and Siberia, then it paid Soviet attackers to begin with the most massive attack possible against the American homeland and against the widest target set of U.S. strategic nuclear forces.

There was no way around the logical trade-off between firebreaks, separating conventional from nuclear war in Europe, and coupling, requiring an indivisible deterrent from the inter-German border to the Great Plains of North America. The United States under the Kennedy and Johnson administrations eventually opted for "flexible response" as a declaratory strategy. Officially adopted by NATO in 1967 at the Americans' behest, it proposed a graduated chain of escalation from an initial phase of conventional war, to the limited use of nuclear weapons in Europe, to the unlimited use of nuclear weapons in global warfare. This great chain of nuclear being was supposed to deter any Soviet aggression in Europe, regardless of its political cause or urgency.

Since no World War III took place between 1946 and 1989, many credit nuclear weapons and nuclear deterrence, as explained above, for the absence of major war in Europe and of world war for a half century. Given the turbulence of the first half of the twentieth century, the pacification of Europe and the absence of world war are singular accomplishments. But are they probative evidence that nuclear deterrence worked? One might argue that the Americans, Europeans, and Soviets had been exhausted by the exertions of World War II and had neither the intent nor the societal stamina to fight another major war after 1945. This argument of postwar political and societal combat exhaustion has some plausibility for the early years of the Cold War, say, until about 1958 or 1959. By then another generation of leaders in the Kremlin and in Washington had come to power, and the economies of the United States, the Soviet Union, and Western Europe had recovered from much of their wartime devastation. Memories of World War II U.S.–Soviet accord were replaced by confrontations between 1958 and 1962 over Berlin and Cuba, the latter arguably the most dangerous confrontation of the Cold War.

It is important for predicting the post–Cold War role of nuclear weapons, and of nuclear deterrence, neither to exaggerate nor to disparage the status of nuclear weapons in keeping the Cold War peace.[4] Any correct assessment of that role runs into an irony: history turned favorably on the difference, instead of the similarity, in U.S. and Soviet military thinking. If the Americans and Soviets had thought alike about nuclear strategy during the Cold War, then Armageddon might have been closer and the likelihood of actual shooting between the two superpowers so much the greater.

Because U.S. notions of nuclear strategy were influenced by technology, military servicism, and social-scientific thinking in a weird-package fashion, they kept some restraints on the buildup of superfluous weapons and on defense spending. U.S. perspectives on defense strategy also kept open the door to U.S.–Soviet arms control negotiations that helped to mitigate some of the suspicions of the Cold War. On the other hand, the Soviet military traditionalist view of the role of weapons in strategy and its assumption of ideologically driven global conflict made the Soviet leadership cautious and pessimistic about nuclear brinkmanship, threats that left "something to chance," and other manipulations of risk that the Brezhnev regime attributed to Khrushchev in retrospect as "adventurism." Risk-acceptant behavior with nuclear weapons was not, in the Soviet view, prudent unless the issue was deadly serious. Using nuclear weapons to send signals of resolve or of tacit nuclear bargaining in crises was tantamount to playing with atomic fire that might bring down the Soviet regime.

There is another important issue here related to the role of nuclear weapons in the Cold War and what it might mean for the post–Cold War world. The Soviet leadership, steeped in the tenets of Lenin and Clausewitz, did not believe in apolitical wars. Wars, even nuclear war, grew from political causes having to do with the conflict between socialism and capitalism. Soviet military "doctrine" was always a much more theoretically embedded notion than its usage in Western terminology, where "doctrine" was characteristically expressed in training manuals. Soviet military doctrine existed at two levels: the sociopolitical and the military-technical. The sociopolitical level of doctrine defined the nature and causes of future war and identified the main enemies of the Soviet Union and their aims. Doctrine at the military-technical level described the ways and means by which Soviet military power could overcome its enemies.[5]

A correct understanding of the role of military doctrine in Soviet policy leads to two important insights. First, the Soviet leadership disbelieved in automated wars. Second, the possibility of accidental/inadvertent nuclear war, while occasionally alluded to in Soviet writing, was not taken as seriously as it was in the West. The differences between the United States and the Soviet Union on these points were more than a matter of semantics. The differences on automatic or accidental nuclear war reflected the differences in the relationship between state and the armed forces in the two countries. The Soviet armed forces were a politicized entity. The leading military cadres were carefully vetted for their Communist Party bona fides and scrutinized by the Main Political Administration with regard to their career patterns. Additional security organs outside the military were also used to establish the sincerity, or at least acquiescence, to party norms on the part of the military leadership. Over time, the Soviet military establishment became more Marxist–Leninist than many members of the party leadership or government, because they identified the survival of the ideology with the survival of the state, their primary mission.

Because of this, it was impermissible, from the perspective of the Soviet political or military leaderships throughout the Cold War, for wars to start accidentally or to run automatically. The notion that political leaders, having decided upon a war, turn decisions about military operations over to the armed forces was simply unacceptable to disciplines of Lenin as tutored by Clausewitz. This was as true of a war in which nuclear weapons might be used as of any other conflict. Soviet leaders were not fools. They knew how destructive a nuclear war in Europe or a larger war might be. But they also believed in their interpretation of the relationship between war and history. War might be unleashed against the Soviet Union at any time. Preparedness for war, including the conduct of a war through its various phases, was necessary in order to ensure the historically necessary triumph of socialism over capitalism.

The notion of accidentally caused and automatically run wars was a Western, not a Soviet, one. Nuclear weapons raised popular fears in the United States and in NATO Europe of a mad general grabbing control of the deterrent and launching a Strangelovian attack against Russia. More realistically, there were from time to time mishaps that took place in the operation of nuclear forces that could have led, under less propitious circumstances, to greater tensions between Washington and Moscow. But this issue was a point of agreement, not disagreement, between the U.S. and Soviet leaderships. Everyone agreed that a mistaken radar warning or a faulty silicon chip in the NORAD computers should not lead to an outbreak of tensions or fighting.

On the other hand, the two states' political and military leaderships were more different in their handling of the issue of automated war. The United States, in order to get around the problem of interservice disputation in the development of nuclear war plans, created the Single Integrated Operational Plan in the late 1950s. The SIOP was a highly technical and closely held document put together by the Joint Strategic Target Planning Staff (JSTPS) under loose policy guidance from the Department of Defense and the Joint Chiefs of Staff. As the numbers of U.S. nuclear weapons expanded into the thousands, and then tens of thousands, the numbers of targets identified as ground zeros in the USSR also increased proportionately. The SIOP eventually became so large and complex that it was a nuclear version of the Schlieffen. To make it workable, the decisions about weapons and targets were worked out in detail and packaged in one or more attack "options" for presidential decision.

In the event of a crisis involving the possible launch of U.S. nuclear weapons, the president would have minutes in which to decide among several major attack or limited attack options. But even the limited options involved large numbers of strikes into Eastern Europe and/or Soviet territory, and there was no opportunity for improvisation of plans or options within the plausible time frame of decision. SIOP targeting decisions were based on the requirement in all instances to attain Damage Expectancies (DE) against various classes of targets. The mechanics of the process drove the compilation of the war plan. Policy planners in the Office of the Secretary of Defense (OSD) supposedly provided substantive guidance within which the target planners at Omaha were to work. In practice, this guidance from OSD was either vague or ineffective. The air force did its thing: It prepared a war plan for the destruction of the Soviet Union's military forces, military-supporting infrastructure, and economy regardless of the exigent circumstances. The president's decision would be an essential yes or no.

The Soviet political leadership distrusted its military and feared the emergence of any Red Napoleons with political ambitions, despite the close monitoring and indoctrination of the military by the party and its security organs. Therefore, the idea of letting a nuclear war run itself by a single predetermined plan was anathema to the party leadership. In contrast to the rigidity of U.S. nuclear war plans (until the very end of the Cold war, in the Bush administration), the Soviet planning process emphasized requisite variety in options and military tasking. Because war might come in many sizes and shapes and unexpectedly from the Soviet standpoint, leaders had to have more than one major attack option and many minor ones as well.[6] Of course, the United States had these additional options *technically*, but the differences in style of thinking are the issue here. The Soviet political leadership expected that the General Staff would run any war hands-on, under the close supervision of the Politburo over the purposes of fighting and over the means of battle. Their model would be the Great Patriotic War and Stalin's oversight of his generals during that conflict. While Stalin was forced to concede some things to the professionalism of his General Staff and leading field commanders if he wanted to win the war, he did not concede his right to determine the sequence of main political and military objectives or the costs that the Soviet Union would be willing to pay to obtain them.

A NEW THREAT ENVIRONMENT

The spread of nuclear weapons is not an isolated danger but one heavily bound up with the proliferation of other weapons of mass destruction (chemical and biological) and of the means for their delivery. Arguments that the spread of nuclear weapons will contribute to military gridlock in East Asia or in the Middle East, as in Europe between 1946 and 1990, ignore the synergistic threat to stability brought about by the lethal combination of chemical, biological, and nuclear weapons, and improved air- and land-based delivery systems, among aspiring regional hegemons or dissatisfied states. That having been said, the problem of nuclear proliferation is sufficiently serious in its own right. Table 5.1 presents a sum-

Table 5.1
Status of Nuclear Proliferation

I. Acknowledged Nuclear Weapons States

China, France, India, Pakistan, Russia, United Kingdom, United States

II. Unacknowledged De Facto Nuclear Weapons States

Israel, North Korea (?)

III. States of Immediate Proliferation Concern

Iran, Iraq, Libya, North Korea (?)

IV. Converts to Nuclear Nonproliferation

Algeria, Argentina, Belarus, Brazil, Kazakhstan, South Africa, Ukraine

---

Notes:

1. India and Pakistan declared themselves nuclear powers after each completed a series of tests in May 1998. India is estimated to have 60 to 80 weapons, and Pakistan, 10 to 15. Neither state is a member of the Non-Proliferation Treaty (NPT).

2. Israel is thought to have between 70 and 125 weapons. Israel is not a signatory of the NPT.

3. North Korea's nuclear program is supposedly frozen under Internationl Atomic Energy Agency (IAEA) safeguards. In 1994 North Korea signed the Agreed Framework with the United States, calling for North Korea to freeze and subsequently give up all parts of its nuclear weapons program. In return, the United States promised to arrange for North Korea to receive two 1,000-megawatt light-water reactors (LWRs), plus annual allotments of 500,000 tons of heavy fuel oil until the first LWR is completed. Implementation of the Agreed Framework has been assigned to the Korean Peninsula Energy Development Organization (KEDO), also including South Korea, Japan, and the European Union.

4. Iran is a member of the NPT. The United States suspects that Iran is developing a nuclear weapons program and has tried to prevent other states from providing Tehran with pertinent technology or know-how. Russia agreed in 1995 not to sell uranium enrichment technology to Iran, and China promised in 1997 to end civil nuclear cooperation with Iran.

5. According to UN Security Council Resolution 687, the UN Special Commission (UNSCOM) for Iraq and IAEA were to verify the complete elimination of Iraq's nuclear, chemical, and biological weapons, its ballistic missiles, and its means for producing these weapons and delivery systems. After U.S. bombing attacks on Iraq in late 1998, Iraqi head of state Saddam Hussein ejected UNSCOM from the country, and it is unclear as of this writing when, or if, inspections can resume.

6. Libya is a member of the NPT, but the United States maintains that the regime nevertheless wants to acquire nuclear weapons.

Sources: Updated and adapted from Arms Control Association, Fact Sheet, *The State of Nuclear Proliferation* (Washington, D.C.: Arms Control Association, May 1998). For a study of Iraq's weapons of mass destruction, see Scott Ritter, *Endgame: Solving the Iraq Problem—Once and for All* (New York: Simon and Schuster, 1999), esp. pp. 217–224. See also Commission to Assess the Ballistic Missile Threat to the United States (Rumsfeld Commission), *Report* (Executive Summary) (Washington, D.C.: July 15, 1998).

mary of the status of nuclear proliferation group states by pertinent categories and offers supplementary notations about selected actors.

The status of North Korea has been mired in a complicated shell game of U.S. political relations with both Koreas, of bureaucratic politics on the American home front, and of a confrontationally oriented U.S. government approach to North Korea, up to the very edge of a near outbreak of war in 1994.[7] North Korea's standoff with the United States and the IAEA over its nuclear production program, culminating in the Framework Agreement of 1994 intended to cap that program, is well known.[8] During the 1980s and 1990s, North Korea was able to develop a complete nuclear fuel cycle, including a capability for the production of plutonium at its Yongbyon nuclear research center. A plutonium production reactor became operational in 1986, with refueling in 1989, making available weapons-grade plutonium for at least one nuclear weapon. North Korea was also building a 50-megawatt reactor at Yongbyon and a 200-megawatt reactor at Taechon before construction was halted under the Framework Agreement. The 50-megawatt reactor could have produced enough plutonium for North Korea to have developed between 7 and 10 nuclear weapons *per year*.[9]

North Korea was also developing a diversified industry for the production of ballistic missiles of various ranges, including missiles for export. North Korea in 1996 deployed with its forces several hundred Scud-B and Scud-C ballistic missiles with maximum ranges of 300 and 500 kilometers, respectively. Its Nodong-1 intermediate-range (estimated 1,000 kilometers with a 1,000-kilogram payload) ground-mobile, liquid-propelled missile was first tested in 1990 and entered service in 1994. By December 1994, according to some reports, between 12 and 18 Nodong-1 missiles were in service.[10] A follow-on Nodong-2, with increased range and reduced payload, has been reported: Its estimated range is 1,300 to 1,500 kilometers with a payload from 500 to 750 kilograms.[11] Also in development are two missiles of longer range than the Nodong: the Taepodong 1 and 2, with estimated ranges greater than 1,500 and 4,000 kilometers, respectively.[12]

During the summer of 1998 North Korea test-fired a three-stage ballistic missile rocket over the Sea of Japan. The Democratic People's Republic of Korea (DPRK) government described the test as an intended satellite launch that was less than completely successful, but some U.S. observers drew the conclusion that North Korea had demonstrated a prototype capability for missile attacks well beyond the tactical or theater range. According to the Commission to Assess the Ballistic Missile Threat to the United States in its 1998 report to Congress, a North Korean decision to rapidly deploy the Taepodong 2 ballistic missile might not be known to U.S. intelligence very far in advance of the decision to launch.

Table 5.2
DPRK Selected Ballistic Missile Capabilities, May 1999

Name	Maximum Range (km)	Warheads (kg)	Initial Operational Capability (IOC)
MRBM			
Nodong 1	1,000	1,000	1994
Nodong 2	1,350	1,200	1997
IRBM			
Taepodong 1	1,500–2,200	700–1,000	1998
ICBM			
Taepodong 1			
SLV*	4,000	50–100	1998
Taepodong 2	4,000–6,000	700–1,000	2000

Note: A space launch vehicle (SLV) capable of placing a 100-kilogram payload into low earth orbit (LEO) is, in theory, able to deliver a 200-kilogram warhead to a range of about 10,000 kilometers.

Sources: Excerpts from a chart originally prepared by Joseph S. Bermudez, Jr., May 11, 1999, via Ed Ivanhoe Website, and *Jane's Strategic Weapons Systems*, September 30, 1998. Available: http://janes.ismc.sgov.gov/egi-bin . . . h_janes/.

The capabilities of Taepodong 2 once deployed, according to the Commission, are potentially strategic in reach and impact:

This missile could reach major cities and military bases in Alaska and the smaller, westernmost islands in the Hawaiian chain. Light-weight variations of the TD-2 could fly as far as 10,000 km, placing at risk western U.S. territory in an arc extending northwest from Phoenix, Arizona to Madison, Wisconsin.[13]

A summary of some attributes of North Korea's missiles of longer than tactical ranges appears in Table 5.2.

An important aspect of North Korea's ballistic missile program is that it is designed for export as well as for Pyongyang's own defense needs. Hundreds of Scud missiles have been provided by North Korea to countries in the Middle East, including Iran, and North Korea is already marketing the Nodong for export. The U.S. Department of Defense estimates that, thus far, North Korea has not become an international supplier of nuclear, chemical, or biological weapons technology, despite its aggressive marketing of missiles and missile technology. Pyongyang has a substantial chemical weapons capability and limited facilities for producing biological weapons.[14]

North Korea's ballistic missile export program has enhanced the threat to stability in Southwest Asia. Iran acquired Scud-B missiles from Libya and North Korea and Scud-C missiles from the latter in the 1980s. During just three years of the Iran-Iraq war, between 1985 and 1988, Iran fired almost 100 Scud-B missiles at Iraq. In addition to obtaining ballistic missiles from North Korea, Iran is attempting to set up its own missile production capability. Acquisition of the North Korean Nodong missile would permit Iran to attack targets in Israel, much of Saudi Arabia and the Trucial States, Turkey, Russia and other former Soviet states, Pakistan, and India.[15] Iran's original reason for acquiring ballistic missiles was to employ them in its protracted war against Iraq during the 1980s. Having acquired the taste for technology and having taken note of Iraq's post–Desert Storm weakness in the 1990s, Iran now reasonably aspires to the status of first among equals among Gulf states. In addition to its ballistic missile capabilities, Iran has Chinese-supplied cruise missiles, artillery and aircraft capable of delivering chemical and biological weapons, and Russian-built SU-24 fighter-bombers that can deliver nuclear weapons.[16] Rumors of Russian-Iranian nuclear cooperation and of leakage of nuclear weapons experts from the former Soviet Union into Iran are frequent in U.S. and other media sources.

PROLIFERATION AND RATIONAL DECISION MAKING

One problematical aspect of complacency about nuclear weapons spread is the question of rational decision making. The assumption of rational decision making is a necessary condition for making testable hypotheses and verifiable generalizations about social behavior. In and of itself, the rationality postulate does no harm. It becomes dangerous, however, when it is assumed that particular notions of rational decision making can be transferred from one culture or society to another. U.S. policymakers have on more than one occasion substituted assumptions for evidence or intelligence about the behavioral propensities or mindsets of foreign leaders. For example, throughout the summer and early autumn of 1962, U.S. leaders simply assumed that Khrushchev would not dare to put Soviet missiles into Cuba because it was illogical and too risk acceptant, by U.S. reasoning, for the Soviet leader to have done so. As another example, American policymakers between 1965 and 1968 assumed that selective bombing of targets in North Vietnam would increase the pressure on the regime in Hanoi to withdraw its support from the National Liberation Front in South Vietnam.

When assumptions based on U.S. decision rationality are not supported by experience, leaders sometimes cling to the assumptions or to their supporting logic and blame the other side for "irrational" or illogical behavior. Khrushchev's deployment of missiles in Cuba in the face of U.S. warnings against doing so has been described as irrational by many American, and even some Soviet, sources. Yet in his memoirs

Khrushchev gives two reasons, equalizing the balance of nuclear power and deterring U.S. attack on Cuba, which make plain sense from his political and military vantage point. Similarly, the North Vietnamese reaction to U.S. bombing from 1965 to 1968 was to increase their support to the National Liberation Front (NLF) and their commitment to ultimate victory over the government of South Vietnam and its American supporters. The U.S. bombing could destroy value targets in North Vietnam, but it could not remove from Hanoi its capability to support insurgency in the South. Nor could bombing impose any unacceptable cost to North Vietnamese military capabilities for large-scale conventional ground warfare, later put to use in the final push by Hanoi against Saigon in 1975.

U.S. policymakers assumed in July 1990 that it would not be prudent for Saddam Hussein to attack and occupy Kuwait. The Iraqi leader was thought by most American prewar assessments to be using coercive diplomacy against Kuwait owing to its uncooperative oil-pricing behavior. Saddam Hussein also miscalculated Bush administration perceptions of U.S. and allied interests in the region, and he misestimated U.S. domestic politics as still being caught up in a Vietnam syndrome that would preclude President Bush from the actual use of force. Even after weeks of pounding from the U.S. and allied coalition air forces in January 1991, Saddam disbelieved that the United States would initiate a ground war because of fear of excessive numbers of American and allied casualties.

Looking inside the heads of enemy leaders, especially those of idiosyncratic and impulsive dictators, is never easy. But the preceding examples hold some pertinent social science lessons. Explanatory and predictive approaches that may suffice for issue areas such as welfare, urban development, education, and other largely domestic matters are not necessarily optimal for explaining behavior pertinent to war and peace. In these other issues with less than ultimate stakes, it makes sense to base predictions of future behavior on *typical* past behavior and on culturally shared norms and values. However, in international behavior related to war and peace, it is more important to be able to explain and predict *atypical* behaviors between states and leaders who do *not share* cultural norms and values. In other words, the marginal utility of being able to explain typical, as opposed to atypical, behavior declines as the situation moves from one of general to immediate deterrence (that is, from a condition of legal anarchy permissive of potential aggression to a more menacing condition in which one state has actually made threats against another).

The marriage of nuclear and other weapons of mass destruction to long-range ballistic or cruise missiles expands the capabilities of aspiring regional hegemons and of state or nonstate actors determined for various reasons to undo the international status quo. Even with short-range ballistic missiles of the Scud-B or Scud-C range and accuracy, states capable of producing chemical and biological, not to mention nuclear, weapons can wreak havoc against their regional neighbors. Iraq's military buildup prior to the Gulf war of 1991 is a case in point. The world was fortunate that Saddam Hussein's exhausted exchequer motivated his attack on Kuwait in 1990 instead of five years later. Iraq's massive military establishment included a multipronged strategy for acquiring nuclear weapons and a substantial chemical and biological weapons arsenal. Iraq's nuclear program was, according to authoritative sources, "massive" and "for most practical purposes fiscally unconstrained."[17] The pre–Desert Storm Iraqi nuclear program was also "closer to fielding a nuclear weapon, and less vulnerable to destruction by precision bombing than Coalition air commanders and planners or U.S. intelligence specialists realized before Desert Storm."[18] Coalition target lists on January 16 included two suspect nuclear production facilities: Postwar UN inspectors uncovered more than 20 sites related to Iraq's nuclear program, including 16 described as "main facilities."[19]

In addition to the uncertainties surrounding Iraq's prewar nuclear weapons program, Saddam Hussein's mobile Scud missiles played havoc with coalition intelligence during Desert Storm and threatened to cause a political crisis within the anti-Iraqi alliance. Scud attacks on Israeli cities created the possibility that Tel Aviv might retaliate, thus bringing Israel directly into the war and giving Saddam a wedge issue to divide Arab members of the U.S.-led coalition from others. According to the U.S. Air Force–commissioned *Gulf War Air Power Survey*:

Efforts by Coalition air forces to suppress Iraqi launches of Scud missiles against Israel, Saudi Arabia, and other Persian Gulf nations during Desert Storm ran into many of the same problems evident in the case of the Iraqis' nuclear weapons program. Key portions of the target set—notably the pre-surveyed launch sites and hiding places used by the mobile launchers—were not identified before 17 January, and, even in the face of intense efforts to find and destroy them, the mobile launchers proved remarkably elusive and survivable.[20]

Soviet exercises with Scuds in Eastern Europe and Iraqi practices during the Iran-Iraq war suggested to coalition air war planners that a sufficient number of prelaunch signatures and adequate time might be available to permit attacks on mobile launchers, before they fired, by patrolling aircraft. Iraqi countermeasures disappointed these expectations: Their Gulf war use of mobile Scuds, compared to earlier cases, reduced prelaunch setup times, avoided telltale electromagnetic emissions that gave away locations, and deployed large numbers of decoys in order to confuse coalition targeters.[21]

The case of Iraq is instructive for optimists about the stability of a new world order marked by proliferation of weapons of mass destruction and modern delivery systems. Consider how different the problem facing the United States would have been if Iraq had invaded Kuwait in 1996 instead of 1990. The United States in 1990 did not face an Iraqi adversary already equipped with usable nuclear weapons. The United States had available for Desert Storm the large, forward-deployed forces built up in the Cold War years for a theater-strategic campaign against the Soviet Union and its Warsaw Pact allies. The Soviet Union under Gorbachev decided with some reluctance to support the UN authorization for the forcible expulsion from Kuwait of its former ally in Baghdad. Iraq's unwillingness to employ chemical or biological weapons against the United States was probably related to its expectation that a U.S. nuclear retaliation might follow, to which Iraq could not respond in kind. An Iraq in 1996 (absent Desert Storm) possessing nuclear charges capable of delivery by air or missile, even over distances of several hundred kilometers, could have posed a threat against outside intervention by the U.S. and its NATO allies, or against regional antagonists like Saudi Arabia and Israel, very different from the threat it posed in 1990.

The preceding statement seems almost self-evident, but there is more than a self-evident point built into it. Iraq successfully concealed from the most technically complex intelligence systems in the world the prewar location of most of the installations related to its nuclear weapons program. Iraqi mobile Scuds confounded coalition air war planners to the extent that there exists not even a *single* documented case of mobile Scud destruction by coalition fixed-wing aircraft.[22] Notably, this level of frustration marked the efforts of the winning side in a very one-sided military contest: an essentially postindustrial strategy for warfare against a static defensive strategy accompanied by political ineptitude in Baghdad of the highest order.[23] In addition, the United States and its allies had five months to build up forces, collect intelligence, and plan countermeasures against Saddam's anticipated moves while Iraqi forces inexplicably squatted down in the Kuwaiti theater of operations. All these considerations point to the uniqueness of the environment surrounding Desert Storm and contain tacit warnings about the potential mischief of a future Saddam, strategically tutored and more decisive.

The U.S. inability or unwillingness to deter Iraq's invasion of Kuwait in 1990 contains another warning against complacency about proliferation. The basic maxims of deterrence learned during the Cold War years may have to be rethought, or in some cases rejected outright, in the remainder of the century and thereafter. Nuclear weapons and war avoidance worked together during the Cold War because U.S.–Soviet strategic nuclear bipolarity enforced a *connection between basic and extended deterrence*. One could predict the degree of vulnerability to coercion to be expected of U.S. allies by deduction from the stability of the

U.S.–Soviet relationship itself. U.S. strategic nuclear forces were coupled to the fates of European and Japanese allies who could not then be coerced into submission by the Soviets, nor by Soviet allies, without risking confrontation with the U.S. deterrent.

The collapse of bipolarity after Cold War diminishes the link between basic and extended deterrence: one can make fewer reliable predictions about states' behaviors on the basis of "system" variables. The significance of this theoretical construct for the practical problem of nonproliferation is illustrated by then-Secretary of Defense William J. Perry's comment that future terrorists or rogue regimes "may not buy into our deterrence theory. Indeed, they may be madder than MAD."[24] Deterrence theory à la the Cold War, based on realist premises that assume risk-averse- and cost-benefit-sensitive leaders, may no longer hold tenable for leaders armed with weapons of mass destruction and motivated by "irrational" or "illogical" objectives by at least U.S. standards. As Keith B. Payne has explained:

Assuming that deterrence will "work" because the opponent will behave sensibly is bound to be the basis for a future surprise. I do not know whether our expectations of a generically sensible opponent will next be dashed by a so-called rogue state, such as North Korea, or by another challenger. That they will be dashed, however, is near certain. As we move into the second nuclear age and confront opponents with whom we are relatively unfamiliar, assumptions of a generically sensible foe almost certainly will ensure surprises.[25]

In addition, most academic or policy analyses have focused on dyadic relationships that are not complicated by triangulation or indirect deterrence.[26] Current U.S. strategy relies upon the ability to conduct two nearly simultaneous major theater wars against rogue states or aspiring regional hegemons by exploiting the superior reach, battlefield knowledge, and striking power of U.S. high-technology conventional weapons. Future rogues or other regional aggressors might seek to neutralize the U.S. conventional deterrent by acquiring weapons of mass destruction and by threatening U.S. forces, regional allies, or even noninvolved states. Threats to use nuclear weapons against noninvolved states' cities might play against U.S. or allied fears of civilian casualties. As Robert Harkavy has noted:

But conceivably, an Iraq or Iran could threaten to use nuclear weapons against other countries—perhaps those not aligned with the United States or nominally under its extended deterrence protection—banking on American reluctance to countenance massive civilian casualties anywhere. Either Iran or Iraq could indeed threaten to attack the other with nuclear weapons. Iraq could so threaten its own Kurdish cities; Iran could threaten cities to its north in the new Central Asian nations.[27]

Another reason why deterrence might not work in a post–Cold War, proliferated world is that reliable and timely intelligence and warning might not be available about the intentions or capabilities of rogues with WMD and ballistic missile capabilities. According to the Rumsfeld Commission, the U.S. intelligence community had great difficulty assessing the pace and scope of North Korea's Nodong missile program and may have very little advance warning of the deployment of Taepodong 2.[28] The commission report states that Iran has a nuclear weapons program intended to produce nuclear weapons as soon as possible and the technical capability to demonstrate an ICBM-range ballistic missile similar to the TD-2 within five years of a decision by Iran to do so. Unfortunately, according to the Rumsfeld Commission, the United States is unlikely to know whether Iran has produced nuclear weapons "until after the fact."[29] An Iranian ballistic missile with a 10,000-kilometer range "could hold the U.S. at risk in an arc extending northeast of a line from Philadelphia, Pennsylvania, to St. Paul, Minnesota."[30] The Rumsfeld Commission concluded, with regard to the possible dangers presented by short or no-warning ballistic missile attacks and WMD proliferation:

A new strategic environment now gives emerging ballistic missile powers the capacity, through a combination of domestic development and foreign assistance, to acquire the means to strike the U.S. within about five years of a decision to acquire such a capability (10 years in the case of Iraq). During several of those years, the U.S. might not be aware that such a decision had been made. Available alternative means of delivery can shorten the warning time of deployment nearly to zero.[31]

The preceding arguments do not prove that deterrence, old style, can never work in the new world order: including deterrence based on nuclear weapons. But deterrence in the next century will be more conditional, culturally driven, and less technology oriented than it was during the Cold War. States owning weapons of mass destruction and ballistic missiles will present a mosaic of hard-to-read intentions that defy easy characterization by standard intelligence collectors. Deterrence, having been overdetermined in the Cold War, may lead the pack of underachievers before the twenty-first century is very old.

CONCLUSION

The slow spread of nuclear weapons during the Cold War has led some analysts and policymakers to unjustified optimism about the manageability of a faster rate of nuclear proliferation in the post–Cold War world. The arguments for a proliferation-acceptant world are based on a model of politics that relies on photocopy policymakers. Optimists about proliferation also expect that deterrence will work as well after Cold War as it did between 1946 and 1991. As the case of India and Pakistan shows, not only are more states acquiring nuclear weapons, but those weapons are showing up in states in which the relationship between the armed forces and political authority is ambiguous—and in the hands of contiguous actors with immediate and unresolved territorial and other grievances to settle. In addition, the possible spread of nuclear weapons along with long-range delivery systems places U.S. allies such as Japan and the American homeland potentially at risk. Among other results, the possible spread of nuclear weapons and long-range delivery systems among antisystemic actors caused the U.S. Congress and the Clinton administration to move closer to a decision in favor of national missile defenses.

In the real as opposed to the academic world, it does matter "who" the proliferators are and what kinds of regimes they have: Proliferation is not all of a piece. And practically speaking, U.S. officials would be sticking their fingers in the proverbial dike if they attempted to prevent any and all possible cases of nuclear, chemical, and biological weapons spread in the twenty-first century. But containment of WMD by means of selective nonproliferation, or counterproliferation in order to undo newly acquired arsenals, requires that the United States act in concert with allies and, preferably, with the approval and support of the international community. It remains one of the more remarkable features of the nuclear history since 1945 that so few states, instead of so many, have acquired nuclear arsenals. This self-denial cannot be explained away only by pointing to fear or deterrence. Obviously, a tacit but powerful international norm now exists in favor of nuclear forbearance: It does not prevent all nuclear weapons spread, but it helps to stigmatize the spreaders and to raise their profiles as targets for intelligence collection.

NOTES

1. Kenneth N. Waltz, *Theory of International Politics* (Reading, Mass.: Addison-Wesley, 1979). See also, and more specifically on Waltz's views of the relationship between nuclear weapons and stability, *The Spread of Nuclear Weapons: More May Be Better*, Adelphi Papers No. 171 (London: International Institute of Strategic Studies, 1981); "Nuclear Myths and Political Realities," *American Political Science Review*, no. 3 (September 1990), pp. 731–745; and his chapters in Scott D. Sagan and Kenneth N. Waltz, *The Spread of Nuclear Weapons: A Debate* (New York: W. W. Norton, 1995). Other arguments for a positive association between the spread of survivable nuclear forces and international stability appear in Martin van Creveld, *Nuclear Proliferation and the Future of Conflict* (New York: Free Press, 1993).

2. The U.S. policy debate is in the process of undergoing a tectonic shift on

this very issue. According to one authoritative study, "It seems certain that active defenses will play a growing role in U.S. strategy and in the strategy of others in the early decades of the next century." See Center for Counterproliferation Research, National Defense University, and Center for Global Security Research, Lawrence Livermore National Laboratory, *U.S. Nuclear Policy in the 21st Century: A Fresh Look at National Strategy and Requirements* (Washington, D.C.: U.S. Government Printing Office, 1998), p. 2.43. For counterarguments skeptical of national missile defenses, see John Steinbruner, "National Missile Defense: Collision in Progress," *Arms Control Today*, November 1999, pp. 3–6.

3. For clarity on this topic, I recommend William E. Odom, *The Collapse of the Soviet Military* (New Haven, Conn.: Yale University Press, 1998), pp. 1–15, and Raymond L. Garthoff, *Deterrence and the Revolution in Soviet Military Doctrine* (Washington, D.C.: Brookings Institution, 1990), pp. 6–28.

4. For assessments of the nuclear past and its relationship to the nuclear future, see Colin S. Gray, *The Second Nuclear Age* (Boulder, Colo.: Lynne Rienner, 1999); Stephen J. Cimbala, *The Past and Future of Nuclear Deterrence* (Westport, Conn.: Praeger Publishers, 1998); and Keith B. Payne, *Deterrence in the Second Nuclear Age* (Lexington: University Press of Kentucky, 1996).

5. On the sociopolitical level of military doctrine, see Marshal N. V. Ogarkov, *Istoriya uchit bditel'nosti* (History teaches vigilance) (Moscow: Voennoe Izdatel'stvo, 1985), pp. 75–76. On the military-technical aspects of military doctrine, see ibid., pp. 76–77.

6. Ghulam Dastagir Wardak, comp., and Graham Hall Turbiville, Jr., ed., *The Voroshilov Lectures: Materials from the Soviet General Staff Academy*, vol. I (Washington, D.C.: National Defense University Press, 1989), pp. 63–78.

7. Leon V. Sigal, *Disarming Strangers: Nuclear Diplomacy with North Korea* (Princeton, N.J.: Princeton University Press, 1998), esp. pp. 3–14.

8. See Michael J. Mazarr, *North Korea and the Bomb: A Case Study in Proliferation* (New York: St. Martin's Press, 1995), passim.

9. Office of the Secretary of Defense, *Proliferation: Threat and Response* (Washington, D.C.: U.S. Government Printing Office, 1996), pp. 6–7, provides background on the North Korean nuclear program.

10. *Jane's Strategic Weapons Systems*, September 30, 1998. Available http://janes.ismc.sgov.gov/egi-bin . . . h_janes/.

11. Ibid.

12. Ibid., p. 9.

13. Commission to Assess the Ballistic Missile Threat to the United States (Rumsfeld Commission), *Report* (Executive Summary) (Washington, D.C.: July 15, 1998), p. 9. Pagination may be inexact due to variations in electronic transmission.

14. Ibid.

15. See map, *Ranges of Current and Future Ballistic Missile Systems* (Iran), in Office of the Secretary of Defense, *Proliferation*, p. 17.

16. Ibid., p. 16.

17. Thomas A. Keaney and Eliot A. Cohen, *Revolution in Warfare? Air Power in the Persian Gulf* (Annapolis, Md.: Naval Institute Press, 1995), p. 67. This is a revised version of the official U.S. Air Force *Gulf War Air Power Survey*, first published in 1993.

18. Keaney and Cohen, *Revolution in Warfare*, p. 67.

19. Ibid.

20. Ibid., p. 72.

21. Ibid., p. 75.

22. Ibid., p. 78. Special forces teams may have destroyed some mobile Scuds.

23. Jeffrey Record, *Hollow Victory: A Contrary View of the Gulf War* (Washington, D.C.: Brassey's, 1993), pp. 71–73.

24. Secretary of Defense William J. Perry, "On Ballistic Missile Defense: Excerpt from a Speech to the Chicago Council on Foreign Relations," March 8, 1995, p. 1 (mimeo), cited in Payne, *Deterrence in the Second Nuclear Age*, p. 58.

25. Payne, *Deterrence in the Second Nuclear Age*, pp. 57–58.

26. Robert E. Harkavy, "Triangular or Indirect Deterrence/Compellence: Something New in Deterrence Theory," *Comparative Strategy*, no. 1 (1998), pp. 63–82.

27. Ibid., p. 74.

28. Rumsfeld Commission, *Report* (Executive Summary), p. 10.

29. Ibid., p. 11.

30. Ibid.

31. Ibid., p. 22. The Rumsfeld Commission cannot be dismissed by skeptics as an alarmist group. Its membership included, in addition to former Secretary of Defense Donald Rumsfeld, who chaired it, noted experts on nuclear technology, strategy, and policy representing a variety of policy views and professional backgrounds.

Chapter 6

Small Wars and Peace Wars: Disarming the Devil

INTRODUCTION

The collapse of states into political and military fratricide since the end of the Cold War has been the defining element of the new world order. In a number of failed or failing states, the U.S military has been required to take on postmodern tasks: border patrolling, establishing civil infrastructure, rebuilding uncorrupted police forces, supervising elections, and returning refugees to their original homelands. And in more than one instance since 1991, the United States and allied peacekeepers have been inserted into hot spots of internecine ethnic or religious conflict and tasked to enforce disarmament of militarized factions without taking sides. By the end of President Clinton's second term, U.S. military leaders were reporting that readiness was stretched to the limit in order to meet requirements for worldwide peacekeeping deployments and still maintain the ability to fight two nearly simultaneous major regional conflicts.

This chapter considers the demands made upon U.S. and allied forces in peace operations and other missions apart from war. We also discuss the difficulty of maintaining a clear demarcation, in principle as well as in practice, between the state of war and the state of almost-war in which peace operators, including humanitarian rescuers, often find themselves. First, we review existing concepts having to do with small wars, including so-called unconventional wars and low-intensity conflicts. Second, we discuss some U.S. armed forces doctrine for organizing and conducting military "operations other than war" (OOTW).[1] Third, we consider the special complexities of urban conflict, since the next century may see more warriors and peace operators tasked to work in urban environments. Fourth, we discuss the problem of conducting small wars or peace operations with allies, using U.S. relations with NATO as illustrative. Fifth, we consider the problem of U.S. public, media, and congressional support for OOTW, especially for those with the potential to turn into wars through inadvertence.

DEFINING THE PROBLEM

Military planners and scholars have been frustrated by the lack of a conceptual framework for understanding how the internal wars of the post–Cold War era are different from the revolutionary wars of the Cold War. Donald M. Snow outlines some of the important ways in which contemporary internal wars differ from traditional insurgencies.[2] First, traditional insurgencies are fought with the object of capturing control over the political system; for many of the new internal wars, this object is absent or secondary. Criminal organizations and narcoterrorists, for example, prefer a weak state, not a strong one, and are comparatively indifferent as to who rules so long as they can escape effective control. Second, contemporary internal wars are often marked by lack of restraint, compared to Cold War insurgencies. Insurgent tactics emphasize winning over the "hearts and minds" of a politically ambivalent population. Internal wars of the 1990s, for example, in Bosnia and Rwanda, were marked by "ethnic cleansing" and other massacres with no apparent object other than killing.

A third apparent difference between Cold War insurgencies and post–Cold War internal wars, according to Snow and others, is that many internal wars are concentrated in the economically least developed states or in politically failed states. Failed states are those in which the government has suffered a terminal loss of legitimacy and effectiveness. Loss of legitimacy means that the state is no longer regarded as authoritative, that is, as entitled to rightful rule. Lack of effectiveness in a failed state is often apparent in the shift of control to local centers of real power and resistance: warlords, clans, criminal syndicates, ethnonational rebels, and others from a list difficult to exhaust.[3] Although a weak or failing state may give the appearance of sovereignty and strength, its durability rests solely on consent. As the weak state increases its level of consent seeking in vain to substitute for lost legitimacy and effectiveness, resistance to state authority also increases. Eventually the state fails of its own apparent incompetence as even its coercive powers dissolve or are overthrown by its enemies.[4]

It may be useful to distinguish between small wars and peace wars. Small wars may be peace wars, and vice versa; but the similarities between the two have more to do with the types of forces engaged or equipment used than they do with the purpose of fighting. *Small wars* are military conflicts in which at least one side employs irregular forces and unconventional methods of battle. Often this side is something other than a politically accountable state authority.[5] Small wars have variable purposes and even more variable methods, especially on the irregular side: terrorism, insurgency, guerrilla warfare, and so forth. The unconventional and usually weaker side in a small war against a state authority wins if it is not defeated as a political force in the society: Absent a decisive political setback, it can live to fight another day and gather new recruits to replace the ones lost.

Peace wars refer to those military deployments, or threats of intervention, that are intended to accomplish some *political purpose other than victory in battle* but that may require *capability for military combat* as well as noncombatant missions. I prefer the term *peace wars* because it emphasizes the two-sided demands placed upon military operators in these situations: Simultaneously, they are diplomats or politicians as well as warriors. These missions, however honorable in intent, (1) force military commanders into political, cultural, and social contexts over which they have partial and often *inadequate* control relative to their assigned mission and (2) within those contexts, may require that commanders and forces be forced to play an undesirable, unaccustomed, or unpopular political part. U.S. forces in Somalia from 1991 to 1994 found themselves in the first situation; French paratroops in Algeria from 1956 to 1958 ended up in the second situation. The verdict on NATO and Russian peace operators in Yugoslavia (Kosovo) in 1999 remains to be seen.

Involvement in small or peace wars by outside powers, especially great powers involved in another state's civil wars, often brings into play the Gulliver effect. The Gulliver effect is the discrepancy between a state's ability to destroy things, on the one hand, and its ability to persuade or coerce its opponent with the use of minimum or no force, on the other. It is not a static measure of winning or losing. The Gulliver effect is a loss-of-strength gradient that, because of the domination of small or peace wars by political/social/cultural and other nonmilitary factors, saps the strength of major powers as their involvement in small wars becomes protracted. The more prolonged the conflict, the more the potential for Gulliver effects. And it is worth noting that, at least in democratic societies, Gulliver-type loss of political and military strength in the field can originate from causes on the home front: as the Americans and the French in Vietnam, and the Soviet Union in Afghanistan and in Chechnya, discovered.

ORGANIZING THE U.S. MILITARY FOR NONWAR OPERATIONS

The U.S. Department of Defense recognizes that its responsibilities now include preparedness for so-called unconventional conflicts, including revolutionary and counterrevolutionary warfare, terrorism, antidrug operations, and peace operations, inter alia. In part, this recognition has found its way into manuals and other publications giving the accepted version of military doctrine and practice. For example, specific kinds of "operations other than war" included in a recent version of army doctrine were (1) support to domestic civil authorities; (2) humanitarian assistance and disaster relief; (3) security assistance; (4) noncombat evacuation operations; (5) arms control monitoring and verification; (6) nation assistance; (7) support to counterdrug operations; (8) combating terrorism; (9) peacekeeping and peace enforcement operations; (10) show of force; (11) support for insurgency or counterinsurgency; and (12) attacks and raids.[6]

Current U.S. joint (multiservice) military doctrine assumes that most peace operations will take place in "complex contingencies." A complex contingency operation is one that responds to a complex emergency. The United Nations defines a complex emergency as

a humanitarian crisis in a country, region or society where there is a total or considerable breakdown of authority resulting from internal conflict and which requires an international response that goes beyond the mandate (or) capacity of any single agency and/or the on-going United Nations country program.[7]

Experts on complex emergencies emphasize that complex emergencies must be distinguished from natural disasters. According to Mark Duffield:

So-called complex emergencies are essentially political in nature: they are protracted political crises resulting from sectarian or predatory indigenous responses to socioeconomic stress and marginalisation. Unlike natural disasters, complex emergencies have a singular ability to erode or destroy the cultural, civil, political and economic integrity of established societies.[8]

According to the U.S. *Joint Task Force Commander's Handbook for Peace Operations*, complex contingencies have the following characteristics:

• Increased use of asymmetrical means by belligerents.

• Dominance of political objectives.

• Presence and involvement of nongovernmental, private, voluntary, and international organizations, media, and other civilians in the military operations area, impacting upon military activities.

• Usually takes place in a failed state, which also implies: undisciplined factions, absence of law and order, numerous parties to the conflict, large-scale violations of human rights, risks of armed opposition to peace forces, and other problems.[9]

Table 6.1
Operations Other Than War and Types of Military Operations

Combat/ Noncombat	Type of Military Operation	General U.S. Goals	Examples
Combat	War	Fight and win	Large-scale combat operations/attack/ defend/blockade
Combat and Noncombat	OOTW	Deter war and resolve conflict	Peace enforcement/ counterterrorism/ show of force, raid, strike/ peacekeeping/nation assistance/ counterinsurgency
Noncombat	OOTW	Promote peace and support civil authority	Freedom of navigation/ counterdrug/ humanitarian assistance/ protection of shipping/ U.S. civil support

Note: OOTW = Military operations other than war.
Source: U.S. Joint Chiefs of Staff, *Joint Doctrine for Military Operations Other Than War* (Washington, D.C.: Joint Pub. 3-07, June 16 1995), p. I-2.

Operations other than war constitute an elastic category. As such, they invite controversy about the boundary line between "war" and "other than war." When, for example, does U.S. support for the counterinsurgency or counterterror operations spill over from non-war (NW) into de facto involvement in a war? The object of insurgents is to blur the line between peace and war until such a time as they are ready to wage open, conventional warfare to their advantage. This is not merely a problem of terminology. Confusion about whether the United States is actually at war invites inconsistency between policy objectives and military operations. A working solution to the boundary problem is depicted in Table 6.1. The U.S. Army codified its doctrine with regard to peace operations in Field Manual (FM) 100–23, *Peace Operations*, issued in 1994. In early 2000, the Army Peacekeeping Institute was revising FM 100–23. The essence of FM 100–23 was to be included as part of an overall doctrine manual FM 100–20, under "Stability and Support Operations." Later editions of FM 100–20 will more specifically consider the techniques for peace operations. Updated army doctrine also incorporates NATO's Allied Joint Publication (AJP)-3.4.1, "Peace Support Operations" (draft). In addition to these army efforts during the 1990s, the Joint Warfighting Center published the *Joint Task Force Commander's Handbook for Peace Op-*

erations in June 1997, with a CD-ROM of papers on doctrine, bibliographies, and other very useful materials.[10]

Clearly: Doctrine on this topic is important, since doctrine tells the troops how to implement or operationalize the goals of policymakers and higher-level commanders. Equally clear: Doctrine on this topic is a movable feast, subject to the vicissitudes of changes in U.S. government administration. And even the best doctrine must speak in glittering generalities. It is up to the field commanders and the plethora of other actors with whom they must work on site in order to bring stability and postintervention-responsive government into war-torn areas. As bitter experience in Sierra Leone in May 2000 showed only too clearly, international and regional military forces cannot by themselves create a legacy of peaceful expectations for conflict resolution. Multinational intervention forces can only influence some of the environmental parameters conducive to, or unfavorable to, lasting pacific settlement of conflicts.

THE STREETS WITHOUT JOY

The last quarter of the twentieth century has shifted the milieu for many intrastate conflicts from rural to urban environments. Twenty-first-century fighting in cities might follow neither the Maoist nor the Leninist pattern of revolutionary war nor prior experience in conventional campaigns against cities. New technologies, forms of organization, and causes of fighting in cities will stress existing templates of military planners and political leaders. For example, future urban revolutionaries may prefer dispersed and decentralized command systems that are harder to identify, target, or destroy compared to cells centralized under a single directorate. According to Gerard Chaliand, an expert on unconventional conflicts,

The new factor in contemporary terrorism as compared with national liberation movements (some of which also resort to terrorism) is the emergence of little groups with no organized links with the masses and no movement worthy of the name to draw up a political program. There has been a massive increase in the number of minuscule groups which see indiscriminate terrorism as both tactic and political line.[11]

Future urban warfare may require more than peace or stability operations against lightly armed, indigenous paramilitary forces. General Charles Krulak has described the diversity of future urban military operations as a "three block war": U.S. forces might be conducting a humanitarian operation in one part of a city, peacekeeping or peace enforcement in another, and fighting a mid-intensity battle in a third sector.[12] Lt. Col. Robert F. Hahn and Bonnie Jezior, of the U.S. Army's After Next Urban Warfare Project, argue that U.S. military planners must exploit new technologies for situation awareness, precision fire, mobility, and other uses if they are to cope with the complexity of urban warfare in the next century.[13] These recommendations will collide with existing U.S. and allied military doctrine that emphasizes the avoidance of fighting in built-up areas. Although cities can sometimes be made to surrender by siege or bypassed and isolated, these favorable outcomes cannot always be assumed.[14]

Both the political and the military operational settings for fighting in urban areas are full of potholes. Combat will be taking place in conditions that impede communications, hamper movement of friendly forces, permit maximum concealment to enemy regular and irregular forces, and commingle noncombatants with combatants. Adversaries will definitely exploit all the opportunities for friction that these political and military conditions make possible. As the analysis of the battle of Grozny in January 1995 by Timothy L. Thomas suggests, urban warfare in the age of information can combine the friction of unconventional and conventional military operations, as well as the frustrations of first-, second-, and third-wave warfare in a single military campaign.[15] The environment of urban warfare is especially unforgiving. Urban combat is three-dimensional in nature: (1) It makes insatiable demands on casualty evacuation and resupply; (2) urban structures block line-of-sight radio communications and create other difficulties that force units to fight in a highly decentralized, separated manner; and (3) situation awareness is limited because the terrain imposes so many constraints on intelligence gathering and troop movement.[16] According to Lt. Col. John F. Antal:

The history of conventional combat in the 20th century proves that single arm solutions in complex, urban terrain almost always fail, particularly if they are hastily prepared and poorly planned. Roof-to-roof, house-to-house, cellar-to-cellar city fighting against a determined foe is grisly business, a business that requires a tough, competent combined arms solution.[17]

Fighting in urban terrain is costly and difficult enough, even if the contestants on boths sides are conventional militaries. When, in addition, at least one of the disputants is something other than a government and employs mostly irregular military tactics, the headaches of fighting in built-up areas are compounded by the overlay of conventional and unconventional military templates. Such was the situation in which Russia's armed forces found themselves between 1994 and 2000 in the North Caucasus.

Chechnya I: Russia Enters the Quagmire

When Russia invaded its rebellious province Chechnya in December 1994, it was expected in Moscow that Chechen resistance would rapidly give way to superior Russian forces. Previously Russian security organs had failed to topple the government of rebel Chechen President Dzhokar Dudayev by working with indigenous forces to attempt a coup. Frustrated by its inability to dislodge Dudayev by other means, Russia escalated and sent in its army and air force. Russia's initial military campaigns in Chechnya were poorly prepared and met with disaster. Instead of fighting for several months, Russian forces were bogged down in Chechnya for two years. Russia was forced to negotiate a peace settlement in August 1996, calling for the removal of Russian forces from Chechnya by the end of the year and leaving the political future of Chechnya open-ended.[18]

Although the combat organization, training, and performance of Russia's forces in Chechnya were unimpressive, these weaknesses were made worse by Russia's failure to correctly forecast how Chechen society and culture would hobble its war effort. Russia's own experience in the previous century against Imam Shamil and other Chechen resistance fighters was ignored.[19] The more recent Soviet combat experience against Afghan resistance yielded little in the way of lessons learned for an overconfident Russian defense ministry in 1994. The ineptitude of Russian combat tactics in Chechnya was compounded by the inability of President Boris Yeltsin and his entourage to make a persuasive case for the legitimacy of the military campaign. Russians, by and large, were skeptical of the entire affair or opposed or tuned out.

Russia lost the battle of moral influence, as the renowned Chinese military philosopher Sun Tzu would have called it, for several reasons. First, the leadership of the Russian armed forces was bitterly divided over the prudence of using the security forces of Russia, especially those of the defense ministry, to impose order on Chechnya. Second, the Russian media covered the war like a proverbial blanket and gave a great deal of publicity to Russian and Chechen opponents of the war. Third, Chechens successfully used psychological warfare, including deception operations, to depict their cause favorably and to attempt to intimidate and deceive their opponents.

For example, a commander of Russia's North Caucasus Military District complained that the Ministry of Defense had almost totally ignored any preparations for psychological warfare in Chechnya. As a result, the Dudayev forces had nearly demoralized the 19th Motorized Rifle Division by sending radio messages to individual officers by name and threatening their wives and children if those officers took part in any attack on Grozny. Another example is the use of Ukrainian nationalists in Chechen deception operations. Ukrainians dressed in Russian uniforms led unsuspected Russian comrades to Dudayev as prisoners of war. Other Ukrainians disguised themselves as members of Doctors without Borders (Medecins sans Frontieres) or the Red Cross in order to question refugees and to obtain other intelligence for Chechen forces.[20] Chechen "psyop" information activities against Russia also exploited perceptions management in order to present the case against Russian military intervention favorably to Russian and other news media. These and other problems that marked Russia's conduct of its disastrous military self-invasion in Chechnya are summarized by the principle of military effectiveness that they violated in Table 6.2.

Chechnya II: Russia Reenters the Quagmire

In late summer and early fall 1999, Russia again invaded Chechnya and determined not to repeat the military debacle of 1994–1996. In its second Chechen war of the post–Cold War era, Russia's military and political leadership threw in some 100,000 troops, a substantially larger force than that committed in the first conflict. Specialized troops and forces available to commanders of the North Caucasus Military District, in charge of military operations in the air and on the ground, included OMON (elite paramilitary troops from the Interior Ministry), paratroopers from the 76th Russian Airborne division, and an elite special unit of the Main Intelligence Directorate of the Russian General Staff (GRU).[21] Tactics and operations eschewed frontal assaults by armored spearheads that had trapped hapless Russian forces in Grozny in January 1995. Instead, the Russians reverted to the "Katyusha" approach. Massive firepower from air and artillery was employed to clear large areas of any resistance fighters and to demolish the infrastructure and sources of supply that sustained them. Russians then moved in and occupied the devastated territory. Having cleared northern Chechnya of effective resistance, Russian commanders proceeded to surround, cut off, and eventually clear and hold the main strongpoints in Grozny by the latter part of February 2000. Shortly afterward, Russia declared victory.

Russia's "victory" in Chechnya in February 2000 was short-lived. Chechen fighters were driven south into the mountains, where they could melt into the population and terrain, gathering strength of numbers and equipment to continue a protracted guerrilla war against Russia.[22] Russia now faced the prospect of stationing a sizable constabulary force in Chechnya that might be cut off in pieces by ambushes or pinned down and discouraged by hit-and-run strikes. As with all irregular forces, so too the Chechens had the initiative: They could take as much, or as little, of the war as they chose.

Russia's tactics in Chechnya II were not as bad as in Chechnya I, but

Table 6.2
Russian Military Fiascoes in Chechnya, 1994–1996

Principle of War or Military Art	Deficiency in Russian Performance
Objective	The stated objective was to preserve the territorial integrity of Russia and reestablish constitutional order in Chechnya. Use of the military was premature, and no real crisis resolution was attempted. Military tactics of massive firepower and killing of civilians alienated the population.
Offensive	Russians launched a hastily prepared offensive in December 1994 with untrained troops and ambivalent commanders. The initial assault on Grozny moved along three different and mutually unsupported axes.
Mass	Massed force and indiscriminate firepower were not appropriate for the situation. Air, artillery, and tanks were of limited value in low-intensity conflict. In addition, the principle of mass requires that forces are closely coordinated: many Russian units, in contrast, failed to cooperate.
Economy of force	Sloppy employment and distribution of forces resulted from poor planning and lapses in control. Russians were unable to isolate and target actual Chechen fighters or to crush the Chechen center of gravity. Instead, Russian forces were responsible for mass fires and destruction of civilian areas.
Maneuver	Chechen knowledge of territory kept Russians off balance. Russians often operate with a "firebase" mentality. Russians lack flexibility in adapting tactics to changed situation (i.e., when unexpected resistance impeded original plan to seize Grosny, Russians continued frontal assault).
Unity of command	Dissension was evident among all levels of command and between field commanders and Moscow. Ground forces, air forces, and interior troops operate as separate forces and distrust one another. No concept of professional solidarity is evident.
Security and intelligence	Chechens were apparently aware of every major Russian military action in advance (except for air) from December 1994 through August 1996. Russians were unaware of Chechen plans for hostage seizures and unable to identify sources of intelligence leaks.
Surprise	Russians expected to catch Chechens unaware in December 1994 but failed. Chechen tactics in Grozny surprise Russians.
Simplicity	Russian forces were drawn from a large number of different security agencies and were unfamiliar with one another's operational modes. The training, coordination, and leadership needed to combine these forces into a cohesive whole were absent.

Source: Adapted from Major Raymond C. Finch III, *Why the Russian Military Failed in Chechnya* (Fort Leavenworth, Kans.: Foreign Military Studies Office, 1998). Available: http://leav-www. army.mil.fmso/fmso.htm (10/17/00).

in both cases, it seemed that Russia repeated many of the mistakes made by the Soviet Union against the Afghan resistance from 1979 to 1989. Blunderbuss attacks not discriminating between armed opposition and innocent civilians only alienated further a population already suspicious of Russian intentions. In Afghanistan, as in Chechnya, Islamic warriors motivated both by religion and by nationalism turned ideology as a weapon against the Soviet Union and later Russia.

The end of the Cold War did not usher in the end of ideology, as some thought. But it did mark the evolution of ideology beyond the arguments about social class or left–right views toward something more identity based. This problem of identity is not so easily comprehended by outsiders, especially if, as in the case of Chechnya and in Afghanistan, indigenous peoples are plural rather than singular in their sense of community. "Chechens" are rooted in their families, villages, and clans; their societies are essentially local, and their nationalism is primarily particularistic. They can cooperate against an outside invader, and have done so against Russians for centuries, but they are not political peas in a pod. In fact, one of Russia's problems in pacifying Chechnya is precisely this diversity of Chechen field marshals and political leaders representing different factions within the same region.[23] There is more religious as well as political diversity among Chechens than is apparent to outsiders: Wahabis, Sunnis, and other branches of Islam compete for the adherence of the faithful throughout the North Caucasus, including in Chechnya.

Russia's conventional armed forces, at least as of the spring of 1999, were ill suited for a protracted conflict of any kind. Military planners were impeded by lack of funds for personnel and equipment, poor morale among officers and rankers, and lack of public esteem and support for the military as an institution. Desertion and draft avoidance remained high throughout the 1990s, and troops sent into the field sometimes refused to carry out their assigned missions even in combat. During Chechnya I the Kremlin was forced to sack several leading generals for refusal to carry out the orders of the Defense Ministry and General Staff. Chechnya II was better prepared politically than Chechnya I from a propaganda standpoint. The Russian government established to the satisfaction of most of the Russian public that, owing to the Chechen incursion into Dagestan in August 1999 and the bombings of Moscow apartment buildings allegedly committed by Chechen terrorists, a casus belli existed for another go at Chechnya. In addition, the Russian military leadership was smarting in 1999 to prove that the setback in 1996, when Russia was forced to settle for a cease-fire with an uncertain political endgame, was exceptional: This time the Chechens would taste the full fury of Russia's armed might.

However, Russia's new version of its official Military Doctrine, approved by President Putin on April 21, 2000, shows that Moscow can expect little of its conventional military forces beyond the conduct of holding operations. The new doctrine is avowedly defensive in character, but it is forced upon Russia by the weakness of its armed forces: They are not capable of large-scale offensives outside of Russia's borders, having demonstrated in Chechnya minimum competency in the conduct of offensives *within* Russia. This is one reason for Russia's departure from the Soviet-era declaratory policy of no nuclear "first use." Russia's current doctrine now envisions that nuclear weapons might have to be used first in response to conventional attacks on vital military or other targets in Russia. And in another departure from former Soviet precedent, Russia now avers that its nuclear weapons might be used in a limited, selective manner in order to deescalate a regional or local war.[24] This proviso of possible resort to nuclear strikes in order to contain or deescalate regional and local conflicts suggests that the General Staff doubts the ability of its armed forces to do more than to fight on the defensive. According to veteran defense correspondent Pavel Felgenhauer, in 1999 he was heavily criticized by Russian generals at a meeting in 1999 for suggesting the possibility that Russia might be involved in a regional or local limited nuclear war. However, he adds:

Today the official line has changed dramatically. This latest war in Chechnya has once again exposed the overall weakness and low quality of Russia's conventional forces. It's not at all surprising that today military authorities have recognized the possibility that they may have to resort to nukes in almost any serious future armed conflict.[25]

The preceding assessment of Russia's military capabilities may be on the extreme end of military pessimism, but regardless, it leans in the correct direction. Russia cannot count on its conventional forces to fight for very long or on more than a single front against any serious opponent. Nor can Russia depend upon allies in order to fight her border wars: Russia's "near abroad" is dotted with potential and actual enemies. On the other hand, as we note in the next section, the availability of allies for small wars and peace operations involves the complications of alliance management and joint command. Alliance management and joint command can challenge even the most powerful and cohesive military alliance of the present day.

ALLIES IN SMALL WARS AND PEACE WARS

Command and Control

Fighting or peace soldiering with allies is one way to blunt the fear of casualties and the risks of wider war. But alliances introduce other complexities, including the question of shared military command. Napoleon is reported to have commented on at least one occasion that fighting with allies was even worse than fighting without them. In the 1994 version of its annual report to the Congress, the U.S. Department of Defense was careful to acknowledge the difficulty of command and control for multinational operations and to offer itself a plausible way out:

The issue of command and control will always be a key factor in deciding whether to deploy U.S. forces as part of a U.N. peace operation. As a practical matter, if significant combat operations are contemplated, and if American involvement is planned, it is unlikely that the United States would agree to place its forces under the operational control of a U.N. commander. In these situations, the United States would prefer to rely either on its own resources, on those of a capable regional organization such as NATO, or on an appropriate coalition such as that assembled for Operation Desert Storm.[26]

The 1994 Clinton administration policy statement on U.S. participation in multilateral peace operations established three sets of criteria.[27] The first set of factors would be considered in deciding whether to vote in support of a UN peace operation (chapter VI or chapter VII). The second set of even more restrictive standards would apply when the participation of U.S. personnel in peace operations is being considered. Third, additional and more rigorous factors would be taken into account if the peace operation is a peace enforcement (chapter VII) exercise likely to involve combat. These criteria reflected a post-Somalia and more cautious view of military intervention, at least outside of Europe, compared to that with which the Clinton administration operated in its first several years.[28]

In the aftermath of NATO's air war (Operation Allied Force) against Yugoslavia in 1999, Clinton officials were less fastidious in their public pronouncements about the criteria for humanitarian intervention than they appeared to be in the 1994 guidelines. National security adviser Samuel Berger indicated that future interventions could be undertaken if: there existed a sufficiently grave violation of human rights; if the United States and its allies possessed the military capability to do something about it; and if other options seemed to have exhausted themselves. It was not clear that Kosovo was more than sui generis in its implications for further U.S. decision making about the uses of force for humanitarian rescue or for peace and stability operations. Much would depend upon the political outcomes in Kosovo subsequent to NATO's 78 days of air war.

Some critics of U.S. and NATO performance in the air campaign against Yugoslavia blamed the need for inter-allied consensus for inept war plans, unwillingness to authorize a ground campaign in Kosovo if necessary, poor communication of signals to the Serbs about probable terms of settlement, and other political and military land mines over which the bombing campaign allegedly tripped. It is not clear that lack of inter-allied consultation caused most of the hiatus between political and military objectives in Operation Allied Force, however. One apparent cost of alliance management of the war did appear: in the area of intelligence. NATO's consultative process for planning the air war leaked important information to the Serbs in the first two weeks of the conflict; numbered among the suspects were the intelligence services of NATO's newly acquired members who were formerly Soviet allies in the Warsaw Treaty Organization during the Cold War. The leaks could not be traced to a particular source, but NATO did narrow the circle of target planners and reviewers after several weeks of war, and fewer leaks resulted.

NATO: Out of Area and into OOTW

One of the earliest tests for the post–Cold War cohesion of NATO, and for the willingness of the United States and its NATO allies to support multilateral peace operations, occurred in the former Yugoslavia beginning in 1991. The breakup of that multinational state into Serbia, Croatia, Bosnia-Herzegovina, and Slovenia resulted in a variety of uncivil wars involving "ethnic cleansing" and other atrocities. Bosnia itself was eventually torn apart by civil strife. A United Nations peacekeeping force was established, and NATO, in support of UN efforts, was tasked to help isolate the battlefields from outside intervention and to maintain as level a playing field as possible among combatant factions. Toward these ends, NATO used its maritime forces to enforce an embargo against the shipment of arms from outside sources into the Yugoslav cauldron. NATO also established a "no fly" zone over portions of former Yugoslavia, especially over parts of the former Bosnia-Herzegovina, to support UN efforts to restore peace there.

It became clear by the summer of 1995 that traditional peacekeeping, based on the assumption that disputant parties are ready to stop fighting, was insufficient as a mechanism for conflict termination in Bosnia. The UN forces were a lucrative target for angry sharpshooters not yet disarmed. Accordingly, NATO resolved its differences of opinion and intervened with massive, and effective, force to establish an at least temporary freezing of the military status quo. By means of the Dayton peace agreement of December 1995, NATO deployed some 60,000 troops, of which about 20,000 were Americans, in Bosnia-Herzegovina with an objective somewhere between traditional peacekeeping and peace enforcement.

NATO's Operation Joint Endeavour tasked its Implementation Force (IFOR) to disarm combatant factions and by other means to support an enforced pause in the fighting among Bosnian factions. At the same time, NATO's diplomacy had obtained the necessary political and diplomatic acquiescence of Slobodan Milosevic's Serbian government in order to ensure the cooperation of Bosnian Serbs. IFOR's mandate was for one year, after which it was supplanted by a smaller NATO contingent Stabilization Force (SFOR) with a mandate permitting more military support for the rebuilding of consensus-based political institutions in Bosnia. SFOR's mission was originally scheduled to expire in 1998, but the actual termination date remains open.

NATO's Joint Endeavour combined peacekeeping and peace enforcement duties with humanitarian assistance in a single, complex contingency operation. *Peacekeeping,* according to the U.S. Department of Defense (DOD), refers to military or paramilitary operations that are "undertaken with the consent of all major parties to a dispute" and are primarily designed to "monitor and facilitate implementation of an agreement . . . and support diplomatic efforts to reach a long-term political settlement."[29]

Peace *enforcement,* on the other hand, involves the application or threat of military force "to compel compliance with resolutions or sanctions" designed to "maintain or restore peace and order."[30] The U.S. DOD terminology is more or less similar to the difference between chapter VI and chapter VII operations according to the UN Charter. Chapter VI operations are carried out "with the *consent* of belligerent parties in support of efforts to achieve or maintain peace, in order to promote security and sustain life in areas of potential or actual conflict." Operations authorized under chapter VII, on the other hand, are conducted in order to "restore peace between belligerent parties *who do not all consent* to intervention and may be engaged in combat activities."[31]

The distinction between peacekeeping and peace enforcement is not semantic only.[32] The availability of consent on the part of local belligerent parties may determine the likelihood of success or failure of an intervention. The difficulty is that consent is not a hard line but a vanishing and reappearing fog of indistinct political and military attributes.[33] The range of the zone of intervention is wide: On one side it is bounded by traditional UN Chapter VI peacekeeping, and on the other, by large-scale but limited wars like Desert Storm. In between lies no man's land with plentiful opportunities for self-deception and wishful thinking on the part of outside interveners and their militaries:

It becomes clear that once one moves into the zone of intervention, anything can happen. It is therefore unrealistic and dangerous to make decisions about the nature of an operation and expect it to conform to one's wishes. It won't.[34]

NATO could argue with some merit that Joint Endeavour had established its competency as a collective security organization, in addition to its traditional mission of collective defense. When this intervention was first proposed, skeptics had to concede NATO's first-round success in dampening conflict. This success was conditional. NATO could not guarantee the transition from military to political and social stability among suspicious and antagonistic political communities. Military stability in Bosnia was the necessary, but less than sufficient, condition for enduring peace among previously warring factions.

The same gap, between the military conditions necessary for postconflict stability and the wider social and political matrix that determined whether stability would hold good after NATO's forces departed, was also apparent in NATO's 1999 war against Yugoslavia. After 11 weeks of bombing the regime of Yugoslav, President Milosevic agreed to accept a postwar peacekeeping force directed by NATO in Kosovo. The immediate tasking for Operation Joint Guardian was to oversee the safe repatriation of Albanian Kosovar refugees who had been victims of Milosevic's ethnic cleansing in 1998 and 1999. However, NATO's approximately 50,000-strong Kosovo Force (KFOR) was also tasked to demilitarize the Kosovo Liberation Army and to protect remaining Serbs in Kosovo from the wrath of displaced Albanians. NATO's period of military stabilization would also be required to permit the secure rebuilding of infrastructure destroyed by Milosevic's armed forces and special policy (VJ [Serbian Armed Forces] and MUP [Serbian Paramilitary Police], respectively). In addition, NATO's postconflict transitional occupation of Kosovo might well include a change of regime and the departure of Milosevic from power.

Professor Lawrence Freedman has suggested that peace and other operations apart from war be defined as "stability support" operations, and in offering this terminology, he also makes an important distinction between "wars of survival" and "wars of choice."[35] Wars of survival are those undertaken against a rising hegemon that threatens an entire region or larger area with conquest and who poses an obvious threat to vital interests. Wars of choice are created by the internal problems of weak states, including civil war and communal violence. Publics understand the necessity for costs, including possible high casualties and economic privations, in undertaking wars of survival. But they do not readily understand or accept the rationale for wars of choice, and the level of sensitivity for even moderate casualties and other costs is apt to be extremely high.[36] The next section considers this factor of expectations about the human costs of war or of military peace operations.

CASUALTIES AND POPULAR EXPECTATIONS

Greater sensitivity to casualties may be a feature of "postheroic" warfare, according to some military theorists and historians.[37] Other experts feel that the U.S. policy process is, because of cultural traditions or media saturation, exceptionally vulnerable to the political impact of casualties. One French commander of UN forces in Bosnia reportedly stated: "Desert Storm left one awful legacy. It imposed the idea that you must be able to fight the wars of the future without suffering losses. The idea of zero-kill as an outcome has been imposed on American generals. But there is no such thing as a clean or risk-free war. You condemn yourself to inactivity if you set that standard."[38] The conclusion of the air campaign against Yugoslavia in 1999 without a single U.S. or allied air fighter killed in action will further solidify a public and media expectation of zero friction in modern warfare. The unwillingness of the United States and NATO even to threaten a ground offensive into Kosovo, despite the deterrent effect this threat might have posed to Serbian President Milosevic, reflects the influence of sensitivity to the fear of casualties in framing military options.

In place of a ground campaign, NATO added spin control to its use of airpower. At the conclusion of Operation Allied Force in June 1999, Secretary of Defense William Cohen contended that NATO "severely crippled the (Serb) military forces in Kosovo by destroying more than 50 per cent of the artillery and one third of the armored vehicles." General Henry Shelton, chairman of the U.S. Joint Chiefs of Staff, estimated that NATO air forces had destroyed "around 120 tanks," "about 220 armored personnel carrier," and "up to 450 artillery and mortar pieces."[39] Later investigations, including some conducted by the U.S. military and NATO, questioned whether the air campaign had even made a dent in Serbian military power. Pilots flying at 15,000 feet to maximize their safety against Serbian air defenses achieved consistently high accuracy only against fixed targets, such as bridges and military installations. Hitting tanks, armored personnel carriers, and other mobile targets from that distance was much more difficult. A U.S. Air Force study at first suppressed and then leaked to the media estimated that 14 tanks instead of 120 had been destroyed by NATO bombing; 18 armored personnel carriers, not 220; and 20 artillery pieces, not 450.[40]

On the other hand, the sensitivity of Americans to U.S. armed force should not be overstated. The majority of Americans, immediately after the deaths of 18 U.S. Army Rangers in October 1993 in Somalia, were in favor of sending reinforcements to capture Somali warlord Muhamad Farah Aideed.[41] U.S. public sensitivity to combat casualties has a direct relationship to at least two other variables: (1) public perceptions of the significance of the conflict and (2) the expectation that U.S. political and military objectives will be accomplished in a timely manner and at acceptable cost. Of course, the U.S. political leadership plays an important role, especially the president, in mobilizing or failing to drum up public support for military intervention. The irony is that the president may have a harder sell for nonwar operations in which significant casualties are possible than for traditional wars, since public understanding of the latter is apt to be more intuitive.

Unconventional warfare, including covert operations of various sorts, by its very nature demands things that do not televise well. It sometimes requires that U.S. policymakers get in bed with disreputable characters among the leaders of other state or nonstate actors. The U.S. government may be required to disown its prior authorship of operations gone afoul of the original intent or to conceal the role of allies.[42] Leaders may have to dissemble for reporters or for Congress while an operation is in the planning and hopeful stages in order to avoid compromising security. All of these possible requirements for the successful conduct of covert operations sit poorly with the mind-sets of many, not only in the U.S. Congress and media but also entrenched in U.S. intelligence bureaucracy.

U.S. military service intelligence, including that pertinent to unconventional warfare and special operations, is as steeped in a legalistic paradigm as is its civilian counterpart. The jurisprudential paradigm for deciding how and whether to engage in unconventional warfare is an understandable temptation.[43] Any officer or policymaker who lived through the 1970s investigations of U.S. intelligence or the 1980s Iran-Contra flap has developed forgiveable protective instincts and a necessary reflex for a backside-covering paper trail. Unfortunately, those behaviors and legalisms that are self-protective in courtrooms or congressional hearings are not necessarily those that are strategically useful in a timely manner. Peace operations and other operations "other than war" will not escape the constraints of U.S. legalism and formalism in policymaking. This means, in all likelihood, that a successful endgame for U.S. participation in peace operations will require the drawing of a clear line between peacekeeping and peace enforcement and staying clear of the netherworld between the two conditions.

There is worse. Operations "other than war" can quickly and inadvertently become warlike. Outside interveners in civil wars need a clear statement of mission and some reasonable expectations about the endgame. One Rand study published in 1996 concluded that, with respect to U.S. and Russian use of armed forces since the end of the Cold War,

intervention decisions have been made in both countries from time to time for no more profound reason than the absence of any better ideas. Both the United States and Russia are configured toward unstructured and often shortsighted policy planning, with a tendency to commit forces without clearly articulated aims. In particular, ad hoc and impromptu assessments of "what is at stake" often decide what ultimately gets placed on the U.S. intervention calendar.[44]

CONCLUSION

Small wars, peace wars, and other military deployments for purposes apart from victory in combat, however necessary they may appear to be for reasons of human dignity, pose unique decision-making problems for policymakers. Operations "other than war" also make demands on the professional self-concept of conventional militaries and often place commanders of "peace wars" on the horns of a dilemma with no text-book solution. Peace enforcement, an assertive form of peacekeeping that NATO was forced to adopt in Bosnia and in Kosovo, is a form of peace war that has deployed highly armed troops into political hotspots with very restrictive rules of engagement. On occasion this has required, as in Bosnia, Haiti, and Kosovo, that forces look the other way in the face of civilian versus civilian atrocities that are better deterred or punished by domestic police forces not yet available. The idea of peace war only sounds oxymoronic until you look closely at what it is U.S. forces did most of the time in their most visible and controversial deployments of the 1990s.

NOTES

1. OOTW is preferred here to MOOTW, for "military operations other than war," as a matter of emphasis.

2. Donald M. Snow, *Uncivil Wars: International Security and the New Internal Conflicts* (Boulder, Colo.: Lynne Rienner, 1996), passim, esp. pp. 144–146.

3. On the concept of failed states, see K. J. Holsti, *The State, War, and the State of War* (Cambridge: Cambridge University Press, 1996), pp. 119–122.

4. I. William Zartman, "Introduction: Posing the Problem of State Collapse," ch. 1 in I. Willam Zartman, ed., *Collapsed States: The Disintegration and Restoration of Legitimate Authority* (Boulder, Colo.: Lynne Rienner, 1995), pp. 1–11. See also Holsti, *The State, War, and the State of War*, pp. 116–117.

5. Charles E. Calwell, *Small Wars: A Tactical Textbook for Imperial Soldiers* (1906; rpt., London, 1990), cited in Colin S. Gray, *Modern Strategy* (Oxford: Oxford University Press, 1999), p. 276.

6. Daniel J. Kaufman, "The Army," ch. 2 in Sam C. Sarkesian and Robert E. Connor, Jr., *America's Armed Forces: A Handbook of Current and Future Capabilities* (Westport, Conn.: Greenwood Press, 1996), pp. 49–50. I have combined two of the items into one from the original list.

7. Bradd C. Hayes and Jeffrey I. Sands, *Doing Windows: Non-Traditional Military Responses to Complex Emergencies* (Washington, D.C.: Department of Defense C4ISR Cooperative Research Program, 1999), p. 2.

8. Mark Duffield, "Complex Emergencies and the Crisis of Developmentalism," *IDS Bulletin*, no. 4 (1994), p. 38, cited in ibid., pp. 3–4.

9. Joint Warfighting Center, U.S. Joint Chiefs of Staff, *Joint Task Force Com-*

mander's Handbook for Peace Operations (Ft. Monroe, Va.: Joint Warfighting Center, June 16, 1997), p. iii.

10. I am very much in debt to Col. William Flavin, United States Army (Ret.), U.S. Army Peacekeeping Institute, for permission to read a draft paper clarifying these points. He bears no responsibility for arguments here.

11. Gerard Chaliand, *Terrorism: From Popular Struggle to Media Spectacle* (London: Saqi Books, 1987), p. 117.

12. Gen. Charles C. Krulak, "The Three Block War: Fighting in Urban Areas," presented at National Press Club, Washington, D.C., October 10, 1997, in *Vital Speeches of the Day*, December 15, 1997, cited in Robert F. Hahn II and Bonnie Jezior, "Urban Warfare and the Urban Warfighter of 2025," *Parameters*, no. 2 (Summer 1999), pp. 74–86, esp. p. 75.

13. Hahn and Jezior, "Urban Wafare and the Urban Warfighter of 2025," passim.

14. For a discussion of the complexity of urban operations and an innovative proposal, see Maj. Gen. Robert H. Scales, Jr., "The Indirect Approach: How U.S. Forces Can Avoid the Pitfalls of Future Urban Warfare," *Armed Forces Journal International*, no. 3 (October 1998), reprinted in Scales, *Future Warfare Anthology* (Carlisle Barracks, Pa.: U.S. Army War College, May 1999), pp. 173–186.

15. Timothy L. Thomas, "The Battle for Grozny: Deadly Classroom for Urban Combat," *Parameters*, no. 2 (Summer 1999), pp. 87–102.

16. Lt. Col. John F. Antal, "A Glimpse of Wars to Come: The Battle for Grozny," *Army*, June 1999, pp. 29–38.

17. Ibid., p. 37.

18. Pontus Siren, "The Battle for Grozny: The Russian Invasion of Chechnia, December 1994–December 1996," ch. 4 in Ben Fowkes, ed., *Russia and Chechnia: The Permanent Crisis* (New York: St. Martin's Press, 1998), pp. 87–169.

19. Anatol Lieven, *Chechnya: Tombstone of Russian Power* (New Haven, Conn.: Yale University Press, 1998), pp. 303–323.

20. Timothy L. Thomas, "The Caucasus Conflict and Russian Security: The Russian Armed Forces Confront Chechnya III. The Battle for Grozny, 1–26 January 1995," *Journal of Slavic Military Studies*, no. 1 (March 1997), pp. 50–108, esp. pp. 60–64.

21. Pavel Felgenhauer, "Elite Units Can't Match Foe," *Moscow Times*, March 16, 2000, from Post-Soviet Armies Newsletter (PSAN) Web site at http://www.geocities.com/Pentagon/Barracks/6122/special.html#top (3/16/00).

22. Pavel Felgenhauer, "Guerrilla War Can't Be Won," *Moscow Times*, March 9, 2000, from PSAN Web site at http://www.geocities.com/Pentagon/Barracks/6122/special.html#top.

23. Lieven, *Chechnya: Tombstone of Russian Power*, chs. 10 and 11 are especially pertinent here.

24. Text of the Military Doctrine of the Russian Federation, published in the Russian newspaper *Nezavisimaya Gazeta* on April 22, 2000, from the PSAN Web site at http://www.geocities.com/Pentagon/Barracks/6122/textdoctrine.html (4/22/00).

25. Pavel Felgenhauer, "Nuke Strategy Is Nothing New," *Moscow Times*, February 2000, from the PSAN Web site at http://www.geocities.com/Pentagon/Barracks/6122/doctrines.html#russ (4/15/00).

26. Les Aspin, Secretary of Defense, *Annual Report to the President and the Congress* (Washington, D.C.: U.S. Government Printing Office, January 1994), p. 67.

27. U.S. Department of State, *The Clinton Administration's Policy on Reforming Multilateral Peace Operations* (Washington, D.C.: State Department, May 1994).

28. See Donald M. Snow, "Peacekeeping, Peace Enforcement, and Clinton Defense Policy," ch. 6 in Stephen J. Cimbala, ed., *Clinton and Post–Cold War Defense* (Westport, Conn.: Praeger Publishers, 1996), pp. 87–102.

29. Joint Warfighting Center, *Joint Task Force Commander's Handbook for Peace Operations*, p. xiv.

30. Ibid.

31. UN chapter VI and VII citations are from Christopher Bellamy, *Knights in White Armour: The New Art of Peace and War* (London: Hutchinson, 1996), p. 156. Italics supplied.

32. My colleague Donald M. Snow objects to the locution "peace enforcement" as an oxymoron. Snow argues that the critical line is between "peacekeeping," which occurs with the consent of previously combatant parties, and "peace imposition," the latter involving a settlement imposed over the objections of one or more combatants by outsiders. See Snow, *Uncivil Wars*, pp. 132–133.

33. Chris Bellamy's discussion of this point is very insightful. See his *Knights in White Armour*, pp. 155–161 and passim.

34. Ibid., p. 160. I have defined the zone of intervention a little more narrowly than does Bellamy, who puts major coalition wars at the other end of the spectrum; but the concept is useful either way.

35. Lawrence Freedman, "Bosnia: Does Peace Support Make Any Sense?" *NATO Review*, no. 6 (November 1995), pp. 19–23.

36. Ibid., p. 20. See also Bellamy, *Knights in White Armour*, esp. pp. 30–35.

37. Edward Luttwak, "Toward Post-Heroic Warfare," *Foreign Affairs*, no. 3 (May–June 1995), pp. 109–122. See also, on the nature of "unheroic" and "post-heroic" military leadership and command styles, John Keegan, *The Mask of Command* (New York: Penguin Books, 1987), ch. 3 and pp. 311–351.

38. General Philippe Morillon, quoted in Keith B. Payne, *Deterrence in the Second Nuclear Age* (Lexington: University Press of Kentucky, 1996), p. 14, note 23.

39. See *Newsweek*, May 15, 2000, p. 23, for quotes from Cohen and Shelton.

40. Ibid.

41. I am grateful to Professor Peter Viggo Jakobsen for calling this point to my attention. He bears no responsibility for arguments here.

42. Roy Godson, *Dirty Tricks or Trump Cards: U.S. Covert Action and Counterintelligence* (Washington, D.C.: Brassey's, 1995), pp. 158–180.

43. The temptation is for scholars as well as for soldiers, with the result that there is little written about the *strategic* character of special operations, covert action, or other unconventional means. A useful corrective appears in Colin S. Gray, *Explorations in Strategy* (Westport, Conn.: Greenwood Press, 1996), pp. 163–188.

44. Jeremy R. Azrael, Benjamin S. Lambeth, Emil A. Payin, and Arkady A. Popov, "Russian and American Intervention Policy in Comparative Perspective," ch. 12 in Jeremy R. Azrael and Emil A. Payin, eds., *U.S. and Russian Policymaking with Respect to the Use of Force* (Santa Monica, Calif.: Rand, 1996), CF-129-CRES, via NetScape, p. 6. Pagination varies with downloading software and printer.

Conclusion

THE FRAMEWORK OF THE STUDY REVISITED

Six cases of security policymaking have been examined: three from the Cold War past and three others pertinent to the present and future. What do they tell us, apart from the individual conclusions or lessons learned within each case? Before summarizing our findings that go beyond the individual chapters and cases, let us recall the typology with which we began. We first laid down definitions for conflict prevention, management, and termination as follows:

- Conflict *prevention* is the avoidance of an outbreak of war that is (1) *undesired* by policymakers on either side, (2) to some extent, *unexpected* in the way in which it develops, and (3) involves a *very short time* for decision on the part of the disputant parties before political disagreement spills over into actual fighting. Conflict prevention, as well as the management and termination of conflict, refers to a *process* as well as to an *outcome*. Of course, conflict prevention is a matter of degree. Sometimes it is necessary to take on a smaller conflict in order to prevent it from turning into a larger and more destructive one.[1]

- Conflict *management* is the control and limitation of a set of disagreements among state or nonstate actors in order to (1) mitigate the *extent of misperception* of one another's motives on the part of states or nonstate actors who are potentially or actually in military conflict, (2) regulate or otherwise *limit the amount and kind of destruction* attendant to warfare or other conflict and attempt to *reduce the intensity of disagreements* that keep conflict going, using techniques such as peacekeeping, peace enforcement, humanitarian rescue, and other means, and (3) create an international, regional, or local *climate of expectations* that war is politically undesirable or morally unacceptable (sometimes called a

Table C.1
Behavioral Space for Type of Conflict Limitation Behavior, Classified by
Time Dimension

	Past	Present-Future
Conflict Prevention	Cuban missile crisis	Information warfare serves as a catalyst for nuclear preemption or accidental/ inadvertent nuclear war
Conflict Management	1983 "war scare"	Nuclear proliferation, together with other weapons of mass destruction and delivery systems
Conflict Termination	Gulf war of 1991	Small wars and military operations "other than war," including peace operations, special operations, and intelligence wars

Source: Author.

"security community") and that its military consequences would leave all or
most disputants worse off than they were without war.[2]

- Conflict *termination* means bringing to an *end actual military fighting* and, preferably, also *concluding the political issues* that gave rise to the fighting. It sometimes occurs that it is necessary to arrange a *cease-fire* or armistice among field
  forces before the final political terms of settlement can be concluded. Conflict
  termination may be *agreed to by the disputants* or *imposed by outsiders*, including
  by international organizations or by state actors singly or in combination. As
  applied to unconventional wars within states, conflict termination can only
  reach so far. It rarely can bring immediate halt to all the shooting and looting
  that takes place among competing ethnic, national, religious, or clan factions.
  Conflict termination is a short-term process for the most part; it cannot guarantee against a replay unless the political, social, and cultural issues that gave
  rise to the conflict are meliorated or unless one of the major disputants ceases
  to exist.[3]

We studied two cases of conflict prevention, two of conflict management, and two of conflict termination: one past and one present and/or
future case in each category. Our behavioral space for type of conflict
limitation behavior, classified by time dimension, is summarized in Table
C.1.

Each of the six chapters included a summary of its own conclusions.
What broader themes are suggested? We are far from being able to advance a scientific theory on these topics: The present effort is a policy
study that is partly guided by, but must of necessity go beyond, the body

of knowledge presently available on the topics of conflict prevention, management, and termination.

WHAT PAST CASES TELL US

Our general conclusions about past cases of conflict prevention, management, and termination are as follows.

Images of the other side, in terms of its objectives, capabilities, and mind-sets, ranged from mildly inaccurate to grossly incompetent or incoherent. Kennedy and Khrushchev each assumed the other sought nuclear superiority with the objective of fighting a world war or coercing the other side out of valued Cold War stake (Berlin, Cuba). Neither understood the domestic forces bearing upon his opposite number. Kennedy took Khrushchev's rocket diplomacy in the years immediately preceding the Cuban missile crisis as an effort at intimidation based on the Soviet leader's excessive confidence in his own military position. Actually, Khrushchev's braggadocio after 1960 was a partial attempt to cover for his comparatively weak military position.

In another case, Iraqi leader Saddam Hussein assumed that the United States was too weakened by the Vietnam syndrome to resist his aggression against Kuwait. U. S. planners mistakenly assumed that Iraq would not actually attack Kuwait, based on reassurances from friendly Arab powers. Hussein allowed the United States six months to build up a force of unprecedented size and power in the Middle East but assumed that the force would not actually be used, even after President Bush obtained a UN resolution authorizing the use of force to expel Iraq from Kuwait and the U.S. Congress had signed on. U.S. officials hoped they could get Iraq to pull out of Kuwait without war, then without a ground war. U.S. assumptions about Iraq's prewar nuclear, biological, and chemical weapons proved to be wide of the mark. In addition, Bush's expectation that, in the aftermath of military defeat, demoralized Iraqi opposition to Hussein would rise up and overthrow him was obviously disappointed.

In the war scare case, U.S. officials were not aware of elements within the Soviet party leadership and intelligence communities that regarded the threat of a U.S. or NATO nuclear first strike as more than hyperbole. Undoubtedly Soviet leaders, especially then-party chairman Iurii Andropov and his KGB leadership in 1983, purposely exaggerated the possibility of a nuclear surprise attack by NATO in order to rally their own military and intelligence forces for active measures against NATO's Euromissile deployments. Granted that assumption of Soviet exaggeration for effect, it remains clear that their leaders did believe in a more than trivial possibility that the United States and NATO were preparing an option for, and perhaps actually rehearsing for, a nuclear surprise strike at the theater or global level under some admittedly unusual, but possible, circumstances. And that belief held by Soviet leaders caused them to task intelligence services to look selectively for information that might have been self-validating with respect to the worst possible intentions on the part of the United States and NATO.

Expert analysts and scholars have identified some of the more important decision-making proclivities that have been related to political or military leaders' faulty assessments or mistaken assumptions about their opponents.[4] Among those dysfunctional behaviors, the following seem to apply to the cases examined here:

Schematic thinking. For example, Soviet leaders in 1983 expected that the U.S. and NATO Euromissile deployments would be followed by other actions deemed hostile and aggressive, possibly including the threat of war. In fact, the NATO deployments were perceived in Brussels and in Washington as attempts to equalize an imbalance in theater nuclear deterrence created by prior Soviet deployments of their IRBM the SS-20. In a similar fashion, the Kennedy administration assumed that Khrushchev would not deploy offensive missiles in Cuba because (it was assumed in Washington) Moscow understood how threatening this would be from a U.S. perspective. To the contrary, Khrushchev convinced himself that he could deploy the missiles without being detected and that the United States would thereafter reluctantly acquiesce to the presence of Soviet missiles in Cuba.

Selective perception. Leaders often perceived what they expected to perceive. One reason for this behavioral syndrome is that first impressions are often lasting, even if they are erroneous. Another reason is the influence of expectations: People perceive what they expect to. The influence of *expectations* on perceptions is different from the influence of *wants*. Wishful thinking is less frequently a cause of faulty analysis or decision than are embedded expectations, hopeful or not.[5] Expectation-driven analysis or decision appears in several of our past case studies and looms over possible futures. For example, in July of 1990, U.S. leaders were reassured by heads of state in Egypt and Jordan that Saddam Hussein was bluffing. This was not just wishful thinking on the part of U.S. or Arab leaders: Saddam had bluffed before, and he had much to lose from actually carrying out his threats. Another example is provided by the 1983 war scare incidents that alarmed some Soviet intelligence principals and some Soviet leaders. These pessimists in Moscow were somewhat predisposed, as a result of a variety of events that took place in the latter 1970s and early 1980s, to perceive U.S. actions as more hostile, more sequential, and more deliberate than they really were. The last point plays directly into the next finding.

Assuming that others are acting dispositionally, instead of situationally. This means that the actions of one side are attributed by the other to a stylized way of thinking or behaving or to a predictable and immutable mind-set. Cold War thinking by American and Soviet leaders often exhibited this behavior pattern, which shows itself in our Cuban missile crisis and 1983 war scare cases. In each case, excessive optimism about the other's apparent weakness and willingness to tolerate being pushed into a corner (Khrushchev on Kennedy in 1962, the early Reagan administration on the Soviet Union) led to an unexpected crisis. In the 1983 case, the crisis was slow to build and was almost invisible to one side until after the fact of its having been defused.

Dispositional thinking also caused the U.S. leadership in late July 1990 to discount intelligence reports of Iraqi troops massing on the Kuwaiti border: It was assumed that Hussein's deployments were a show of force in order to coerce Kuwait into compliance with Iraq's desire for oil price increases. It was also assumed that since U.S. relations with Iraq had been on good terms in the 1980s, Hussein would not commit aggression in the face of assumed U.S. displeasure. In part based on this assumption, U.S. leaders and diplomats were more equivocal in stating their objections to any aggression in the region than they should have been.

Adhering to misleading probability estimates. This is another kind of decision pathology that is related to faulty comprehension of the "other." In this case, leaders assume that typical past behavior will be repeated indefinitely, even if conditions and circumstances have changed. Saddam Hussein's troop movements near the Kuwaiti border in late July 1990 also fit this category as well as that of dispositional thinking. Another example not studied here is the assumption by the United States and Israel that Egyptian leader Anwar Sadat was bluffing in October 1973: His maneuvers were not a prelude to an actual attack on Israel. This mistaken assumption cost Israel heavily in the early stages of the October war.

Kennedy and Khrushchev also failed on this attribute or decision proclivity in 1961 and 1962. Khrushchev, having seen Kennedy's indecisive handling of the Bay of Pigs, having seemed to intimidate the youthful U.S. president at Vienna in 1961, and having observed Kennedy to have accepted the construction of the Berlin Wall between the Western- and Soviet-dominated parts of the city, assumed that Kennedy would also swallow missiles in Cuba. Kennedy also failed to adjust probability estimates. He and his advisers assumed that since the Soviet Union had not previously dared to introduce offensive, nuclear-capable missiles into the Western Hemisphere, they would not do so in 1962.

Allowing certain kinds of information to have an emotional impact on decisions. Khrushchev was highly affected by the presence of U.S. medium-range ballistic missiles in Turkey, although these missiles were obsolete and the United States had already planned their eventual withdrawal. Kennedy was personally offended by Khrushchev's willingness to deploy missiles in Cuba in the face of repeated reassurances by Soviet diplomats and by secret intelligence back-channels between Moscow and

Washington that this would not happen. Saddam Hussein was angry at Kuwait for its refusal to support oil price hikes to bail out his economy from its prolonged war against Iran. Arab leaders in the Middle East in August 1990 felt that the norm that one Arab state should never attack another Arab state would hold in the case of Iraq's dispute with Kuwait.

Fixation on early assumptions or initially visualized scenarios when they are no longer relevant. Leaders have a propensity to stick with preferred visions or desired end states despite evidence that the goal is no longer attainable by the available or preferred means. Robert E. Lee's invasions of the North in the American Civil War offer vivid examples. In our study, Khrushchev visualized favorably the results of his missile deployments in Cuba in the spring and summer of 1962. When political tensions with the Americans heated up in the autumn and the possibility of Soviet missiles in Cuba became a matter of partisan U.S. domestic political debate, Khrushchev took no actions to delay the process of deployment or to improve the probability of its concealment. Kennedy stuck with his preferred vision that the Soviets would not double-cross him on missiles in Cuba until he was presented with the hard satellite photographic evidence to the contrary.

Saddam Hussein judged that Americans would not fight in the Middle East despite their enormous buildup of military power near his borders, because, from his perspective, the United States was a weak society that could not stand large numbers of casualties. He had apparently never heard of the American Civil War or seen *Natural Born Killers*. Iraqi foreign minister Tariq Aziz judged in January 1991 before the outbreak of war that the United States would not go to war because American forces were not trained to fight in deserts (U.S. Army and Marine national training centers are located in California deserts).

In another example of this proclivity from our study, the United States and NATO were determined to go through with the Euromissile deployments beginning in December 1983 regardless of Soviet reactions. NATO saw the issue as a matter of alliance solidarity: Equalizing the balance of medium-range nuclear firepower deployed in or near Europe was a secondary objective for the alliance. The Soviet Union saw the Euromissiles as a putative first-strike capability against vital Soviet military and command targets and based in Europe. The Soviet leadership also saw the Pershing and GLCM deployments as components of a larger pattern of NATO and U.S. intimidation, including the U.S. Strategic Defense Initiative, U.S. public diplomacy over the Soviet shootdown of Korean Air Lines Flight 007, NATO military exercises close to Soviet borders and military installations, and other indicators understood as threatening by the Kremlin.

What implications do these summary findings from the past have for the present and future of theory and policy related to the starting, management and limitation, and termination of wars? In the remainder of the chapter, we expand on that topic, but a brief preview here may whet the appetite for more.

First, the hardest problems in preventing, managing, and ending military conflicts are not posed by the asymmetries in power among states or by the unbridled lust for power in international politics. Instead, conflicts often get started and resist limitation because of leaders' misperceptions of their own and others' political objectives and military plans.

Second, a preponderance of military power, such as is attributed to the United States in the first decade of the twenty-first century, does not guarantee that wars can be avoided or that they can be successfully managed or terminated to political advantage. An enormity of power tends to dull the senses to the nuances of policy and strategy, and these subtleties may make the difference between marginally successful and unsuccessful conflict resolution.

Third, wars and crises are easy to get started, harder to stop, and even harder to resolve on terms that are regarded as equitable by all disputants. Crises with nuclear weapons involved are the most dangerous of all. The Cold War track record of "successful" nuclear crisis management between Washington and Moscow cannot serve as a precedent for the twenty-first century. The spread of nuclear weapons and long range delivery systems to states with regional scores to settle, or to those with diffuse grudges against the existing international order, opens the door to "heavy" intimidation. The information superhighways created by the Internet and other aspects of the globalization of information technology offer the opportunity of "light" coercion. Whether subject to intimidation by brute force (Dark Beer) or by the threat of rendering one's brain and central nervous system confused and paralyzed (Light Beer), policymakers and military planners will have to think quicker and move faster than hitherto.

ADDITIONAL INSIGHTS ABOUT DECISION-MAKING PAST, PRESENT, AND FUTURE

If these are the conclusions from past cases, with regard to the effectiveness and validity of images of the "other" that decision makers have held in time of peace, crisis, and war, what of the present and future?

The cases that interrogated present and future issues (obviously) remain unresolved: Decision-making deficiencies may or may not impede efforts to arrive at a valid image of the other side that leads to the successful attainment of U.S. policy objectives (or vice versa: to future opponents' superior reading of the United States). Although the outcomes for the present-future cases are indeterminate, we can hypothesize some arguments of interest about future possibilities based on past findings.

These *arguments of policy interest* admittedly fall short of theory—therefore, the less ambitious label "argument of interest" is used to imply that a good case for alternate points of view could probably be made by the astute reader. All in social behavior is contingent, and policymakers have shown a remarkable propensity over the years to confound scholarly prediction. The arguments of interest are listed below.

1. *The most overworked word in the U.S. national security policy lexicon for the past 40 years or so has been* "deterrence." Deterrence has been made into much more than it was intended to be by those analysts who first propounded it in the 1950s. It evolved into an all-purpose solvent for U.S. defense and foreign policy problems that were difficult to manage. Deterrence was first applied to the relationship between nuclear armed states, then to situations of conventional dissuasion. Eventually it became a competitor for "containment," the paradigm first articulated by diplomat George F. Kennan to serve as a basis for U.S. policy formulation throughout the Cold War. Because it meant all things to all users, it became distorted as a concept and as a shorthand for strategy.

The essential question relative to deterrence is: Who is deterred by whom from what? Deterrence is a form of applied psychology based on a combination of will and capability. For deterrence to work, the threatener must make the threatened party believe that he has the capability and the will to carry out the threat. On the evidence, and apart from nuclear threats that are a special case, threats based on the ability to deny the opponent his objectives by defeating his forces in battle, or by destroying the cohesion of his military organization, are more persuasive than threats to inflict allegedly unacceptable or intolerable degrees of punishment to his society or armed forces. Defeating the opponent's forces in battle may require high levels of casualty. Therefore, modern military thinkers, including those who fought the Gulf war on the winning side, have emphasized in recent years the possibility of decisive attacks against the enemy's military brain and central nervous system, or system for command, control, and communications. Decapitation is therefore posed as an alternative to deterrence by punishment or by denial, as perhaps a composite form using both punishment and denial threats.

However, decapitation is not always easy to define in practice or to ascertain as an accomplished fact. The "brain" of the opposed system may be difficult to locate and even more difficult to hit. Iraq's political and military leadership structures were attacked repeatedly in the Gulf war of 1991, but Saddam Hussein and his principal court retainers survived. Between the end of the Gulf war in 1991 and the end of President Clinton's second term in office, the United States launched various cruise missile attacks against military leadership and command-control targets in Iraq. In 1999, NATO's air strikes included attacks on Yugoslav President Milosevic's residences in addition to hits on military bunkers where the Serbian high command was thought to be entrenched. In neither case was anything decisive accomplished.

Military scorpions, especially if they are large and complex organizations, have the capability to regenerate their heads as well as the nerves of communication and control necessary to prosecute a war. Even the U.S. and Soviet nuclear command and control systems during the Cold War dedicated considerable effort to this problem of "postattack" survivability. Neither government wanted an accidental or unauthorized launch of a nuclear weapon; both wanted to guarantee that authorized launch commands would be carried out promptly and successfully. Therefore, each built "fail safe" procedures against accidental or inadvertent war, but each also guaranteed that if the head of state or government and/or the topmost layer of military command were destroyed, assured retaliation would nevertheless take place. The United States guaranteed this latter result by establishing a clear order of presidential succession and, along with this but not identical to it, a succession chain of military command below the president and the secretary of defense. If necessary, the commanders of unified or specified commands actually holding nuclear weapons could, if higher levels were incapacitated, fire back at an attacker.

2. *U.S. and Soviet leaders in the Cold War frequently failed to understand one another's short-term political objectives and the motivations behind those objectives.* With equal frequency, they misunderstood important aspects of social and political culture in the United States and among the various Soviet nationalities. With even greater frequency, each of the Cold War superpowers misestimated the capabilities and intentions of states outside of Europe, especially "Third World" leaders and the mind-sets of their militaries. The United States plunged into Vietnam with misconceptions about Vietnamese politics, society, and culture that defy caricature. Nor did U.S. military experts have a clear picture of the military strategy and tactics being followed by North Vietnam and the Viet Cong (South Vietnamese National Liberation Front). The Soviet Union was equally misinformed and hubristic about its intervention in Afghanistan, to a comparably dismal dénouement for its political leadership and armed forces.

3. *Nuclear weapons are dangerous instruments that few, if any, heads of state or leaders of armed forces are competent to play with.* U.S. and Soviet Cold War experiences, some described in this book, are replete with instances of atomic bluffing to the detriment of sound policy. Nuclear danger was thought to be a tool by which adversaries could be intimidated, and it can be argued that it was intimidating when used in a one-sided manner: by a nuclear power and against a state without nuclear weapons. But confrontations between U.S. and Soviet leaders during the Cold War

were made more dangerous and less manageable by nuclear weapons. The argument that nuclear weapons "prevented" World War III in Europe is comparable to the argument that the possibility of getting AIDS prevents unsafe sex. Unfortunately, not always and not everywhere.

The relationship between nuclear weapons and Cold War politics might better be described as analogous to the role of air bags in automobile safety. Air bags, under some collision conditions, can mitigate the effects of impact, just as nuclear weapons can in some conditions sober up leaders in the middle of a crisis. On the other hand, we know that air bags can cause injuries to small children in the front seats of cars or to shorter adults. Nuclear weapons, like air bags, involved a willingness to run a higher risk of a Type II error (the null hypothesis is valid, but we assume it is wrong) than of a Type I error (the null hypothesis is invalid, but we assume it is true). That is: We assume that nuclear weapons will work most of the time the way they were intended to, as we assume that air bags will. We accept a small probability that occasionally they will not and have undesired side effects.

Of course, the difficulty with this reasoning is that the consequences of nuclear deterrence failure are more drastic than the consequences of premature or unnecessary air bag explosion (quite literally). Nuclear weapons placed the fates of entire societies, and perhaps the survival of the Western Hemisphere, at risk to the crisis management skills of policymakers. And some of these policymakers were demonstrably unprepared for their jobs. Robert McNamara, secretary of defense under Presidents Kennedy and Johnson, is one of the few who have been very candid about the lack of preparedness of policymakers for many of the decisions they will have to take in public life. "What," he once told a public forum, "did I as a former automobile executive know about national defense? Absolutely nothing."

4. *The process of selection, recruitment, and training for U.S. and other major power political leaders and for the top bureaucrats who advise them has numerous shortcomings.* Apart from the vagaries of electoral politics that are necessary in a democracy, the recruitment of cabinet and other officials is a process that is overdosed with cronyism (called "networking") and sycophancy. Acolytes of powerful Beltway power brokers bubble to the top of the U.S. policy advisory pyramid as a result of their ability to buff the prose or analysis of military leaders and politicians. Leaders become so dependent on these advisers that the leaders' own thoughts are often menu driven and choreographed. When off their prepared scripts, some U.S. presidents, defense secretaries, and other cabinet-level officials were simply lost. At least one national security adviser in the Reagan administration was widely acknowledged to know absolutely nothing about national security.

Of course, the situation was even worse for the Soviet leadership in the Cold War. Some of the troglodytes in command of the world's largest nuclear arsenal challenged the imagination of creative fiction writers. Leonid Brezhnev's last years before his death in 1982 were particularly gruesome. Russians joked openly about Brezhnev's physical and mental infirmities. A typical story told by Muscovites went as follows. Brezhnev is informed by one of his aides: "The media are saying that you never show yourself outside the walls of the Kremlin. They report that a dummy has taken your place in the back of the official Presidential limousine." Brezhnev's angry retort: "Put out a directive immediately correcting this lie: say that I am the dummy."

Although there are no textbook solutions by which any state can guarantee improved quality in its policymakers, an alarming trend in the past two decades has been the number of persons holding key positions in the U.S. executive branch and in Congress related to military affairs but without any personal military experience. This is not an argument for a return to conscription in the United States, neither a necessary nor a desirable policy choice. But the peacetime draft did acclimate persons across the spectrum of society to the norms, expectations, and culture of the armed forces. There is a growing danger that the American military, high tech and proficient in combat as it has thus far proved to be, will become sociologically and politically separated from the cultural mainstream. If so, a vital connection between the armed forces and its democratic nutrients in civic culture will have been severed, to the detriment of the military and the American people. One sign of this growing divergence between the armed forces and society is the public (and congressional and media) expectation that all conflicts involving U.S. combat or peacekeeping forces will be short, casualty light, and television friendly.

5. *The Gulf war of 1991 was not a triumph of technology.* It resulted from the favorable correlation of political and military forces as well as from the technology advantage favoring the United States and its allies. The United States had lined up some 30 states including Arab powers against Iraq, thus isolating Saddam Hussein from meaningful political support. The United States also had the advantage of Soviet cooperation to a point: The Soviet Union signed onto the United Nations resolution in favor of expelling Iraq from Kuwait by force if necessary. Saddam Hussein also "cooperated" with his adversaries by allowing them time to build up their defenses in Saudi Arabia and by permitting them additional time to prepare for an offensive air and ground war. Third, Hussein played his cards prematurely. If he had waited until his fledgling nuclear weapons program had come to fruition, he would have been in a stronger position to coerce his immediate neighbors and to deter any U.S. counterintervention to stop Iraqi aggression.

That having been said, the U.S. and allied air and ground campaigns failed to destroy most of Iraq's prewar nuclear complex; failed to destroy most (if any) of Iraq's mobile ground-to-ground Scud missiles; and left the hard core of Hussein's crack Republican Guard forces free to fight another day by terminating the ground war after only 100 hours. In the first year of the twenty-first century, Saddam Hussein was still in power in Baghdad and President George Bush's son was elected president of the United States. Should the United States and its coalition allies have extended the war fighting in February 1991 into a march to Baghdad to dislodge Hussein from power?

The answer is: arguably not, based on historical precedent. George Bush chose not to run the same risk that President Harry S. Truman ran in September 1950. After General Douglas MacArthur's dramatically successful landing on the coast of North Korea at Inchon and the subsequent rout of the invading North Korean forces from South Korea, President Truman agreed to adjust the goal of the American and other UN forces from restoring the status quo ante to liberating all of Korea, north and south, to the Chinese–North Korean border. This decision did not sit well with Mao Zedong and his regime in Beijing. The Chinese intervened with massive numbers of "volunteers" in November and drove the Americans and South Koreans back out of North Korea to well below the 38th parallel, where subsequent fighting eventually stabilized. The United States then reverted to its original war aim and settled for a negotiated peace. General MacArthur and President Truman clashed over the decision to settle for the status quo ante, and their public argument led to MacArthur's dismissal in 1951.

Had President Bush insisted upon extending the Gulf war into a march to Baghdad with the objective of deposing Hussein and installing another regime, he would have met resistance from other members of the anti-Iraq coalition. Most prominently, Saudi Arabia might very well have dropped out, depriving the United States of its logistics base for further warfare and of its legitimacy in most of the Arab world. In addition, there was not any serious planning in the United States or elsewhere for the post-conflict governance of a state such as Iraq. In the aftermath of its military defeat and Hussein's political deposition, Iraq could have been torn apart by civil war including Kurdish factions in the north and Shi'a Muslims in the southern part of the country. The United States and its allies would have been in charge of something analogous to southern Lebanon in 1983, but now in Baghdad and the surrounding countryside in 1991. The willingness of the American public and of the U.S. Congress to support an indefinite occupation of Iraq was doubtful, to say the least. That the United Nations would have supported an American and allied occupation of an Arab country was even more doubtful, amid the cries of "colonialism" that would have echoed through the halls of the UN General Assembly.

6. *The idea of establishing "information dominance" in warfare is probably overrated and misleadingly dangerous if taken literally.* The process of "friction," as Clausewitz called it, ensures that in any war many things will go unexpectedly wrong. The effort to establish information superiority over the opponent is laudable, but it will be wise to plan for disappointment. Information warfare has both defensive and offensive aspects, and things can go wrong quickly on both ends of the equation. Offensive information warfare aims to destroy, negate, or exploit the enemy's information systems, communications, and command/control for U.S. purposes. Defensive information warfare protects the same systems and processes from enemy manipulation or destruction. Obviously this is a two-sided game and one that depends upon strategy as well as technology.

For example, NATO had an overwhelming advantage in the pursuit of information dominance against Yugoslavia when NATO undertook its punitive bombing campaign against Serbia in the spring of 1999. NATO had the high-tech information systems, and its systems were not vulnerable to outright attack and destruction, as were those of the Milosevic regime in Belgrade. In addition, NATO chose to fight an air war without a ground war component, thus putting at risk fewer of its forces that might be killed, captured, or wounded to the advantage of Serbian propaganda. Finally, NATO had as its leader the United States, where a great deal of military thinking had been done in the preceding decade about the importance of information warfare and how to conduct it.

Although NATO did have some success in carrying out information warfare against Serbia, its success was partial, despite its lopsided advantage in technology and casualty-avoidant strategy. One might argue that Serbia, playing very few cards, played them as well or better than NATO did. First, Serbia initiated a fairly sophisticated public information campaign telling its side of the story, providing nearly real-time images for Internet consumers and video for the world's television networks. These pictures of destruction to civilian infrastructure in Belgrade and elsewhere in Yugoslavia made NATO's air attacks appear heedless of collateral damage, despite NATO's desire and effort to hold down incidental destruction.

Second, Yugoslav President Slobodan Milosevic manipulated the negotiating process so that he was able to continue his campaign of ethnic cleansing against Albanians in Kosovo right up to the end of the bombing campaign. It took 78 days of bombing and ground operations by the Kosovo Liberation Army, as well as mediation by the president of Finland and the former prime minister of Russia, to bring about a cease-fire acceptable to both sides. By then most Albanians had been driven from Kosovo and NATO faced the hard work of mounting a peacekeeping operation to bring them back and to reintegrate them into their former society. For many of the departed this would be impossible. In addition, Milosevic remained in power in Belgrade and maintained control over a state media and security services, placing himself as the Saddam Hussein of the Balkans and perhaps just as durable in the short run. Milosevic was only deposed in the fall of 2000 after suffering electoral defeat.

Postconflict bomb (or battle) damage assessments (BDA in military jargon) became a matter of significant controversy within the U.S. government and NATO. There was disagreement over how many Serbian tanks and armored personnel carriers NATO air strikes had actually destroyed. Several estimates were ordered up by NATO commanders, but the numbers produced by different studies were widely divergent. Some of the more optimistic estimates of Serbian armored vehicle destruction had been based on wishful thinking, much like some of the more optimistic estimates during the Gulf war about the numbers of Scud missiles killed by air strikes or by Patriot air defense interceptors. Despite NATO's claim that this was the most precise bombing campaign in history, it was self-evident that targets not on the authorized list received NATO ordnance when the Chinese embassy in Belgrade was bombed. So overconfident was NATO based on its own info-hype that some of its supporters even theorized that the attacks on the Chinese embassy must have been deliberate—no mistake of that proportion was possible, given U.S. and NATO information superiority!

7. *Information superiority would in all likelihood be even more difficult for the United States or another major power to establish in the asymmetrical conflicts termed "low-intensity conflicts" or unconventional warfare, as compared to the difficulty in doing so in conventional warfare.* Unconventional warfare includes a broad spectrum of types of fighting. Here we employ the term to mean a conflict in which at least one major party to the conflict is not a conventional armed force paid, trained, and ordered into action by an accountable state government. In these types of conflicts, superior information technology may be useful for logistics, administration, and reconnaissance/command-control. But at the sharp end of the spear, where conventional militaries must take on warrior bands with a different idea of war, the pertinent information may not be the kind that comes out of fiber optic cables or computer terminals.

In Somalia in 1992–1993, the United States lacked essential information about the culture and society that proved to be self-defeating for its military effort. Somalia's political legitimacy and authority were fragmented among disparate clans and clan leaders. Clan allegiances were shifting sands, and clan promises to cooperate with outsiders such as UN peacekeepers were matters of short-term tactical expedient. The major concern of each clan leader, relative to the impact of the U.S. and UN intervention with the initial objective of preventing mass starvation, was:

Will this intervention leave me and my followers better off, or worse off, compared to our competitors?

The United Nations and the United States expanded their political objective from peacekeeping for food distribution (humanitarian rescue) into the more ambitious aim of quelling civil strife and brokering a lasting peace settlement among Somalia's clan leaders. When the most powerful clan leader, Muhamad Farah Aideed, decided it was no longer advantageous to emphasize a cooperative strategy as defined by the United States and United Nation, the American government and the head of the UN mission to Somalia authorized military escalation: the attempted capture of Aideed and the destruction of his leadership cadre.

Toward this end, a U.S. Army military operation to capture Aideed and many of his principal associates was approved in October 1993. Reminiscent of the ill-fated Carter administration attempt to rescue American hostages held in Tehran, Iran, in 1980, the raid against Aideed's supposed headquarters in downtown Mogadishu was a military and public relations disaster. First, the raid was based on faulty intelligence, and perhaps deliberate disinformation, about Aideed's whereabouts and vulnerability. Second, insufficient firepower was allocated to carry out the mission successfully if anything went wrong (as something always does). Third, the timing and character of the raid were leaked to Aideed by some process still not fully explained. The result was that the U.S. forces ran into unexpected and well-planned military resistance, resulting in the deaths of 18 U.S. Army Rangers in an urban firefight.

Worse for the American government, Aideed used the embarrassing military setback for the United States and the United Nation to conduct his own form of information warfare. The body of a slain U.S. serviceman was dragged through the streets of downtown Mogadishu with global media coverage. Cheering Somalis dominated the background. In addition, the Clinton administration, faced with an uproar in Congress against the expanded military mission and its aftermath, decided to set a firm date for eventual withdrawal of virtually all U.S. military forces from Somalia. The United States and the United Nations then backtracked and determined that they would have to work with Aideed if there were to be any hope of pacification and stability in Somalia before the major military forces of foreign powers were withdrawn. So the recalcitrant Somali warlord of June through October 1993 became the cooperative partner of the United States and the United Nations in 1994 as they sought to extricate themselves from Somalia with dignity.

The Russian armed forces in Chechnya from 1994 through 1996 demonstrated, in fighting on their own state territory with superior firepower and technology, a remarkable incapacity for doing battle against highly motivated irregular forces. Russian command and control was abysmal from the top (President Yeltsin) to the bottom of the military command structure. Russian tactics in attempting to storm Grozny in January 1995 ignored everything learned by the Soviet armed forces in the Great Patriotic War of 1941–1945 about urban combat. The Chechens even won the information war: Prominent Russian generals and politicians publicly opposed the war, others chose retirement in preferment to military command in the North Caucasus, and soldiers deserted en masse or sold off Russian equipment to Chechen resistance fighters. Russia negotiated a face-saving cease-fire in August 1996, and Chechnya acquired de facto independent status as of the following January.

Russia's war against Chechnya beginning in August 1999 was more popular among Russians and better planned from a military standpoint. Russian Prime Minister and later Acting President Vladimir Putin gained at least temporary political ballast as Russian forces, relying mainly on air strikes and artillery firepower, cleared and held Chechnya north of the Terek river and then proceeded south to attack the major urban areas of the rebellious republic. After a brutal battle for control of Grozny lasting several months, Russian forces ran up a flag in the central square of the Chechen capital and declared it theirs. A city that once housed a prewar population of 400,000 had been bombed and strafed to rubble, and now 40,000 or fewer citizens, mostly Russian civilians, remained. Figure C.1 captures the essence of Grozny as it appeared to a photographer in early February 2000: An ironic foreground shows a Russian soldier, as if preparing to dine, amid the ruins.

The Russians had perhaps gained a Pyrrhic victory in Grozny in February 2000, as they had in the first Chechen war of post-Soviet Russia. In the earlier war Russia finally took Grozny in the spring of 1995, only to lose it again to a Chechen offensive in August 1996. Even if Russia held onto the major cities and roads of Chechnya, Islamic resistance fighters would remain in the mountains of southern Chechnya to fight another day. For several centuries, the obdurate Chechens had fought against the imposition of Russian military power and political control: against imperial Russia, against Soviet Russia, and now into the twenty-first century against democratic Russia.

Russia, in order to deal with future Chechnyas, would have to learn the tools of the trade of what I have elsewhere referred to as *armed persuasion*.[6] Armed persuasion means the use of armed forces for purposes other than destruction. Destruction is what most military hosts have been trained to accomplish throughout history—and with good reason. Until the armed forces of the other side were utterly destroyed or thoroughly disarmed, the opponent's territory that they protected could not be invaded, its riches plundered, or its government deposed. Nuclear weapons rewrote the rules of war or threat of war precisely because they overturned, or seemed to overturn, the maxim that one must first defeat

Figure C.1
Devastation in Grozny, February 2000

Sources: alm@znet.com and http://naqshbandi-sa.org/chech.htm#top (February 2000).

the opposed military force before one could attack the society of the enemy.

RESOLVING FUTURE CONFLICTS

There is another purpose for which militaries can be used, equally with destruction of the opponent's order of battle or disarming of the opposed force. The other purpose is to *induce* the other side to cooperate in disarming itself or in sheathing its own sword.[7] Rules of chivalry related to battle between mounted knights are only one example of the kind of convention that warriors have frequently established to legitimate fighting for less-than-total objectives. The duel is another convention of this sort, as was the custom of potlatch among aboriginal tribes of the American Northwest. In fact, the twentieth century is unusual in its lack of restraint upon the use of military power for political purposes. It was Clausewitz, that greatest of Western military thinkers and close student of the Napoleonic wars, who admonished that war was not a thing in itself: It had a political purpose, and the military instrument had to be subordinated to politics as defined by the head of state.

Clausewitz's admonition about the control of force by policy was balanced on a precarious fulcrum, however, for several reasons. First, he wrote before the most modern technologies of his own century, let alone those of a century later, appeared to increase the rate at which mass destruction could be accomplished. Second, Clausewitz, having observed Napoleon's wars against Russia and Prussia from the other side of the hill, repeatedly expressed admiration for Napoleon's ability to mobilize the French nation for total war. Third, Clausewitz's ideal type of "absolute" war lent itself to misconstruction at the hands of both his devotees and his critics. Because of the friction that bogs down war plans and war machines, as well as the requirement that war must be limited by policy, Clausewitz recognized that actual wars would be limited in fact if not by desire. World War I showed the willingness of the heads of state in Europe to wage total war by standing Clausewitz on his head, as Lenin had done to Marx. Instead of insisting upon the subordination of war to policy, the leaders of the Triple Alliance and Triple Entente presided over the subordination of policy to war. And nowhere was this reversal of Clausewitz more apparent than in Germany, where Generals Erich von Ludendorff and Paul von Hindenburg became, in effect, a state within a state.

World War II seemed to approximate the standard for absolute war, and nuclear weapons that exploded at the end of it were premonitory of the ultimate capability for global destruction that science had now bequeathed to the military. But the reaction, among military professionals and political leaders alike, was one of horror, not enthusiasm. Recall that the United States had a monopoly on nuclear weapons from 1945 until the first Soviet atomic bomb was detonated in 1949. The United States had a virtual monopoly longer than that, because it deployed a bomber force with global reach that could have inflicted total devastation on the Russian heartland without fear of comparable retaliation. Not until the Soviet Union began to deploy long-range ballistic missiles, in the late 1950s, was the mechanism of mutual deterrence set in motion. The U.S. nuclear hand was not stayed by the prospect of assured retaliation in the latter 1940s or early 1950s. It was held back by American values (against committing an American version of Pearl Harbor), by the relative scarcity of nuclear weapons (until Eisenhower's first term in the White House), and by the awareness of politicians and military professionals that nuclear war even on a small scale would not be war but genocide. Having recently witnessed the Holocaust in Europe, the postwar leaders of Europe and North America had no desire to repeat the experience and call it "victory."

The self-contradictory status of any nuclear "war" was the first clue to the Americans, to the Russians, and to others that limited wars, including subconventional conflicts not necessarily fought by the rules of the Geneva Convention, were going to challenge military art in the remainder of the twentieth century and beyond. French social theorist Raymond Aron termed the twentieth century the century of total war, and he was correct. But, because of that experience, states and their leaders had had enough—and more important in the economically advanced democracies of Western Europe, North America, and Japan, so had their publics.

Then, too, the political causes for war in Europe had faded into a geopolitical global joust between America and Russia that, as Alexis de Tocqueville had foreseen, was inevitable, once the age of colonial expansion and dominion by Britain, France, and Germany had come to an end. Of course, the U.S.–Soviet global rivalry was couched in the ideological garb of communism versus capitalism, and no doubt sincerely for all of that. But it was also, and mainly, about power and position, about the right to rule and to determine the rules of the international power game. It ended not when one side defeated the other in battle (nuclear weapons precluded that, at least at an acceptable cost to either side, for most of the Cold War) but when the Russian people had had enough of Sovietization, Marx, oppression, and poverty. There is nothing like stores with empty shelves to concentrate the mind of the voter on the absurdity of his or her political system. In the information age, Soviet citizens could see that their system had failed and capitalism had succeeded, and once glasnost permitted open acknowledgment of the failures of Sovietization, all bets were off.

The Russians now find themselves driven back to the Soviet achievements in World War II (the Great Patriotic War, or Fatherland War, in Russia) in order to build ersatz legitimation for their cash-starved armed forces. For historians the mining of World War II experience is a plausible treasure trove. But that war was arguably the last of its kind. It was certainly the last of its kind in the century of total war. A repeat of global war is even more unlikely at the turn of the century for a number of reasons. First, the end of the Cold War and the demise of the Soviet Union remove the proximate political tensions between East and West that might, albeit inadvertently, have escalated into global war. Second, nowadays the major military powers are mostly aligned with one another under the command of NATO. Outside of NATO, Russia, China, and India are major powers with nuclear arsenals, and other states (Pakistan and Israel) have either declared themselves nuclear or are widely acknowledged as such. The non-NATO great powers and nuclear powers are not in alignment: To the contrary, they eye one another suspiciously (China and India; India and Pakistan), although some post-Soviet political rapprochement is now going on between Russia and China. Israel's nuclear arsenal is intended to deter regional aggressors, as is Pakistan's and India's.

If global war is unlikely, the possibility of large-scale regional war (without nuclear weapons) cannot be dismissed so easily. The Gulf war of 1991 is an example of the kinds of stakes that can lead states into major coalition wars: oil, nuclear weapons (future tools of Iraq unless destroyed), and naked aggression. On the other hand, the Gulf war is exceptional in the numbers of participants, in the lopsided alignment of the major powers on one side against Iraq, and in the celerity with which Saddam Hussein was forced to withdraw from Kuwait. Iraq faced an overwhelming U.S. force fighting with a template of "AirLand battle" developed for war in Central Europe against Soviet armored regiments and maneuver battalions. This template and the forces trained to fight it simply crushed the comparatively smaller mini-Soviet force of Iraq. Another regional war on a large scale, such as one in the Middle East or Northeast Asia (Korea), would not necessarily find that political alignments were so one-sided in favor of the status quo ante, nor that the United States and allied NATO publics and parliaments were as eager to support the government war aims. The first test of the twenty-first century would probably come when China first coerces, and then openly threatens, Taiwan. On the evidence, although China will certainly wax its military power and political influence in the Pacific basin, it will steer shy of any direct military clash with the United States. It neither needs nor wants a major regional war in order to accomplish its near-term political and economic objectives in Asia.

A regional war is thought by some to be the possible result of a "rogue" state such as Iraq, Iran, or North Korea acquiring weapons of mass destruction, including nuclear weapons, and firing them at targets of opportunity. But notwithstanding the unpredictable character of some of the rulers in these countries, it would be self-defeating for any rogue regime to attack U.S. or allied NATO territory. A WMD attack would virtually guarantee a U.S. or NATO nuclear response capable of annihilating the offending regime and destroying its entire military capability, if not more. The argument that religious or ideological fanatics in control of nuclear weapons are capable of nonrational thinking (i.e., defined in Western culture as not within the cost-benefit model of evaluating outcomes) is certainly true—and sobering. It is also the case that the relationship between the armed forces and society in some of these newer nuclear powers is an uncertain one. Nevertheless, history shows that few heads of state or chief warlords prefer to accomplish their own certain death and destruction when alternatives present themselves. Hitler, perhaps, is the exception that proves the rule, but Hitler's philosophy was a pathological and peculiar mix of Norse mythology, Wagnerian opera, and racism. There will not be many leaders in the twenty-first century who are preparing for entry into Valhalla on the installment plan.

Since global war is nearly impossible to imagine and major regional wars are improbable, then "war," or the use of force by professional militaries to accomplish the aims of state policy, is more and more the fighting of small conventional conflicts, of unconventional wars, and of military commitment to peace operations intended to prevent war, enforce cease-fires, and deescalate conflicts. This, to return to our earlier argument about the relationship between force and policy in the new world order, means that military persuasion will become more important than military destruction. Of necessity, the *capacity* for military destruction will have to support the ability to employ military persuasion. For example: NATO's ability to act as a pacifier in Bosnia after December 1995 was based not only on that alliance's diplomatic skill but also on its preponderant military capability in Europe.

The new world order of the twenty-first century will pose significant security challenges for the United States, for its NATO allies, and for other major power militaries that will clash with some of their policy instincts and professional military ethos. First among these will be the challenge of military intervention to stop genocide or other atrocities in failed and failing states. These interventions will be controversial for a number of reasons: (1) They will usually take place in parts of the world that are non-Western, offering cultural and social barriers to understanding; (2) Western armed forces may confront irregular forces or unruly mobs who play by no particular rules of war currently enshrined in manuals; (3) ubiquitous television coverage of peace operations or other conflict prevention or mediation missions may distort images and misshape priorities; and (4) worst of all, the expectation on the part of the U.S. public, media, and Congress that military operations are casualty free can be self-inhibiting against constructive military engagement, where risk factors exceed the trivial.

These preventive or meliorative interventions, so-called, will not exhaust the kinds of challenges to U.S. and allied national security in the early decades of the twenty-first century that require skills in conflict prevention, management, and termination. The second kind of challenge appears at the other end of the force and policy spectrum: the use of weapons of mass destruction in order to intimidate and coerce other states or, if necessary, to inflict destruction on them. The spread of nuclear, biological, and chemical weapons after the Cold War has been much remarked upon in the literature and in policy debates. There is some false comparison of apples, oranges, and tomatoes here: Nuclear weapons are in a class by themselves, and chemical weapons are far easier to make and to employ for military purposes compared to biologicals or nukes. Nonetheless, all qualify as weapons of mass destruction that, in all likelihood, would be threatened or used against cities or objects of social value more than they would be used to destroy armies, fleets, and air forces.

The problem of "deterring" the spread of weapons of mass destruction and ballistic missile delivery systems is that *deterrence* is probably the wrong word to use to describe the problem or the solution. The process of proliferation is driven by both "hard" and "soft" variables that are difficult to put into any calculations of military deterrence. The "hard" variables driving proliferation forward are the economic incentives of the supplier states to sell weapons and delivery systems in order to earn hard currency. Along with the hard currency may also go a bonus of political influence: Russia, China, and North Korea have all benefited financially and politically from arms transfers to the Middle East and South Asia and elsewhere.

The "soft" variables pushing proliferation are related to the prestige value of nuclear weapons among states that are currently nonnuclear. Whereas most states have agreed to extend the Nuclear Non-Proliferation Treaty indefinitely, a significant minority have refused to do so, and some members of that minority (India) are now acknowledged nuclear powers. The United States and its NATO allies are apt to assume, on the basis of their Cold War experience and post–Cold War hopes, that nuclear weapons are at best a necessary evil, to be marginalized as instruments of influence in favor of information-based, advanced conventional forces. This may not be the perception everywhere. In some regions weapons of mass destruction may combine with feelings of nationalistic assertiveness and/or resentment at past treatment by the West.

For example, in Asia some states wishing to flex their military muscles may see nuclear and other weapons of mass destruction as components of a broader military modernization.[8] This broader military modernization may also be designed to change geostrategic space in Asia. India and China, for example, may combine weapons of mass destruction with ballistic missiles and some enhanced C3I (space reconnaissance, modern communications) to extend their military reach well beyond previous confinements. In so doing, they would force the United States, Japan, and Russia to recalculate their estimated costs and risks from military deployments or interventions in the Pacific Basin.

Another reason for the increasing relevancy of military persuasion in the twenty-first century, and related to the potential for nuclear weapons spread, is the repolarization of politics after the Cold War. The demise of the Soviet Union transformed a bipolar distribution of global military power into something diffuse and uncertain of its direction. If we make the reasonable assumption based on history that there is an eventual correlation between economic and military power, then the twenty-first century will witness, at least, a five-sided multipolar power system: the

United States, NATO Europe, Russia, China, and Japan. Japan is the negative case: It ended the twentieth century as an economic superpower but one content to remain among second-tier military powers. Japan's experience from 1946 through the end of the century will not be normative for the next century, however. Japan lives in a dangerous neighborhood and an unpredictable neighborhood since the end of the Cold War; during the Cold War it was also dangerous, but the nature of the threat was predictable. Now Japan must consider an ambitious China, more assertive North and South Koreas, Indonesia, Taiwan, and India as considerable players in the Pacific littoral and/or the Indian Ocean. This new geostrategic neighborhood may force Japan into two decisions: to develop a more blue water navy capable of military power projection; and to attempt to deploy with American assistance (and over Chinese objections) a ballistic missile defense system for its national territory.

The preceding arguments suggest that the spectrum of weapons and conflict types that the U.S. and other militaries will face in the new world order might be charted and summarized along the lines of Table C.2. The table represents a continuum of types of weapons and/or varieties of military coercion, from left to right, and it identifies for each weapons type/form of coercion five aspects: the distinctive features and tasks appropriate for each type of weapon or use; its most plausible purpose; the most likely user or users; the expected cost of buying into this particular capability; and finally, the C4ISR support requirements for this combination of weapon type and conflict mode.

Each cell entry is the cross product of column and row headings. Each is therefore a highly nuanced behavior space. Each of these behavior spaces represents ideas about the uses of force as well as prevalent tools that go with, or are expected to go with, those kinds of ideas. The continuum from left to right might appear at first blush to be based only on the degree to which force is calibrated and selective (or massive and indiscriminate). Although discrimination and precision are important variables, an additional and more fundamental component determines one's place in the table: the relative importance of brain compared to brawn in carrying out military operations to a successful conclusion. Thus, for example, although cyberwar might involve no actual killing of human beings and it might be contended that this is the most precise and discriminating form of war, cyberwar does not necessarily require sophisticated "soft" knowledge about a society and culture (granted: the more you know about a target state's society and culture, the better your cyberwarriors will do). But wars and weapons of the mind are placed to the right of cyberwar in this chart because they require nuanced perceptions management and behavior modification of leaders and others in non-Western cultures: One must get into the deep structure of meanings

Table C.2
Spectrum of Weapons and Conflict Types

	Distinctive Features and Tasks	Purpose
Nuclear/Chemical/ Biological Weapons/ Mass Destruction	Difficult to impossible to use without unacceptable collateral damage or side effects	Avoid war by means of deterrence
Precision Conventional Weapons and Supporting C4ISR/ Precision Conventional Warfare	Precision-guided munitions, stealth, and advanced C4ISR make possible long-range destruction of high-value, protected targets while minimizing collateral damage and own losses	Deter or fight regional conflicts on a large scale or other war at acceptable cost
Nonlethal or "Less than Lethal" Weapons/ Nonlethal Uses of Force	Avoids deliberate killing or serious injury while stopping undesired behavior	Subdue hostile elements without making situation worse
Information Warfare and Weapons (including electronic warfare and cyberwar)	Attacks focus on information systems, communications, and electronics but may involve side effects on civilians or infrastructure	Confuse or disrupt opponent's ability to collect and analyze information and to act on it in a timely way
Wars and Weapons of the Mind, Psyche, and Spirit (including wars of identity)	Range from propaganda, psychological operations, terrorism, guerrilla warfare, and other unconventional means, including competitive intelligence	Confuse or disrupt opponent's decision making; manipulate enemy's mind-set and perceptions, including intimidation of authority

Who Uses	Cost of Entry	C4ISR Requirements
State actors so far, but terrorist use of weapons of mass destruction is a worry for state actors	Very high in money and equipment, and draws attention of skeptical international community and possible enemies	Expensive technical intelligence and well-placed human intelligence
State actors	Very high—prohibitive for all but a few advanced "third-wave" economies	High-end technical intelligence plus considerable human intelligence
State and nonstate actors	Low to moderate, but need military mind-set adaptable to nonlethal uses of force as part of tool kit	Understand cultural and social milieu
State and nonstate actors	Low to moderate, but need brain power, freedom to create and adapt outside of regulations	Mapping the enemy's "Info-infra," especially that related to its military
State and nonstate actors	Low to moderate in monetary expenses, but high in psychic disruption of some professional military and political mind-sets	Understand how the enemy thinks, what it values

Notes: Info-infra = information-infrastructure; C4ISR = command, control, communications, computers, intelligence, surveillance and reconnaissance.

and symbols that motivate warrior societies, for example, and technology may be more help than hindrance in doing so.

GRACE NOTES

The reader does not have to endorse this particular frame of reference in order to see the larger point: that the prevention, management, and termination of all conflicts, including wars, are as subjective as they are "objective," if not more so. Part of my purpose in this study is to argue a larger case for the importance of subjective factors than is customary in U.S. military-strategic culture and in U.S. policymaking. I will cite two apparently unrelated studies that actually support my point very well.

The first is Richard Shultz's historical investigation of U.S. covert special operations missions (SOG, for Studies and Observation Group) against North Vietnam from 1964 to 1972.[9] In this study, Shultz shows that these missions were crippled in their effect, not as much by lack of personnel or funding as by the conventional mind-set of the Pentagon. The U.S. Army leadership of the time was suspicious of special operations and regarded SOG missions against North Vietnam as of marginal or no significance. After first attempting to duck responsibility for these missions and pass it on to the CIA, the Joint Chiefs of Staff finally acquiesced in accepting the assignments but only after absorbing them within a rigidly controlling and bureaucratically stifling structure.

The second study is on the topic of complex interdependence and the information revolution. Robert O. Keohane and Joseph S. Nye, Jr., accept that information, communications, and electronics technology has made it possible for state and nonstate actors to create networks and political communities that cross state borders and to enhance the influence of those transnational cybercommunities.[10] However, they caution against deriving from this situation the conclusion that states are being displaced or superseded as key political actors or that security and armed forces are becoming less important in world politics. What has changed, according to Keohane and Nye, is the relative importance of "soft power" compared to "hard power" in world politics. Hard power is the ability to get others to do what they might otherwise not do by means of coercion: rewards mixed with threats. Soft power is the ability to get others to want the same outcomes that you do. Soft power includes the appeal of a state or nonstate actor's ideas, culture, values, society, and political system.

In an electronically borderless world the ability to get the most from a state's soft power may be closely related to the ability to limit the use of force or to tailor the uses of force more precisely to the exigent situation. The United States discovered in Somalia in 1993 that the failure to convince public, media, and congressional audiences of a credible policy story in support of military intervention did more to force an American military withdrawal from that troubled country than did lack of firepower or insufficient tactics. In contrast, NATO's military implementation force in support of the Dayton Peace Agreement in Bosnia was preceded by extensive documentation and publicity about the humanitarian disasters there and about the stakes for NATO if the war were to spread beyond Bosnia proper. NATO's soft power was not capable of disarming and separating the contending factions in Bosnia—its Implementation Force some 60,000 strong at the outset, was tasked to accomplish that. But soft power did help to maintain alliance unity and determination to back up the peace agreement with a quantity and quality of force that said to the "bad guys" on all sides: It is to your advantage to step down, not up, the ladder of escalation.

Historians of the Cold War now acknowledge that soft power had as much to do with the eventual "victory" of the West and the demise of the Soviet Union in 1991. The important point about the end of the Cold War is that it occurred peacefully. Few, if any, experts in the United States or in Russia foresaw this. Some predicted the *eventual* doom of communism in the same way that Ronald Reagan did: as an article of faith, not as a social science prediction. Most U.S. experts on the Soviet Union, in academia and in government, recognized that the Soviet system was sclerotic. It was running on borrowed time economically and politically. What kept it going was the political mythology of Marxism–Leninism, the military power of the Soviet Union, and the grip of the Communist Party on the reins of power. When Gorbachev dissolved the party's monopoly on political power and demythologized the history of communism, a Potemkin village devoid of substance was exposed to Soviet citizens and to the world. Seeing their opportunity at least, the non-Soviet nationalities of the Soviet Union claimed their political rights to abdicate. When the Russian Federation declared itself out of the Soviet Union, all was lost.

It was ideas, those of Lenin and his contemporaries, that allowed a fanatical party of conspirators to seize power in Petrograd in November 1917. It was the ideology of Leninism and Stalinism that cemented Soviet power over millions of Russian and non-Russian citizens, to their detriment for most of the twentieth century. And it was the fateful irrelevancy of those ideas, in a post–World War II setting of spreading international democracy and capitalism, that doomed the Soviet system to extinction. The Soviet regime might have carried on for a decade or so longer than it did, at least officially; it might, that is to say, have carried on a nominal existence as a party and bureaucracy out of touch with the world and with the reality of Russia until the year 2000 or even a few years afterward. But Leninism, a program and philosophy rooted in Marx's anger against the ravages of nineteenth-century capitalism, had been overtaken by events. People simply did not believe in the Soviet version of socialism any more than they believed in the phlogiston theory of matter.

Soft power is not disconnected from hard power, however. The Soviet system was able to outlive its "expected" lifetime because of its military power, including its nuclear weapons. The United States was able to resist Soviet coercion of Western Europe during the Cold War because of its military power and that of its NATO allies. And both the United States and the Soviet Union preferred to terminate the Cold War without firing a shot across the Elbe because, in an age of nuclear plenitude, neither could guarantee that any shooting war could be stopped short of mutual assured destruction. Here soft power counted, too: In the shared understanding that gradually developed between two very distinct strategic cultures—the American and Soviet ones—nuclear weapons were something different from other military means for resolving political disputes. In the aftermath of any major nuclear war between the Americans and Russians, the postwar peace conference would have to be held in hell. So soft power helped to maintain the Cold War without hot war for 45 years or so, and it helped to end the Cold War without a shooting war, but it worked with hard power to do so.

In the future, as in the past, ideas and hard power will matter. If the United States retains a political system and culture that others find attractive, this form of soft power will obviate the need to rely on hard power for some kinds of conflict prevention, management, and termination. The twenty-first century will surely see the rise of some unanticipated challenges to U.S. military and economic supremacy: The nature of international relations is that crowns rest precariously on the heads of leading state actors. The United States cannot deploy its military power or even threaten to use it for every international crisis, and it does not want to become a de facto international gendarme or "911" number.

Soft power, including the power to persuade others of the need for commitment to international peacekeeping, can help to "multilateralize" the costs of international commitment and make those costs more acceptable to the American people and to Congress. For the United States to play a major role in conflict prevention, management, and termination in the twenty-first century, as in the previous one, the jury of American public opinion must be involved in the taking of this stance and provide its approval. U.S. presidents who understand this will do well; those who do not will fall through the gap between public skepticism and political ambitions.

The point here, however, is not restricted to the prudential application of soft power for political survival. Ideas matter. They matter in and of themselves. Political ideologies also matter. They motivate people to do things that they would not otherwise do: a traditional measure of power among social scientists. The twentieth century was a Wagnerian opera of major coalition wars fought on behalf of one or more political ideologies. It was the political genius of Winston Churchill that he understood this with exceptional clairvoyance before the fact of World War II and with unwavering commitment to purpose during it. Not all of Churchill's contemporaries understood the same situation. A British Foreign Office spokesman, having just been informed of the nonaggression pact between Hitler and Stalin in 1939 that opened the door to World War II, remarked with cynicism: "All the Isms are Wasms."[11] This view of the obsolescence of political ideology has now taken hold of another generation since the end of the Cold War: With communism in its grave and the Soviet Union defunct, liberal democracy reigns supreme alongside capitalist economics.

To the contrary: Liberal democracy as practiced in the United States and in much of Western Europe is a precious value based on traditions of the rule of law, individual rights against the state, and religious values that cannot be transferred along with bombs and bullets to other cultures. From the end of World War II to the end of the century, U.S. and other Western military interventions in non-Western cultures have resulted in a trail of tears. If high-technology civilizations cannot comprehend the ideas, including cultural hatreds, that motivate unconventional warriors in Third World societies, their likelihood of success in peacekeeping or peace enforcement is nil. Even within a single country, as in Russia from 1994 to 1996 and again in 1999, clashes of culture provide the nutrient from which wars fought between Russians and Chechens continue into the twenty-first century. If the Chechens have to fight the Russians with sticks and stones, they will do so. Some say the Chechens are motivated by religious as much as political factors, but in the present context, that is a distinction without a difference.[12] So it was between the English and the Scots, between Palestinians and Israelis, and for that matter, in the Crusades fought during the Middle Ages for control over Constantinople and the Holy Land.

The assumption that technology itself, innocent of military strategy and supported by economic supremacy, can win wars and enforce peace settlements is the most dangerous of many notions that have captivated audiences of CNN and some policymakers in the post–Cold War era. The sudden collapse of communism was wrongly taken to show the end of ideology; instead, it demonstrated the folly of buying into an erroneous political belief system. The end of Soviet communism was the end of one kind of ideology: totalitarian and world aspiring. Now political ideologies, commingled with communal and cultural values, have returned from the global to the regional or village level: Tip O'Neill's comment that "all politics are local" certainly resonates in Srebrenica, in Grozny, or for that matter, in Belfast. The wars since the end of the Cold

War have demonstrated the irrelevancy of "systems of systems" and the limited suasion of bayonets and bullets absent comprehension of what it is that people are fighting for. If, for example, they are fighting for identity ("none of your ancestors lived in this village, and neither will you"), the option of conflict containment, of preventing the conflict from escalating across state boundaries, may be the most that outsiders can accomplish. In a hard world that is not to be despised.

NOTES

1. In addition to sources cited earlier, a study pertinent to the problems of conflict prevention, management, and termination is Fred Charles Ikle, *How Nations Negotiate* (New York: Frederick A. Praeger, 1967), esp. pp. 26–42 and 87–121.

2. See Edward A. Kolodziej, "Thinking about Coping: Actors, Resources, Roles and Strategies," ch. 15 in Edward A. Kolodziej and Roger E. Kanet, eds., *Coping with Conflict after the Cold War* (Baltimore, Md.: Johns Hopkins University Press, 1996), pp. 363–394, and I. William Zartman, "Bargaining and Conflict Reduction," ch. 11 in ibid., pp. 271–290. Also pertinent to the management of conflict is some of the literature on coercive diplomacy and bargaining, especially in crisis. See, for example, Alexander L. George, "The Development of Doctrine and Strategy," in Alexander L. George, David K. Hall, and William E. Simons, *The Limits of Coercive Diplomacy* (Boston: Little, Brown, 1971), pp. 1–35.

3. In addition to sources cited in the introduction on this topic, see Colin Gray's comments on the relationship between political and military objectives in strategy and in war in Gray, *Modern Strategy* (Oxford: Oxford University Press, 1999), pp. 57–64, and his discussion of the "arrhythmic pulse" of major conflict, pp. 182–185. See also Karl P. Magyar and Constantine P. Danopoulos, eds., *Prolonged Wars: A Post-Nuclear Challenge* (Maxwell Air Force Base, Ala.: Air University Press, 1994).

4. Paul K. Davis's research on these issues as applied to national security problems is exceptional and informative. See, for example, Paul K. Davis, "A New Analytic Technique for the Study of Deterrence, Escalation Control and War Termination," ch. 3 in Stephen J. Cimbala, ed., *Artificial Intelligence and National Security* (Lexington, Mass.: D. C. Heath, 1987), pp. 35–60; Paul K. Davis, *Studying First Strike Stability with Knowledge-Based Models of Human Decisionmaking*, R-3689-CC (Santa Monica, Calif.: RAND, 1989; Paul K. Davis, Steven C. Bankes, and James P. Kahan, *A New Methodology for Modeling National Command Level Decisionmaking in War Games and Simulations*, R-3290-NA (Santa Monica, Calif.: RAND, 1986); and Paul K. Davis, "Behavioral Factors in Terminating Superpower War," ch. 6 in Stephen J. Cimbala and Sidney R. Waldman, eds., *Controlling and Ending Conflict: Essays Issues before and after the Cold War* (Westport, Conn.: Greenwood Press, 1992), pp. 165–182. Other important contributions include: Robert Jervis, Richard Ned Lebow, and Janice Gross Stein, *Psychology and Deterrence* (Baltimore, Md.: Johns Hopkins University Press, 1985); Robert Jervis, *Perception and Misperception in International Politics* (Princeton, N.J.: Princeton University Press, 1976); Graham T. Allison, Albert Carnesale, and Joseph S.

Nye, Jr., eds., *Hawks, Doves and Owls: An Agenda for Avoiding Nuclear War* (New York: W. W. Norton, 1985); Patrick M. Morgan, *Deterrence: A Conceptual Analysis* (Beverly Hills, Calif.: Sage Publications, 1983); Irving L. Janis, *Groupthink*, 2nd ed. (Boston: Houghton Mifflin, 1982); and Thomas C. Schelling, *Arms and Influence* (New Haven, Conn.: Yale University Press, 1966). With regard to separating the wheat from the chaff in matters of military strategy, see Gray, *Modern Strategy*. In a better world, one might have expected that the "rational choice" theorists so in vogue in much of political science would have applied their talents to national security problems, but for the most part, they have not chosen to. See, however, on the problem of rationality in deterrence theory: Morgan, *Deterrence: A Conceptual Analysis*, ch. 4, and Richard Ned Lebow, *Nuclear Crisis Management: A Dangerous Illusion* (Ithaca, N.Y.: Cornell University Press, 1987).

5. Richards J. Heuer, Jr., *Psychology of Intelligence Analysis* (Washington, D.C.: Center for the Study of Intelligence, Central Intelligence Agency, 1999), p. 9.

6. For arguments specific to this issue, see Stephen J. Cimbala, *Russia and Armed Persuasion* (Boulder, Colo.: Rowman and Littlefield, 2001).

7. The seminal statement on this, which has not been improved upon since, is Schelling, *Arms and Influence*, passim. Also very important are the contributions to political psychology by Jervis, Lebow, and Stein, cited above, and the work on crisis management and/or coercive diplomacy by Alexander L. George, Ole Holsti, and Lebow. See Alexander L. George, ed., *Avoiding War: Problems of Crisis Management* (Boulder, Colo.: Westview Press, 1991), especially George, "The Tension between Military Logic and Requirements of Diplomacy in Crisis Management," ch. 3, pp. 13–21; George, "A Provisional Theory of Crisis Management," ch. 4, pp. 22–27; and George, "Strategies for Crisis Management," pp. 377–394. See also George, "The Development of Doctrine and Strategy," in George, Hall, and Simons, *The Limits of Coercive Diplomacy*, pp. 1–35; Ole R. Holsti, "Crisis Decision Making," in Philip E. Tetlock, Jo L. Husbands, Robert Jervis, Paul C. Stern, and Charles Tilly, eds., *Behavior, Society and Nuclear War*, Vol. 1 (New York: Oxford University Press, 1989), pp. 8–84; and Lebow, *Between Peace and War: The Nature of International Crisis* (Baltimore, Md.: Johns Hopkins University Press, 1981).

8. For an expansion, see Paul Bracken, *Fire in the East* (New York: Harper-Collins, 1999), passim.

9. Richard H. Shultz, Jr., *The Secret War against Hanoi: Kennedy and Johnson's Use of Spies, Saboteurs, and Covert Warriors in North Vietnam* (New York: HarperCollins, 1999), esp. pp. 266–306.

10. Robert O. Keohane and Joseph S. Nye, Jr., "Power and Interdependence in the Information Age," *Foreign Affairs*, no. 5 (September–October 1998), pp. 81–94.

11. Cited in Bruce Page, David Leitch, and Philip Knightley, *Philby: The Spy Who Betrayed a Generation* (London: Andre Deutsch, 1968), p. 292.

12. One expert argues that the motivation of Chechens fighting against Russians in 1994–1996 was more political than it was religious, although both factors mattered. See Anatol Lieven, *Chechnya: Tombstone of Russian Power* (New Haven, Conn.: Yale University Press, 1998).

For Further Reading

Alberts, David S. *Defensive Information Warfare*. Washington, D.C.: National Defense University, Directorate of Advanced Concepts, Technologies and Information Strategies, August 1996.

Andrew, Christopher, and Oleg Gordievsky, eds. *Comrade Kryuchkov's Instructions: Top Secret Files on KGB Foreign Operations, 1975–1985*. Stanford, Calif.: Stanford University Press, 1993.

Arquilla, John, and David Ronfeldt, eds. *In Athena's Camp: Preparing for Conflict in the Information Age*. Santa Monica, Calif.: RAND, 1997.

Cimbala, Stephen J. *The Past and Future of Nuclear Deterrence*. Westport, Conn.: Praeger Publishers, 1998.

Craig, Gordon A., and Alexander L. George. *Force and Statecraft: Diplomatic Problems of Our Time*. New York: Oxford University Press, 1983.

Denning, Dorothy E. *Information Warfare and Security*. Reading, Mass.: Addison-Wesley, 1999.

Gaddis, John Lewis. *We Now Know: Rethinking Cold War History*. Oxford: Clarendon Press, 1997.

Garthoff, Raymond L. *Detente and Confrontation: American-Soviet Relations from Nixon to Reagan*. Washington, D.C.: Brookings Institution, 1985.

George, Alexander L., ed. *Avoiding War: Problems of Crisis Management*. Boulder, Colo.: Westview Press, 1991.

Gordon, Michael R., and General Bernard R. Trainor. *The Generals' War: The Inside Story of the Conflict in the Gulf*. Boston: Little, Brown, 1995.

Gray, Colin S. *Modern Strategy*. Oxford: Oxford University Press, 1999.

Gray, Colin S. *The Second Nuclear Age*. Boulder, Colo.: Lynne Rienner, 1999.

Ikle, Fred Charles. *Every War Must End*. Rev. ed. New York: Columbia University Press, 1991.

Joint Warfighting Center, U.S. Joint Chiefs of Staff. *Joint Task Force Commander's*

Handbook for Peace Operations. Ft. Monroe, Va.: Joint Warfighting Center, June 16, 1997.

Kolodziej, Edward A., and Roger E. Kanet, eds. *Coping with Conflict after the Cold War.* Baltimore, Md.: Johns Hopkins University Press, 1996.

Lebow, Richard Ned, and Janice Gross Stein. *We All Lost the Cold War.* Princeton, N.J.: Princeton University Press, 1994.

Libicki, Martin. *What Is Information Warfare?* Washington, D.C.: National Defense University, ACIS Paper 3, August 1995.

Lieven, Anatol. *Chechnya: Tombstone of Russian Power.* New Haven, Conn.: Yale University Press, 1998.

Payne, Keith B. *Deterrence in the Second Nuclear Age.* Lexington: University Press of Kentucky, 1996.

Snow, Donald M. *Uncivil Wars: International Security and the New Internal Conflicts.* Boulder, Colo.: Lynne Rienner, 1996.

Volkogonov, Dmitri. *Autopsy for an Empire: The Seven Leaders Who Built the Soviet Regime.* Harold Shukman, ed. and trans. New York: The Free Press, 1998.

Index

About the Author

STEPHEN J. CIMBALA is Professor of Political Science at the Pennsylvania State University (Delaware County). He is the author of numerous books and articles in professional journals on topics related to national security. His most recent books include *The Past and Future of Nuclear Deterrence* (Praeger, 1998) and *Nuclear Strategy in the Twenty-First Century* (Praeger, 2000).